121
Eb39t **Ebersole, Frank B**
  Things we know; fourteen essays on problems of knowl-
edge, by Frank B. Ebersole.   Eugene, Or., University of
Oregon Books, 1967.

  viii, 304 p.   23 cm.

  Bibliographical footnotes.

  1. Knowledge, Theory of·
phy   I. Title.   2. Philoso-

BD161.E23   121   68–63599

71-20

750

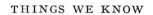

THINGS WE KNOW

THINGS

WE KNOW

Fourteen Essays on Problems of Knowledge

BY

FRANK B. EBERSOLE

UNIVERSITY BOOKS
OF OREGON

Eugene, Oregon
1967

PREFACE

Here is a collection of fourteen essays on problems of knowledge. They deal with related topics, but each is a self-contained discussion and will stand (or fall) by itself. Therefore, any one of them may be read without any of the others.

I wrote these pieces over a period of more than seven years. Although those written last show considerable philosophical progress over those written first, I have not arranged them in chronological order. They are arranged by topic.

The first essay deals with the question of whether the words for simple visual characteristics (e.g., "red") must refer to things (red things) because they share some characteristic (redness); also whether one can see the characteristic which they are expected to share.

Essay II is concerned with the appeal to hallucinations and after-images as support for a sense-datum analysis of perception.

Essay III deals with the time-lag argument for sense-data or immediate objects of perception. We "see" stars which no longer exist. *Ergo,* we cannot be seeing physical objects.

Essay IV is an attempt to raise the philosophical question which leads to the so-called causal theory of vision, i.e., the explanation of vision in terms of light rays, chemical changes in the retina, and electromagnetic currents in the optic nerve.

Essay V examines the traditional appeal to dreams as experiences in which we are acquainted with direct private objects of perception. The things we see when dreaming are the same intrinsically and qualitatively as the things we see when awake.

Essay VI explores some of the problems created by a prehensile or causal model of feeling (tactual perception). Pains are objects we feel; but then, they are such very extraordinary objects.

Essay VII is about a mystery which can arise in trying to describe memory: we must have direct acquaintance with things which no longer exist (the past). But we couldn't: the past does not exist.

Essay VIII deals with another philosophical memory-mystery. My memory must be of my own experiences. Its full or proper object must be some experience in my own past. Yet it is not so.

Essay IX examines this predicament: since it is conceivable that there is no past, our direct memory objects must be in the present. But that cannot be.

Essay X is concerned with the old argument: the future must be fixed or determined since every proposition about it is either true or false.

Essay XI examines an opposing argument: the future cannot be knowable in detail. If it were, it would be not future, but present; and time would be unreal.

Essays XII and XIII are concerned with the question of whether human reason, without experience, is capable of knowledge of existence: and that notorious effort to show that it is, the ontological argument. These essays make a pair, although either can be read without the other. Essay XII is concerned with whether existence is or is not a predicate, and Essay XIII is an inquiry, in connection with the ontological argument, as to whether existence is or is not a perfection.

Essay XIV is addressed to the philosophical difficulty of finding a place in the physical world for human actions. It raises the old free-will question in present-day language: how are "bodily movements" related to "human actions"? It is concerned mostly with two things: (1) the kind of words we use to refer to "bodily movements," and (2) what is involved in seeing "bodily movements," and in "seeing bodily movements as actions." The main part of the essay consists of topics usually counted among the problems of knowledge.

I think of these as some of the principal, perennial philosophical problems of knowledge. In that way the essays form a unity: they deal with main topics of that well-known area of philosophy. They also make a unity in other ways: they originated in the same way, and they had the same pedagogic purpose. With the exception of Essay XII, they were prepared in connection with my courses, most of them for my seminar "Problems of Knowledge" at the University of Oregon. They are not lectures, and while they took form in connection with class discussions, they are not idealized discussions either. They are philosophical monologues. In part, I wrote these pieces out of a conviction that neither the lecture nor classroom discussion is of much philosophical worth. I tried, in them, to give students something else—of my own. I had most of them duplicated, and gave them to students; but, with the exception of Essay IX, I never discussed them in my classes. I wanted the essays to show that though it may be provoked by lecture or begin in discussion, philosophy must be carried out in solitude. (There is a bit of fudge in this: I am making my purpose look much clearer than, in fact, it was.)

In giving these things to my classes, I hope I did not treat my students with disrespect. I never intended to. I thought of the essays, always, as contributions to philosophy. At the time I was writing each of them, I thought I had something fresh and original to say on the topic. My students have now handed these essays about for several years, and compared various versions of them. Some of my colleagues profess to have found a use for some of them in their courses. Students and colleagues put in my mind the idea of bringing them together in a volume.

The essays are also unified, I suppose, by being similar in method and philosophic aim—although they also differ. On this matter I cannot think of anything useful to say by way of introduction. Unless this: I sought behind each problem to expose a picture or model which I believe gets us into the problem. I assume, I suppose, that we think in a graphic or quasi-graphic way when we are in philosophical moods. But I do not ask why that is so. I do not want to ask any such question. What kind of answer could one give to such a question? We think with spatial models because we have sacrificed our instinct to intelligence? Because we seek theoretical simplicity? Because we are inclined to extend our categories beyond the field of their proper application? Because we seek (or act as though we seek) a theoretical defense against our fears of death? Because it is just part of being human? What would a helpful answer be? I try only to work through some of the ways that pictures or models control our thinking.

Three of the essays have appeared as journal articles. Essay III appeared in *Mind*, October 1965. Essay V appeared in *Mind*, July 1959, under the title "De Somniis." Essay XII was published in *The Journal of Philosophy*, August 1963. Also, part one of Essay II is removed from an article, "On Seeing Things," which appeared in *The Philosophical Quarterly*, October 1961, but I have changed it a great deal. I have made lesser changes in the others. I have made small changes throughout Essay III and have added a few footnotes. For Essay V, I have written a new introductory section. I have restored a few paragraphs to Essay XII which were removed in preparing it for journal publication. Although many of the changes may seem insignificant, I think they are important. So I want these present essays to supersede their original journal versions. None of the pieces was written with the idea of journal publication in mind. For that reason I want especially to thank the editors of *Mind, The Philosophical Quarterly,* and *The Journal of Philosophy*: first for publishing some of these things in their journals, and again for permission to reprint them here.

Many people: friends, students, colleagues, have read one or a few of the essays in this collection, and they have made many helpful criticisms. Arthur Cody, San Jose State College, read nearly all of them at some stage in their preparation—and with great care and understanding. He always gave me heart. Sue Townsend suffered through all of them (some many times)—both as typist and salutary critic. After I had selected these particular essays and brought them together in a package, James Kellenberger read through them all—in their present order. He helped me with many details at that painful time when I was fussing over the question of how they fit together. I am greatly indebted to Catherine Lauris, managing editor of University of Oregon Books. She saved me from all kinds of bad things. Lastly, and with a very special affection, I want to thank Laurence Ebersole for helping me with the astronomical stuff in Essay III.

FRANK B. EBERSOLE

CONTENTS

PERCEPTION

AND LANGUAGE

I

SEEING RED IN RED THINGS:

The Question of Common Properties

We commonly assumed that a word was used to refer to a group of things because those things had some common and peculiar property or properties, that is, there were properties which those things shared and which other things did not have, other things not called by the same name. Then we were led to see that all the things referred to by the same word had at most "family resemblances." All pencils, shoes, games do not share common and peculiar properties.[1] We do not find it difficult to accept this, but we feel it is a superficial observation about language. The "family resemblance" feature may describe the way referring words are sometimes used. But as philosophers we are not interested in *describing* language, or not interested in describing it in that way. That words refer to things with no more than family resemblances has to be a derivative feature. Moreover, *all* referring words simply could not work in that way. Within each branch of any family the members *must* share common and peculiar

---

[1] One has to begin philosophizing somewhere. I do not want to worry over this myth now, so I shall start from it. Of course, we learned no such thing, namely, that all pencils, shoes, games, do not share common properties. What are the *properties* of a pencil, or of a shoe (any pencil or shoe)? "Characteristics" or "features" might be better words. "What characteristics (features) must something have to be a shoe?" The question makes it sound as if learning the word "shoe" were like learning to identify birds. "What are the distinguishing features of the nighthawk (or the fox sparrow)?" Here perhaps we do learn, in the process of learning birds, that all glaucous gulls do not have the same identifying characteristics. There are immatures, first and second year plumages, females. (Also there are nestlings, albinos, melanistic varieties, but we would not have been concerned with those.) Is it a characteristic of a bird that makes it a juvenile glaucous gull? Is it parentage, mostly? ("What characteristics do all juvenile glaucous gulls have?" However, we did know what we were asking and we did get a helpful answer to the question, "What are the distinguishing characteristics of the nighthawk?" To ask such a question about pencils or shoes would be so wild a misunderstanding that it is unimaginable. Although we might want to ask, "What are the characteristics of an oxford (a pump, a loafer)?", this, like "What are the characteristics of a nighthawk?", is not a request for a philosophical definition.

characteristics, or, if that is not true, then we must subdivide the family further until we arrive at groups which do. This is the point at which to make important philosophical observations.

Take some word which refers to groups of things which have family resemblances to each other. Say "pencil." Pencils are implements made to write and draw. Some have graphite cores. Some are colored. Some are wax. (How are they distinguished from crayons?) There are grease pencils and even liquid pencils. Colored pencils may be watercolor pencils, or indelible pencils, or wax pencils. There is no one set of characteristics common and peculiar to all these; but what, for example, of watercolor pencils? They are intended to make colored marks soluble in water. Consider these. Are they marked by common and peculiar properties? Or do they only form a family? They are intended to make colored marks, but some are defective. Consider only those which work, those which make colored marks. Are their colored marks characterized by common and peculiar properties? Do the colors share common and peculiar properties? (The family resemblance metaphor is not helpful here.) Say the answer is "no." Say the colors have family resemblances. Then we have the following groups of marks: violet, blue, green, indigo, yellow, orange, red, white, black, etc. Take red ones. Now we are down to red watercolor pencils. Do red marks have a common and peculiar property? They are red. Isn't that the peculiar property? Surely now we are down to a group of things, the red marks, which share and are uniquely distinguished by the property red. And we are down to the simple words, those through which language makes its contact with the things of the world, and through which language acquires meaning.

We reason this way to lend support to our idea that the fundamental words get meaning in referring to things because those things share common and peculiar properties. The "family resemblance" story is not only superficial, it is not a conceivable alternative to the common-property story. If we try to think that all words refer to things with family resemblances, we are in a spin. The idea is self-annihilating. For example, "All pencils do not have anything in common. Some, but not all, are graphite; some, but not all, have paper exteriors; some are wood, etc." But when we say not all are graphite we mean not all have the characteristic of having a graphite core. Is "having a graphite core" a property? If so, it refers to things by virtue of the fact that they have that property.

If not, then when we say that not all have a graphite core, we do not deny that there is a property which all have.

This argument, too, supports the view we do not easily give up. Metaphors may die: they may die and remain dead. And by that means and others, words become applied to new things. But originally they were not applied to these new things. In the beginning they must have referred to things with common properties. How else could language have come to be? By what other method could we have general words—words which refer to more than one thing? Some words must remain as originals. How else could language be acquired?

This fits the picture. When you consider very simple words, those whose application is completely mastered in early childhood, you can see that they refer to things in virtue of the fact that those things have common and peculiar properties. Take color words. The word "red" is applied to many things, the red things. But those red things, wherever they are, have one common property, being red. We have only to look and we shall see that they do. If asked what property red things have in common, we must say, "They are all red. All red things are red." Of course, this is a philosophical thing to say. We say it only when trying to disclose the basis of our language. Its air of triviality is not merely because red is a simple property, and we have no other word with which to refer to red things. We take it that being properly called red and having the property of being red are distinguishable. We are quite convinced that the second is the basis of, the reason for, the first. "All red things are red" is thus a way of saying that the words "red things" apply to the things they do on account of the possession by all these things of the property, red. Although the sentence looks suspect at first, after some thought it does not seem more queer than "All brothers are male siblings" or "All bachelors are unmarried men" when these things are said as part of an exercise in philosophical definition.[2]

---

[2] "Except where a word is patently ambiguous, it is natural for us to assume that the different situations or types of situations, to which it applies have a distinctive common feature. For otherwise why should we use the same word to refer to them? Sometimes we have another way of describing such a common feature; we can say, for example, that what irascible people have in common is that they are all prone to anger. But very often we have no way of saying what is common to the things to which the same word applies except by using the word itself. How else should we describe the distinctively common feature of

The important thing is this: we can look and see the common property. We have to be able to see the property by reason of which we call them "red." All the red things, regardless of what shade, are supposed to be alike (they *must* be alike)—in being—red. We think we can see that property and see that they are therefore appropriately "called by the same name."[3]

Consider a long line of bits of cardboard, each a different color, and arranged in spectral order: indigo, yellow, orange, red, violet, blue, green. A certain number of them in the middle are red. Now look at the property they share by virtue of which they are called "red." Can you see it? This one has it, the one five steps down does not. The ones in between do not clearly and definitely have it; they do not clearly and definitely not have it. All of the red ones must have the same property. Which ones do have the same property? Consider what properties colored things can have.

(1) Suppose that I have just been studying the technique of an artist who

---

red things except by saying that they are all red?" A. J. Ayer, *Problems of Knowledge* (Baltimore, Penguin Books, 1956), pp. 10-11. "... If things resemble one another sufficiently for us to find it useful to apply the same word to them, we are entitled to say, if it pleases us, that they have something in common. Neither is it necessary that what they have in common should be describable in different words, as we saw in the case of 'red'. It is correct, though not at all enlightening, to say that what games have in common is their being games." *Ibid.*, pp. 11-12.

[3] Not only does one have to begin somewhere, but one cannot explore in every direction simultaneously. I ignore the problems behind the word "property," and the phrase "common property." (1) "Property" belongs with a picture of things. Everything sayable consists of two parts: Thing talked about, and what is said about the thing. Anything that can be said about anything refers to a "property." A property is one part of a fact. As soon as we think of the world consisting of things and properties, the common theory of meaning is inevitable. Words surely refer to groups of things. And why one group rather than another unless these, and not those, share common and peculiar properties? I want to get at just one of the ways this picture is confusing. And for this purpose I need only to take it for granted that having the same color, for example, red, is a case of having a "common property" namely, the color. (2) "Common property" is a solecism which does not strike us while we are philosophizing. When "common" is an adjective, what is common is not a "property." Man and monkeys have a common ancestor." "These several trees have a common root system." In connection with properties we use the phrases "in common" or "common to" (depending, it seems, on whether the "property" is object or subject). "A certain characteristic madness is common to all dictators." "Dictators have that trait in common." Why do we think that "common property" and "property in common" are the same? Why do we not feel "common property" solecistic? Of course we are far removed from the details. Also, perhaps we do think of things and properties as connected in the way trees and roots are connected.

produces a strangely muted and tame shade of a color by mixing it with a little of its exact complement and the nearest ground color. I notice three such shades in a group of samples. What property do they have? They create a feeling of rest, immobility. They give a static character to the region they cover. We might say they have the property of creating this feeling. (2) I have just been immersed in a reading on the theory of color. I point to the saturated hues. What property have they? They jump off the surface. They make one perk up and take notice. We might say they have the property of bringing one to attention. (3) I point to the warm shades of each color. They give the impression that the surface they cover would be warm to the touch. Would we say they have the property of giving that impression?

What am I asking here anyway? What am I doing? I suppose I am to imagine myself teaching someone painting. I am trying to enliven his awareness of the effects one can create by using different colors. It need not be just that. I needn't be a painter. I can just be talking with someone and through the talk trying to sharpen his sense of colors and my own. I shall talk with him about the color of the sky and of the wine in a clear bottle. These colors are alike in a way. What property do they have? They have no definite place. They are thick. Would we say they have that property? When philosophizing about the meaning of the word "red," I am not trying to awaken a sensitivity to colors in others or in myself. I am not trying to teach painting. It is more as if I wanted to teach someone to say, "All reds have the same property—just in being red." Suppose I do try to teach someone—someone named Seward—to say that, namely, those colors have the same property. How shall I do it? I shall exhibit objects of different colors and pick out some of them. Laura: "These have the same property. Do you see it? They are red." Seward: "What are you driving at? You mean they are the same color? They're all red." Laura: "Yes. Red is a property. Everything red has the property of being red, therefore everything red has the same property." Seward: "You mean 'all red things are the same color.' But they aren't, that is, they aren't necessarily."

Seward is right: there isn't any one thing that "same color" comes to. (a) "Let's try the chips from the Nu-Crome Enamel line. Why, this one called 'sagebrush' is the same color as the faded wall." The color of a faded plaster wall and a color chip are not the same because they are both green. (b) "Membership in the Chattanooga golf club is limited to people of the same color." This includes people whose skin color ranges all the way from reddish brown to albino white. In fact, this is not a question of skin color in that sense at all. (c) "When I weep, my tears are salty, and when I am cut, I bleed, and my blood is the same color as yours." Here it sounds as though two things are counted as the same color because they are both red. But if my blood were maroon and yours pink, would I say this? I appeal to a fact about human blood to bring out the common nature of man. If the shades of red were very different, I would not have the fact to appeal to. (d) "Part of the 'feel' of the Pacific is that the sky and sea are the same color." This does seem to be a matter of their both being blue. It may be in this way that I want to say you can see that all red things are the same color. Can't you see that the ocean and the sky are the same color?

You understand what he is calling your attention to when you realize that though the sea and sky may both be blue they are not always the same color in this way. Of course, you can see they are the same color here, if you have ever seen the Atlantic, and you realize that he is making a contrast with other seas and skies. (e) Neither the sea nor the sky have their colors on a surface. I can mix paints on a pallette, and of course these colors are on a surface. When I have mixed successfully, I may say, "There, that's the same color as the sky," or, "There, that's the same color as the sea." And these two colors on the pallette may not be the same color even when they are mixed to match the very sea and sky of the Pacific, the ones that "are the same color."

Now can't you look at all sorts of red things and see they are the same color? What gets in the way here? Aren't they the same color? What am I to say? They aren't the same color the way the Pacific Ocean and sky are the same, that is, it is not something you can notice, it is not something that when noticed explains a difference in feel, as we explain how the Pacific feels different from the Atlantic partly because one has the same blue above and below, because one is surrounded by the same color. You cannot imagine another possibility. (f) "I notice that Sally and Ann just bought coats of exactly the same color. That's funny : they will both be very uncomfortable. I wonder what they will do about it." I notice it because it is not a desirable thing for them. It will have sad consequences. I do not notice all reds are red because it is a bad thing for anybody. It will have no sad effects. (g) I can learn to notice all sorts of color things. "Since I have been painting, I have noticed that the color of fall beech leaves and of faded daffodils is the same. I notice they are the same because mixing colors has led me to compare things I never before thought of together. Have I never before thought of red things together? When I think all red things are alike, is it something new to me? Do I ever notice, or have I learned to notice that all red things have something in common—in being red that is? No. Still I want to say so: I must have learned to notice this, but what I noticed in learning color words has somehow become swallowed up in the use of the words. It is now lost from sight. All the same I can *see* it. It is before my eyes. I can see all red things have the same color.

(h) I go to a rubber ball factory. It makes, red, blue, green, and white balls: a hundred red, then a hundred green, and so on, throughout the day. But today they are using up a surplus of red coloring. "All the balls we made today are the same color: all red." They are all on the drying tables. You can see they are all red. Can't I imagine that all red things are on a cosmic drying table. Then I could see they were all red. Yes, if normally some were green, some white. But no red things can be "normally green." "All red things are the same color" is not like "All today's balls are the same color."

(i) We could be having a sort of philosophical treasure hunt, and my team might be sent to get all the red things in the block. Now, in imagination, the problem would be to get all the red things in town, in the country, and in the universe. All right. But that doesn't help understand the idea that they are all the same color. The problem would have to be posed with this order, "Get everything the same color as this" and a red object would be designated. That would not be enough to make the order clear. Perhaps I am to take the designated sample as a color chip, perhaps not. If the sample is the color of wine in a bottle, perhaps I am only to get colored liquids, perhaps not. Suppose the same order were given to other teams," . . . same color as this" and green was pointed out for one, orange for another, etc. Still I would not know what my team was expected to do. The order would have to be "Get the same color as this, namely, red—any shade of red, any sort of thing." Then what on earth was the point of designating an object and chanting "same color as this"?

But when I say all red things are the same color or have the same property

I mean they are red: they have that color, they are alike in their possession of the property of being red. "The balls manufactured today are all alike; they are red." I want to speak of the respect in which all red things are alike, and I want their being red to be that respect. Is it like the riddle "What is spotted and eats rocks?" Answer: "A spotted rock-eater." "In what respect are all red things alike?" Answer: "In being red."

It must not be like the riddle. The riddle leads me to think about the animals I've seen and I try to remember which is spotted and eats rocks. Then I learn that something which is spotted and eats rocks would be called a spotted rock-eater. I am led to think about all sorts of red things and I try to think in what respect they are alike. I am told, "They are alike in being red." All pencils are alike in being pencils, and so with shoes and games, but they do not share common and peculiar properties. Is there something we can notice or discover about red things, something which because of *that* we properly call them red? I want to concentrate on what we can see with the eyes in a red thing in virtue of which it earns the right to be called red. It must be the same in each red thing.

I suppose this must be observed when one learns the word "red." But how can I know? I certainly cannot remember. We cannot learn from children. What would we ask a child? What could we make of his answers? Perhaps a man who has been blind all his life and has just gained his sight would be in a position to observe the required sameness. Imagine such a man: call him Bennett. Now suppose Bennett is to be taught the color words. He must learn to pick the reds out of all the colors. If it would get any results at all it would get the wrong results to tell him to pick out those with the same property as, or the same color as *this* (and show him a red). I don't see how he could be expected to understand "same property," and if he did he could not tell what property. Perhaps the property of exciting anger, or jumping, as it were, from the surface, or being deep like the color of the sky or one of the colors in a rainbow. How would he understand "same color as this"? That is the question. He must be taught.

Here is the home for the relevant use of "same color as this": the games we play with children. We have a supply of blocks of many colors, many shades of red, blue, green, orange, yellow. "Put all the blocks this color in one pile." Having always been blind, Bennett has gained his sight. Such games can be used for his lessons. Now suppose he makes a mistake: he starts to pile the yellows with the reds. I shall say to him, "No. This is a different color. Can't you see, these are alike, but this is different from the others?" What is he to say? Perhaps he will get the idea. He says, "Yes, I see." What is the philosophical purport of this? He must have seen the difference before; he just didn't know it was an important difference. That is the philosophical observation I want to make. That is what my picture dictates: one can see the color all red things have, the color in them which makes it proper to call them "red." But do I understand what I am saying? I want to say Bennett saw the difference but did not know it was a relevant one or a significant one. But he was learning at the same time what counts as the same color and what counts as a difference between colors.

I come home from a walk around the lake and I say, "I saw two water birds floating just beyond the end of the dock." Later I read a book about waterfowl, and I learn one of these birds was a grebe, the other a coot. Now, when I recall that walk, I shall say, "I saw a grebe and a coot. Of course I did not know what they were when I saw them." In learning, I had to remember what they looked like or I could not later have learned that one was a grebe and the other a coot. And I had to learn a great deal more than the names of the birds that were floating on the lake. Suppose someone else had followed me on the walk, had seen the birds, too, and had told me what they were. If that is all that I know, I might say, "I guess I saw a grebe and a coot; at any rate, that's what I was told." Of course I could say, "I saw a grebe and a coot," but it would be with the same force as ". . . so I was told." The relevant case is the one where I learned to distinguish and identify them. I had to learn a lot besides names, and also I had to know *something* about birds when I saw them. Surely I had to know something about the way birds are classified, what sorts of features are apt to count, and I had to remember these things. If that were not so, I would not say in retrospect, "I saw a grebe and a coot."

I try to imagine that Bennett gains his vision after a life of blindness, and he puts the yellow with the red. How am I to describe his mistake? Did he see the difference, just not know it counted, just not know how the color words fit the difference? But he knows nothing about how colors are classified. He knows nothing about what is apt to count and what not.[4] With the waterfowl

[4] Part of the difficulty with this example is that I am thinking of a blind adult who has

I had to know the sort of thing to look for: shape, neck, beak. When learning the color words, that is precisely what Bennett does not know. Rather: what could he look for? Not the beak or the way the tail is held. There is nothing like that: just the color. Isn't that what he was looking at all the time? Bennett was not looking for anything—except the blocks of the same color. Well, when he put yellow with red, did he see the difference? After he learns the color words, will he say, "I saw the difference"? Certainly not as I would say I saw a grebe and a coot. It could not be like that. When Bennett put the yellow with the red what kind of mistake did he make? After I learned the waterfowl, I might have said, "I saw two waterfowl on a walk, but I don't know what they were. I didn't notice. I didn't know what to look for." Is that the sort of thing he would say about the colors? "I saw two. They looked alike. I didn't notice any difference." How could he not notice? There was nothing special to look for: just the color. He was looking at the colors of the blocks. But he knew nothing of colors. He had never seen colors, never seen anything before. He did not know how colors were distinguished, how many dimensions, facets, features they had. He could not have known what to look for. And if he could not have known at all what to look for, how could he have seen the difference between red and yellow?

Perhaps the trouble is with the comparison. When we learn to recognize a coot we learn its identifying characteristics. We learn what to look for and what to notice. I have already seen that there is trouble with the idea that we notice what all red things have in common. Having certain characteristics makes a bird a coot. Having certain characteristics does not make a color red. Consider another example. I am a visitor from a primitive part of the country.

gained his sight. He has a command of English: otherwise I could not use him in my experiment in imagination. Then he has heard and read about colors and he does, of course, know something about colors and and color distinctions. Also he knows many different ways that different sorts of things are "same," "alike," "different." I really do not want him to know much of these things. I really want the child, but I do not know what to say at all about the child, the child just getting his conceptual bearings, still in process of acquiring some of the basic distinctions.

There is a wonderful opportunity here for all sorts of silly speculation, and for philosophical jokes. Perhaps for this experiment one needs a child raised by wolves. Suppose we get a child from the wolves at age ten. We have reason to believe wolves do not distinguish red from yellow and green. We shall now teach the child English and he will learn color words along with all the rest. Will his early life with the wolves make it hard for him? Will he now say, "I always wanted to tell the wolves they were not distinguishing colors?"

I see a strip of bright-colored cloth about four feet long. I am informed that it is a tie. I learn what a tie is, and then I say, "On my first day here, I saw a tie lying across the chair." Learning what a tie is is partly learning how the cloth strip is used, posibly also the intention of its maker, and many other things. It is learning what role it plays in life. Does learning what red is involve anything analogous? What shall we say of this case? "I saw a tie, but at the time I didn't see it as a tie"? When learning colors, will Bennett say of his mistake, "I saw a difference, but at the time I didn't see it as the difference between red and yellow"? With the tie case, I can say what I saw before I knew it was a tie, namely, "I saw a strip of cloth." There are simpler words and I have already learned those. In the color case, there are no simpler words. How could Bennett say he saw a difference when he had no idea what it is to see a difference?

Many animals can distinguish between red and yellow. Surely, then, an adult blind man who has gained vision can distinguish similarly. I say that my pet crow sees the difference between red and yellow. It is easy to teach him to open the yellow box, not the red one, if he wants food. That is part of what is involved in my saying he can see the difference. He does not say or learn to say, "I see red," "I see the box is bright red today," or anything like that. He never acquires a language. One might be inclined to say that this is because of, or associated with, the fact that he can't learn to "see" in the right way. If Bennett made the color distinctions as a crow does, he could not learn the words "red," "yellow." Before he learns the color words, maybe he sees colors as a crow does. After he has learned, will he say, "Now I see the difference as a man sees; before I saw the difference as a crow sees"? How could a person know that he saw as a crow sees? There is no first person use of "see" in the crow sense, only a third person use. How could one invent for himself a first person use in such a case? He would not say, "I saw the difference," because he had evidence in his own case of the kind he has for the crow's making a color distinction. He has not observed that, when hungry, he goes to a red, not a yellow box. In the circumstance we are concerned with, his learning colors by matching blocks, he did not distinguish red from yellow. He put the two colors together.

There are two ways to go here. We might be inclined to say of the blind man who had gained his sight that he noticed the differences, and the common properties before he learned which were significant.[5] He could "see" the difference between a warm and a cold, a surface and a film color, a saturated and a greyed, a red and a yellow. He did not yet know how to classify, what to call them. While we say he "noticed" or "saw" the difference we shall have to admit that he did not notice or see the difference. This, together with the fact that there is another way to go, might alter our inclination.

We can also be inclined to say that the world does not present our animal eyes with the distinctions: warm, cool; saturated, greyed; red, yellow. These distinctions are imposed by us, rational, language-using beings. They cannot be seen or noticed until the "form" is present, that is, until we have mastered the outlines of the relevant portion of our language.[6] Colors as we know them—and that is what we are talking about, the colors referred to with the words "red," "green," etc.—these colors do not exist apart from the use of the words. And here we shall have to agree, too, that we are saying very extraordinary and puzzling things.

[5] "... White is a name of all things whatever having the color, a name, not of the quality whiteness, but of every white object. It is true, this name was given to all those various objects on account of the quality, and we may therefore say, without impropriety, that the quality forms part of its signification..." J. S. Mill, *A System of Logic,* Bk. I, ch. II, No. 4. "The only names which are unsusceptible of definition, because their meaning is unsusceptible of analysis, are the names of the simple feelings themselves. These are in the same condition as proper names. They are not indeed, like proper names, unmeaning; for the words *sensation of white* signify that the sensation which I so denominate resembles other sensations which I remember to have had before and to have called by that name. But as we have no words by which to recall those former sensations, except the very word which we seek to define or some other which, being exactly synonymous with it, requires definition as much, words cannot unfold the signification of this class of names, and we are obliged to make a direct appeal to the personal experience of the individual whom we address." *Ibid.,* Bk. I, ch. VII, No. 2.

[6] "Man evinces reflection when the power of his soul acts so freely that it can segregate from the whole ocean of sensation surging through all his senses *one* wave, as it were; and that it can stay this wave, draw attention to it, and be aware of this attention. He evinces reflection when from the whole wavering dream of images rushing through his senses he can collect himself into a moment of waking, dwell on *one* image spontaneously. observe it ... and abstract characteristics showing him that *this* and no other is the object. Thus he evinces reflection ... when he can *recognize* one or several ... distinctive qualities ... Now by what means did this recognition come about? Through a characteristic ... which, as an element of consciousness, presented itself clearly ... This initial character of consciousness was the language of the soul. With this, human language is created." Herder, *Uber den Ursprung der Sprache* (1772), "Werke," ed. Suphan, V, 34 ff., translated in E. Cassirer, *An Essay on Man,* (New Haven, Yale Univ. Press, 1944), p. 40.

Thus we have two pictures of the workings of language : one, the first, easy thing to think when we make our earliest attempts to theorize in terms of a simple model which the details suggest. And immediately we are in trouble. Still yearning for theoretical simplicity, we adopt the other as a refuge from the confusions of the first. But it brings new, and even stranger difficulties. Both pictures split my dealings with the world into two parts. In the first, the part which I see, or do not see, eat, kick and bump against, is waiting to be confronted. I confront it in the way of any other animal : I perceive it. Language, an implement of civilization, has been invented to aid my intercourse with the things and events of the world. As my ancestors before me, I notice things and events, and rebaptise them for my own use with the names they gave me. That two things are the same, for example, is simply a fact presented to my animal eyes; and once this fact is observed, I naturally use the same name for each.

In the second picture, the split is made in a different place. The senses are brought in on the side of language. What is on the other side is outside our reach completely. Language is like a television screen upon which insensible beams and signals form a familiar picture. The invisible beams represent the "physical world" as it affects my sense organs : it is nothing to a human being, nothing understandable until brought to focus upon the screen of language. According to this story, I do not see that two things are the same until I can use the words "same" and "different." Thus, same and different, red and yellow, I, and the things I see, come into existence together. This picture is more sophisticated : it takes a long time to work out the details. It challenges the philosophical mind to exciting work. Its difficulties, while deeper, are more apparent. This picture forces us to talk about what the world is "in reality" : it is not furnished with the mountains, trees, flowers, colors we see. (We must not be confounded into thinking of molecules, atoms, or electrons here.) At the same time it takes away all possibility of saying what things are "really" like. By this picture we are led very quickly to say what cannot be said. It is not easy to find the way out of this philosophical dilemma. It is worth remembering that both these pictures result from the idea that words must be used to refer to things in virtue of their common and peculiar characteristics. That idea requires continual re-examination. If we could see that we should say neither "yes" or "no" to that, perhaps we could accept language as the pefectly natural thing that it is.

What we were after philosophically was some summary way to put the essential thing about language. We think it has to do with meaning; and in turn we think that somehow, through meaning, language is connected with reality. How could it be other than this: that we give the same words to things which have the same observable features? We must take note that these features may not be the same in all things denoted by the same word. We give the same word to many things which are related to each other in many different ways ("family resemblances"). But this is a superficial correction. It leaves us still with the idea that words are essentially connected to things because of observed similarities of things. We are left with the source of our trouble. Much more philosophical talk is needed. As a guide to the talk, we could say, "Language is connected to reality the way language is connected to reality," but this is a tired and unhelpful philosophical joke.

In the meantime, perhaps, we can restrain our inclinations to think either picture by returning to the details of the imaginary experiment with Bennett. In truth, I simply do not know what a blind man who has gained his sight would do or say. If he were to say anything when pressed with philosophical questions, I would not know what to make of his answers. "This (red) and that (red) are the same color," we shall say to him. "This (red) and that (blue) are different. Now pick the ones the same color as this (red)." I suppose he would quickly do it right. Does he see that each of the reds is red? Will he say, "I see what color that is: it is red. And I see that is red, and that too"? I suppose if he did say this it would be to delight and revel in his new powers of vision. It surely would not be to mark something that he noticed in the way we often do. A person has been sitting back in a deep sofa for an evening of drinks and conversation. The sofa faces an old granite fireplace with a rough chestnut mantle. "I just saw for the first time what has been right before my eyes all evening: the worm marks in that old chestnut mantle make the word 'Peace.'"

The reds are alike, and the red and yellows different. I wanted to say that Bennett notices this, or learns to notice it. But that is not something one can notice. He will not learn to notice that all the reds are red; he will come to notice that all the balls manufactured today are red, or that the willow leaves are yellow, and this only August. It is not right to say that he sees likenesses and differences before he knows the color words. I have no doubt a deaf-and-dumb man, one who has not yet learned sign-language, could learn to pick strawberries, pulling the red ones, leaving the green. It is not right to say one cannot see likenesses or differences in color until he knows the words. It is certainly not right to say: in nature or in reality there is not a difference between red and yellow; that comes only with language.

Bennett, the blind man who gains his sight, was to be me. He was to be all of us, looking fresh upon the world of colors. Through him we were to see the connection of our language with reality. And he is all of us. After he learns the color words, he will speak as we do. By "same color" he will refer to the color chip and the wall, or to the feel of the ocean and the sky. He will say the saturated colors have the property of commanding attention, and the colors of a rainbow a quality of depth. He will not forget that he was once blind, but after a while no one would guess it from talking to him.

II

SEEING THINGS

There used to be some interesting problems about perception, problems about how we can gain knowledge of the "physical world" from the thin data given to our senses. How are "physical objects" related to sense-data? How do people form a public world out of private data? These problems have been banished from the realm of philosophy by recent criticisms of sense-data. The main criticism of sense-data has been this: we must talk of them as if they were objects, but we do not want them to be objects. This is a devastating criticism, yet sometimes we are uneasy about it. We are not convinced that it is final and conclusive. The problems of perception need not be about the relations of physical objects to the objects (or nonobjects) given. We think that we could restate the problems as concerned with the relations between what we say about physical things and what we say about the sense-given. What we say at any one time about the sense-given need not be broken into subject and object: it could simply be taken as a whole, simple, unanalyzable thing said. As opposed, therefore, to the things we say and write about the "outer," "physical" furniture of the world, we need only to envision some things we could say or write which are confined to the direct evidence given to us when we perceive physical things.

These things we might say or write would have to play a role in a philosophical theory of perception analogous to the role played by "sense-datum" statements." They would seldom, perhaps never, be statements. They would simply be some thing we might say or write. The president makes a statement to the press. The doctor sends statements to his patients. Still it will not hurt, I suppose, to use the word "statement." I shall do so, then, and disavow any of the logico-philosophical associations it has gained—along with its companion word "proposition." So for simplicity I shall refer to the things we might say or write about the given in perception as "statements of immediate experience."

Then we need to see when and how we can make a statement of immediate experience. We know what role it is to play in a theory of perception. We know the kinds of questions we want to ask about it and its relations to the things we say about physical things. In order to determine when and how we might make such a statement it may help to set out the conditions it would have to fulfill:

(1) It must concern what we experience now, in the present; and it must be confined to the present in such a way that one cannot think it mistaken because of anything which happens afterward or on the basis of anything which happened before. I shall refer to a statement which meets this condition as one which is "insulated in time."[1]

(2) Some statements of immediate experience will concern objects. If a statement is of this kind, it must not imply anything about the material existence of its object: (a) it must not imply that the object exists in the material world. Also it must not imply that the object does not exist in the material world. (b) Nothing that is known about physical things and happenings (including human bodies and their changes) can be relevant to the correctness of a statement of immediate experience. I shall call a statement meeting these conditions "physical object neutral."

(3) It must, as philosophers generally say, be "private." By this they seem to mean it must not in any way be subject to correction, emendation, reinforce-

[1] This is very hard to state succinctly and accurately. One might once have said something or written something in a diary. He might have thought he was "describing immediate experience"—whatever that comes to. Now, many years later, he could be reminded of what he had said or he could be shown the page of his old diary. At this later time he could call it into question in many ways. (a) He might now think he had been drunk or temporarily out of his mind when he said or wrote the thing. He would now wonder whether anything could be made out of what he had said or written. Although he might question what he had said in this way, he would not find it mistaken. The main thing here is to bring out that a "statement of immediate experience" cannot be mistaken in the usual ways. The speaker or writer cannot have got it wrong. (b) Years later he may come to think he had been joking or lying. He now decides that his "statement" was not true. He has *not* determined that he was mistaken or that he got it wrong.

[This is the oldest essay in the collection. (At least the first version of it was.) I now regret very much having taken on so much heavy philosophical baggage here in the beginning of it. Had I been more skillful, perhaps I could have made these conditions emerge one by one as less jargon-filled discussions called for them. I am now quite incapable of trying.]

ment, or corroboration by anyone other than the person making the state-ment. (Although it may in certain cases be subject to correction by the person himself. "Statements of immediate experience" do not need to be absolutely incorrigible.[2])

(4) It would have to be such that it is in some way implied by statements like "I see X" where X is a physical object. In what way it is implied remains an open question, indeed one of the main questions to be answered by philo-sophical inquiry, but in any case it must be implied in such a way that it con-stitutes in normal cases:

(5) Part of the evidence for a claim that I see a physical object, that is, when taken with other statements of immediate experience or with statements about physical objects.

We must now find some statements which either fulfill these conditions or else come close to satisfying the conditions. Philosophers who have given an analysis of perception have suggested many areas where such statements could be found. They have called attention to occasions on which people are extra-ordinarily cautious about saying what they see, or to situations in which people are subject to perceptual errors, illusions, hallucinations. They have appealed to our understanding of familiar idioms such as "looks like," "appears to be," "has the appearance of," and have directed attention to Macbeth's talk to his dagger, to experiences of seeing spots before the eyes, and other perceptual situations where no "physical object" is being seen.

I shall try to get this suggested rehabilitation of the theory of perceptual knowledge off to a start by looking as closely as I can at one group of state-ments which philosophers have sometimes supposed were statements of imme-diate experience, or else supposed were very much like them. These statements are the ones which we make using a certain sense of the verb "to see," a sense we are told which does not imply that any physical object is seen. In that sense we can use the word "see" correctly even when our eyes are closed and we know that they are closed. Macbeth's question, "Is this a dagger which I see before me?" is frequently cited as an example of this use of "see." I shall try to pursue the inquiry in such a way that, if these statements do not fulfill all the requirements, it can be seen where and how they fail. So that we may learn

2 The types of self-correction permissible are discussed on pages 43-45 of this Essay.

to produce the required statements by changing the meanings of certain words, or by introducing whatever new terms are called for.

In what sort of perceptual situation can I find an example of this use of "see"? Suppose that I am well-known among my friends for keeping an odd assortment of many pets: a gibbon, two crows, several squirrels, and a black skunk. I give these animals the run of the house. Now suppose I have contrived that a group of lights and shadows will fall across the bottom of my large living room wall in such a way that they give the appearance of several rats running back and forth. I seat an old friend at the proper place in the room and ask, "Do you notice anything new?" "Why, you have some new pets," he says. "They're rats and they look red." Now I turn on the ceiling lights and banish the illusion. Suppose he comments, "I saw rats there—red rats—as clearly as anything!" What he says will not do as an example of the requisite use of "see," because it comes very close to "I would have sworn I saw red rats," that is, it comes close to being an amazed exclamation that he thought he saw—in a sense of "see" which implies there were red rats there. Also, he did not speak about the present.

Now I shall dim the lights again, and ask what he sees. "It's amazing," he says. "I see red rats moving about there next to the wall." The trouble with this is that it is so very close to, "It looks exactly like there are red rats there." It is very close to a statement about the way things look, one which does not have the required privacy. I could walk over behind him and agree, "Yes, startling, isn't it? It looks exactly like red rats."

Suppose now that when the lights go up again, and I say, "Now they're gone," he looks very puzzled and says incredulously, "But I still see them there." Is this the example I want? Not yet: he may be making a mistake. I again take a position behind him and say, "I don't understand. The illusion is gone." Suppose, in a tone of some alarm he repeats, "But I still see them." Is this what I want? I can't tell; as I said, I do not understand. Is the illusion different for one who does not know exactly how it is created? Is it more difficult to dispel? Is he beginning to believe there are real rats there? Is he having an hallucination? An hallucination seems the only thing that will give me the right use of "see." When a person suffers certain perceptual aberrations, when he "sees things" he knows are not there, he could tell what he sees without implying that there were any physical things.

Let's suppose that this experience begins my friend on a career of hallucination. From now on I shall call him Ellis. This delusion in my house was his first unnerving, fearful experience—with red rats. This first experience will not give me the right use of "see." While suffering his first hallucination, if he said "I see rats," he would think he saw rats. He would be horribly wrong. He probably would be quite upset. I might try to show him again that there were no rats, but it would do no good.

I must imagine that he continues to see those rats off and on over a long period of time. He consults doctors and gets no help. He adjusts to an occasional run of "seeing red rats," as a rheumatic does to his pains and stiffness in the joints. He learns to live with it and make of it the best he can. He comes to make very sophisticated remarks about the red rats he sees. I shall suppose he remains my friend, and I learn all about his recurrent experiences and his attitude toward them. One day, I am walking along the street with him, and he says, "Oh, I see those red rats again." Is this, at last, the required use of "see"? Will this remark do as a statement of immediate experience? I must find out exactly what he is saying. Couldn't he, a few minutes later, say— maybe with relief—"I was wrong. I didn't see the rats again"? Also maybe, "I thought I saw those rats again. It was just like it." Suppose he had a few red spots before his eyes, and he thought he recognized the symptoms of an onset of the usual hallucination. Then the hallucination does not come, and the red spots disappear—instead of becoming red rats. Surely in this case, a person would say, "I *thought* I saw rats" (where he now knows there were no rats). If so, what he says anticipates certain future developments and is not properly "insulated in time." Can I really imagine Ellis saying, "I see red rats," without any expression of fright or bewilderment? If not, then I who am his friend, when I see that the usual following expressions or symptoms are not forthcoming, may be in a position to suggest, "I guess you didn't see the rats after all. You must have been mistaken." In this case, his statement will not be properly private in order to qualify as a statement of immediate experience.

And I who make the suggestion am not regarding the statement as physical object neutral.

I have not yet found the right example. His tone of voice and his behavior must be a little different, and he must say a little more. Calmly he says to me, "I see those red rats again. The sidewalk is covered with them and they are jumping up and down in a crazy dance." He walks right on with no hesitations, no signs of bewilderment. Now, what is he saying? He is talking to me, but what is he telling me? At least, he is surely informing me that he is having one of his spells of abnormal vision. To the extent that he is letting me know of his abnormal state, he is not making a statement of immediate experience.

All right, he is letting me know that he is having one of his bad perceptual times. But I want to say he is not *telling* me that. Primarily and directly, he is talking about what is given to him in immediate experience. He informs me of his defect *by way* of certain statements of fact: the facts of immediate experience. I want to get at these direct, primary statements of fact. I want to isolate them, to examine them by themselves. I feel that there is some informational core hidden away in what they say. It seems terribly difficult to strip away the secondary and indirect and get down to the primary and direct element in communications like these.

But why should it be difficult? What I seem to have in mind here is the most common of things. He is telling me something, citing a fact—for *some purpose,* some purpose which can be achieved by citing that fact. All I am thinking of here is that facts are stated for some point or reason. When someone states a fact and the point is not clear, we ask, "Why did you tell me that?" Many, many different kinds of answers can be given in order to re-establish understanding. I may tell my mechanically-inclined neighbor that my car won't start this morning in order to get him to help me with it. I may tell my boss the same thing in order to let him know I will be late for work, or in order to excuse myself for being late. Again, I may tell the man who sold me a battery just last week the same thing for still another purpose. When I tell my neighbor that my car won't start, in addition to that primary fact, I obliquely inform him that I want his help. When I tell my boss about my car, I indirectly inform him that I shall be late for work. To the battery salesman I indicate that I suspect his product.

It is by analogy with the car-trouble case that I want to construe Ellis's words. Here is a kind of tandem-telling: One fact stated directly in order to inform someone of another. I say my car won't start in order to inform my boss that I'll be late. Ellis says he sees red rats in order to inform me he is having a spell of hallucination. I tell my neighbor that my car won't start. He infers I want his help. Ellis is telling me about his experience. I want by analogy to say that I infer he is having an hallucination, but the cases are not parallel. Why do I think that I can't isolate Ellis's red-rat fact as I can the fact that my car won't start? For one thing, I cannot *infer* that Ellis is having an hallucination. I do not learn that he is having an hallucination the way I learn from seeing the milkman with his cheeks red and his ear-muffs on that it must be cold outside. "It must be cold outside," I say to him as he comes into the hall. I do not say to Ellis, "You must be having one of your spells again." If Ellis had not spoken to me, but oblivious to my presence, had gasped, "Red rats," then I *might* infer that he was having a spell. I might ask, with concern, "Are you having one of those hallucinations?" Secondly, the two statements can't be misunderstood in the same ways. I call my boss and say, "My car won't start." He says, "That's too bad, Frank, but why are you telling me that?" "I want you to know, Brian, that I'll be late for work." "What happened to your calendar, Frank? This is Sunday, and I'm down here only because I couldn't get all my letters written on Friday." There is no analogous context-mistake for Ellis's remark. When could one say to Ellis in a similar way, "That's an interesting fact, but why are you telling me?" The boss can understand the fact I state, but not know why I told him. I cannot understand what Ellis says without understanding the reason for his saying it. If anyone does not get Ellis's point in saying, "I see rats," or if anyone misunderstands it, he simply could not understand what Ellis was talking about.

I can't detach the informational core of Ellis's remark from its point; I can't understand what the one is without the other. What leads me to say I can get at the primary information given by "My car won't start" is exactly what leads me to say that the same fact can be cited for many different reasons. I can see what the fact is in the one case, just because I see that it would be the same in others. I can't state it in complete independence; I can't state the information for no point at all. An absolutely pointless utterance is an absolutely incomprehensible one. While I am philosophizing, I can say, " Common to all the car-trouble cases is the same piece of information, the fact that my car won't start this morning." But I can give this no interpretation except on the basis of my understanding that a speaker of English can say "My car won't start . . . " in the circumstances I have mentioned, and in many, many more circumstances somewhat like these. When philosophizing, I may think that when I say, "My car won't start," I am primarily stating a fact about my car. I do not mean one can say something just anywhere or anytime and make sense. I only mean that since there are lots of reasons why certain people might want to know about my car troubles, regardless of which reason anyone has, I can say to him, "My car won't start," because that is the truthful and pointed thing to tell him.

If I am to isolate a statement of immediate experience behind its point, or behind the secondary information it conveys about perceptual defect, I need to see that the same information can stand behind several different points. The hallucinator Ellis might say, and say truthfully, "I see red rats," in order (1) to frighten away a nuisance, (2) to excuse himself from continuing a conversation, or (3) to get sympathy from a very stern teacher. However, these examples will not serve to isolate the statement of immediate experience from its communication of perceptual abnormality because it could not accomplish the various things without conveying that the speaker was again having an hallucination. The statement of immediate experience seems securely attached to this point. I cannot think of examples which will enable me to detach it.

Perhaps I am having this trouble isolating a statement of immediate experience because the description was not sufficiently elaborate or complete. Ellis didn't say enough. Suppose he says, "I see those red rats again—running all over the sidewalk." I've now got the point that he is having a bad perceptual spell. So he goes on. He wouldn't go on to make the same point again. He continues, "Now some of the rats are turning green. This is unusual: they are fading away, rear end first, into the sidewalk." Would he be informing me that this is a more severe or a different kind of spell? In order to get away from that interpretation, I shall ask him questions, prying but friendly questions. "What do they look like?" "Well," he might say, "they are queer. They are always a little blurred, never have distinct edges. They are blurred now, and the red ones have a pink halo-like fringe."

Let's assume he is saying this—honestly and sincerely, of course—in order to amuse me or to satisfy my puckish curiosity. Now *that* is a different point. One can tell the truth, describe something honestly—just to entertain or to satisfy curiosity. Although I succeed only in boring people, I tell them what I saw in my travels with the intention to entertain. This comparison inclines me to ask about the description of red rats, just what facts does it tell me? What is the information about? But these questions are not allowed; I am not trying to dissect immediate experience into lumps or sense-data; I am not trying to find out what such statements are about. I am just told facts about what is given in the hallucination; or better, I am just given something said about immediate experience. That telling about nonexistent red rats is not like telling about my car trouble is no objection to telling about nonexistent red rats.

Still I do not feel satisfied that I have isolated the statement. I have not found it behind many points, only behind two; and it's not behind them in the same way. The first point is to let me know of the spell of perceptual delusions; the second is to entertain. But I can be entertained only if I know his words result from a benign delusion, only if I know they are the outcome of this special kind of abnormal perception. What Ellis says can accomplish the second only if the first has been accomplished. I need to find two points in parallel, but these are in series. So, I can not isolate what Ellis says about his immediate experience as I can isolate what I say about my car trouble. I have not found Ellis's description behind even two different points on a par, and so I haven't been able to get the statement right myself.

Maybe my demands are unfair, maybe I'm assuming that there *ought* to be rats to tell about—nonexistent rats to describe. Ellis did not cite a fact about rats as I did about my car. He said, "I see red rats," and this tells me about his disease; or if I already understand all about his perceptual ailment, he can say this to amuse me. For a parallel case I should have considered, "I *see* my car has a flat tire." Now I *could* say this to someone—someone who was suspicious about my eyesight—in order to let him know that my vision is normal. This could be the point of my saying it. And I could also say it for the other points; the other points could be made only if people had no doubts about my eyesight.

Even so, if there were suspicions about my eyesight, I could quickly allay them. And the suspicions having once been put away, I would be free to say, "I see my car has a flat tire." I could say this in making many different points, and I could say that what was common to the different utterances was the information that I see the flat tire. If I did not understand that Ellis was "seeing things," he could let me know, and then he could go on to answer my questions with the strange details about rats with pink fringes. Still I cannot isolate this fact, "seeing rats," behind different points because there is only one point—to amuse me. At any rate I cannot think of another.

Still, isn't this unfair? I have given up the search for any private entities and with it, presumably, the picture that statements of immediate experience are descriptions of anything. But I persist in trying to isolate some statement behind what Ellis says. Now I see that this also is illegitimate. My desire to isolate something comes entirely from my slavery to analogy. I expect there to be isolable statements "of the given" as there are such statements about cars, or planes, or what I see in the neighbor's garden. I am surprised that there are none. But why should there be? Statements of immediate experience are just what they are, and none the worse for not being analyzable in terms of bits of information. Henceforth the statement I must consider is the whole of what Ellis says in some situation in its entirety.

Yet there is something I have overlooked. I am not allowed to say that there is nothing that can be done with statements of immediate experience except entertain, or satisfy idle curiosity. If that were so, they would not satisfy requirements (4) and (5): they must be implied as part of the cash-value of claims to see physical things, and they must be capable of being cited as part of the evidence in claims to see physical things. So my desire to find separable statements of the given is not dictated entirely by some illegitimate analogy: it is given in the very requirements for a statement of immediate experience. Now I am at an impasse. Nothing like Ellis's talk about seeing red rats is implied by talk about seeing real grain-eating rats around the silo. He would never say something about "seeing red rats" or anything like that in support of a claim that he sees rats leaving a quarantined ship.

This is not surprising, because Ellis's talk is about "wild data." I need to make sure that something like what he says satisfies the other conditions.

Then perhaps I can make the changes necessary to assure that the data are not wild. In order to see what changes might be necessary, I must consider someone who says something like Ellis, but he must not be hallucinating and he must not think he is hallucinating. But I have already discovered that such things as Ellis says cannot be said in more normal situations. If I am to get something to satisfy the first three conditions (that is, to be insulated in time, to be physical object neutral, and to be private), I cannot take what Ellis says at the occurrence of his first hallucination because that is about the physical world. I cannot take his later "I see rats again," because that is expectant of future developments, and tells me that he is having an abnormal visual spell. I must take his whimsical fairy-story-like answers to questions. But I can understand these only if I know he is having his strange visual experiences.

Maybe that is too strong. I would not need to know that the *particular* experience was abnormal. I would need only to know that the person was frequently subject to hallucination and had adjusted to it. It is enough if the person thinks he is seeing rats or pink snakes, and tells me that he is seeing things. This could all be so even if he were not hallucinating at all. How could I arrange such a situation? Having already learned that Ellis sees red rats with fuzzy pink edges, I obtain some white rats, dye them red, and glue bits of pink Christmas-tree "snow" to their backs. I turn them loose in a room, and dimly light them from behind so they appear to have pink halos. Now I bring Ellis into an adjacent room—pour him tea containing some mild drug which will make him slightly giddy—and at the proper moment have him turn and look through the doorway into the dim room containing the rats. Suppose he says, as on former occasions, "I see those red rats again." As before I ask him about them, and he tells me, "They appear very fuzzy, with pink glowing rims around their backs. I see about a dozen of them."

Of course he is not claiming to see my dyed rats with pink fuzz glued on. Quite the contrary, he thinks he is "seeing things." I want to know whether the sort of thing he says is implied by a claim to see physical objects. I want to know whether what he says about "seeing those red rats" would be implied by any claim he might make to see real red rats. I must imagine what the logical situation would be (this is a supposal within a supposal) if he were to say, "I see real red rats." Well, I *will* imagine that; I am afraid I shall have to play another rat trick on poor Ellis. I walk into the next room, pick up one of the rats by the tail, and bring it in to him. What will he say? Most likely he will faint or scream. But since I am imagining so much, I'll imagine that the drug in his tea makes him calm, and he catches on right away. He appreciates that my rat experiments with him have come full circle. I cannot think of his saying anything except, "Oh, I *wasn't* seeing things after all. I was wrong. I was *really seeing* red rats." So what he said about really seeing rats does not imply that he sees (nonexistent) red rats. Quite the contrary, it shows that he was wrong in thinking that he was seeing those red rats again. And of course, if I ask him how he knows he is really seeing rats, he would not think of saying, "Part of the evidence is seeing those queer old (nonexistent) rats." So what he says will not qualify for conditions (4) and (5).

Worse than that. Now it is clear that what he says will not qualify for (1), (2), and (3). What happened later showed him wrong. What happened in the next room showed him wrong. What he said was not insulated in time and it was not physical object neutral. And, of course, I knew he was wrong all the time and was prepared to show him that he was. So what he said was not properly private. I have come to the sad conclusion that such things as he says will not qualify as statements of immediate experience in any way. Also, I have managed to get a likely statement to consider—one that did not inform me of some perceptual abnormality—only by letting it be understood that Ellis was perceptually abnormal. But when it is understood that Ellis is perceptually abnormal, then what he says implies there are no rats. I mean to say here the sort of thing a logician might say. Ellis said, "I see red rats." He discovers there are rats; then he says he was wrong. Discovery of the existence of red rats shows that when he said, "I see those red rats," he was mistaken. Therefore, what he said "implied" that there were no rats.

This is the critical weakness with the red-rat statement, that it implies there are no red rats and so is not physical object neutral. There is asimilar statement which philosophers have supposed not to have this failing. Philosophers quote Macbeth's question, "Is this a dagger which I see before me?" as something close to a statement of immediate experience. One difficulty here is that it is a question and cannot qualify as a statement. Perhaps G. E. Moore's comments explain how this is supposed to yield a statement of immediate experience:

Macbeth is represented by Shakespeare as having directly seen an "object" (though of course not a physical object ...) to which he referred by the word "this" and about which he asked, "Is *this* which I see before me a dagger ?"[3]

Moore entertains the possibility of a statement like "This is either a delusive dagger or a real one." This statement is not to imply that there is a dagger, and it is not to imply that there is not a dagger. Thus it will be physical object neutral. The trouble is, any such statement of Macbeth's would be thought of in this way only by someone who had a philosophical theory of sense-data, or immediately given objects. In more aseptic terms, Macbeth seems to be represented by Shakespeare as being in serious doubt as to whether he is having an hallucination or not. Macbeth suspects that he may be "seeing a dagger," that he may just be seeing things. Poetic considerations aside, he might be asking, "Am I just seeing a dagger or do I see a dagger?" He does not know whether he should say, "I am 'seeing' a dagger," or "I see a dagger." Therefore the statement he might make which gives the presumption behind the question is "I am seeing a (nonexistent) dagger or I see a strange dagger here before me."

Now I do feel inclined to think that what he says implies either that there is or is not a physical object, and this is the same as not implying anything about physical objects. His statement is not dependent upon whether any object does or does not exist. But I am misguided. Macbeth makes no assertion. He tortures himself with a question, "Is there a dagger ... or is my brain oppressed by heat?" It is fantastic to imagine him expressing some kind of logical neutrality, "Well, one or the other; no matter which." He wants nothing more than to be in a position to say which. Even if Macbeth is fantastically represented as asserting this disjunction, "either dagger or hallucination," it could not be used as a logic-textbook example of a "tautology" because it clearly implies something about the material world. It implies something about the material world because each of the disjuncts implies something about the material world. The first implies that the material world contains a dagger here, the second implies that it does not contain a dagger here. Since either of these implications disqualifies its implicants as a statement of immediate experience—each fails to satisfy condition (2)—the disjunction as a whole is disqualified.[4]

[3] G. E. Moore, "A Reply to My Critics." *The Philosophy of G. E. Moore*, (Evanston, Northwestern Univ. Press, 1942), p. 630.
[4] I discuss this at greater length on pages 35-39.

The thing we are inclined to put into Macbeth's mouth is a tempting candidate just because it suggests Moore's analysis, and because as it stands it seems not to depend upon whether a dagger exists or not. On the same point, Ayer says:

> In the sense in which I now have this piece of paper in sight, it can equally well be said of Macbeth that he had his dagger in sight. If we are to speak for this purpose of having things in sight, the expression must be understood in such a way that the existence of the physical object which appears to be referred to remains an open question: There is no implication either that it does exist or that it does not.[5]

If forced to consider Macbeth's statement in its expanded form, "Either I am seeing a dagger, or I see a dagger," there is an inclination to want to go on and say, "In any case, I am ——" What is wanted is a phrase for the blank, a perceptual verb together with the word "dagger" which has the required features. Ayer fills it in with "having a dagger in sight," a phrase which he thinks can be used to describe immediate experience. Of course, if this is meant to be equivalent to Macbeth's statement, it will not do. If it is not equivalent, it is hard to see how Macbeth's statement can be of any use in teaching how to use it. This must be a statement of immediate experience. Macbeth's is not; it is not clear that it fills any of the requirements.

Yet I still want to say that Macbeth—before resolving his doubt—was having some perceptual experience, and that if he had described that, it would have been a description of the given. The experience was neutral as to whether there was or was not a dagger. But what is it that I want? I already know how to describe that experience: it was one of doubt as to whether he was or was not seeing a dagger. I feel somehow that the doubt should not figure in the experience. It should be what is experienced (doubtfully). What can that be except what Macbeth was in doubt about? And what he was in doubt about was whether he was or was not seeing a dagger, whether he was or was not having an hallucination.

Even so, I have a philosopher's feeling that Macbeth's question is close to what is immediately given. Maybe a reply which answers his question is not, but the question is. There is something in some way before him, and it is not clearly

[5] A. J. Ayer, *The Problem of Knowledge* (Baltimore, Penguin Books, 1956), p .101.

either a physical object or "...a false creation, proceeding from the heat-oppressed brain." One who is subject to delusive spells like Macbeth's might indeed ask such a question. Ellis might sometimes ask, "Are those real rats?" He might blink his eyes, change his position—or reach to make a tactual test. He might even call in someone else. I feel inclined to ask Moore's philosophical question, "What is it that you are *referring* to by the word "these,' when you ask 'Are these red rats?'"

As soon as I think of asking Ellis, the philosophical spell of the question is dissipated. I ask, "What were you referring to by 'these'?" He says, "That is exactly what I was asking. Now that you are here you can tell me. Are there any rats there on the floor?" "Yes, there are," I say. "Two of my joke-rats must have escaped." So, what he was referring to were these two dyed rats, and they are not samples of immediate experience. He didn't know what he was referring to. It was rats; it could have been rats he saw while suffering hallucination. Never for a moment did he think of a third possibility, something that encompassed "seeing red rats" and was part of seeing real rats.

MORE ELABORATE HALLUCINATIONS

If Macbeth's question will not qualify, perhaps a similiar question will. Macbeth asks, in effect, "Do I see a dagger or am I hallucinating?" If he were to comment calmly on his dilemma, I imagine that he would say, "I am seeing a nonexistent dagger, or I see a strange dagger here before me." One thing: some such comment might satisfy condition (5), that is, that comment or a similar one might be made in giving evidence that there was a dagger suspended in the air (perhaps by a thin wire).

Since there is no way of finding out about Macbeth's frame of mind, I had better return to my own fabricated example. Suppose then that Ellis were to make a similar comment. It has been demonstrated to Ellis that in certain situations he cannot tell whether he is hallucinating red rats or whether he sees red rats. Imagine him in such a situation: he says, "I either see red rats there, or I am seeing red rats." Suppose Ellis has just wandered into my living room, looking for me, and in the usual place he has this now-familiar experience: he either sees my red rats or he has his usual hallucination. Before he can decide, he is called away. His wife calls in alarm, and he hurries off to take care of a family emergency. Later I say to him, "My red rats have escaped from their cage. Have you seen them?" He replies, "They may be in your living room. I was there a little while ago, and either I saw them, or I was hallucinating, I don't know which." Here, "either I saw them or I was hallucinating" is taken as providing some evidence that there were rats there. So it satisfies condition (5).

But does it satisfy any of the other conditions? What about (4): is it "implied" by comments about red rats? I say to Ellis, "My red rats must have escaped. I just saw them romping in the corner of my living room." What will Ellis now reply? Suppose he says, "Ah. Then I did *see* your red *rats* when I was there." When Ellis thinks this over will he agree that his "I did see your red rats" implies his "I either saw or hallucinated your red rats"? The only reason that Ellis knew he saw rats is that he was assured rats were there at the time he was either seeing or hallucinating. He *concluded* that he saw red rats. He reasoned, "When I either see or hallucinate and red rats are there, I see." And I want to know whether he can correctly reason, "When I see, then either I hallucinate or see." Since "I see" in this case amounts mostly to "Either I hallucinate or see and rats are there," then from "I see" perhaps "Either I hallucinate or see" follows in the required way. A "statement of immediate experience" ought to follow from "I see" in the normal sense. Normally we do not *conclude* that we see. Ellis has no visual abnormalities in connection with dogs. He has absolutely no reason to question his ability to see dogs as does everyone else. When Ellis says, "I see my dog coming up the walk," does this imply "I either see or hallucinate my dog"? If it implies anything relevant, his "I see" in this case surely implies "I am not hallucinating." It would imply "I see or I hallucinate" only in the logician's curious sense, that is, it "implies" this only because it "implies" itself, and because any alternation is correct if one of its alternates is correct. But that is not Ellis's kind of alternation. I doubt whether it is anyone's kind. Ellis would not have much of a problem if that was all there was to his alternation. What Ellis says when he says, "I either see or I am hallucinating," is surely not implied by "I see." His alternation means, "Either I see or I hallucinate. I can't tell which." Not only is this not implied by "I see," it is inconsistent with it. ("I see but I can't tell whether I see or hallucinate.") Ellis's alternation is not implied: but we feel that if we could collapse the alternation somehow and weaken it we would get to a comment on a "visual experience." Thus we would get a statement implied by "I see." We need a report on the "experience" one is supposed to have even when he sees in the normal way: "I had a red rat visual experience." Suppose Ellis says, "Ah. Then I did *see* your red rats when I was there." In order to get a "statement of immediate experience," we must somehow collapse the disjunction into a comment on a visual experience: "I had a red-rat visual experience. I don't know what kind." The problem is to find a situation in which it is clear that Ellis can do that.[6]

Ellis has become accustomed to the idea that he cannot tell whether he is seeing rats or whether he sees real red rats. One time when he is hallucinating rats, I shall release some red rats upon the rug before his eyes. "There," I shall tell him, "I've just put two rats where you can see them." He says "I count six in all, and I can't tell which I see and which I'm hallucinating. One is climbing the lamp cord. Is that a real one?" No," I say. "One is now washing his face. Is he real?" "Yes," "I simply can't tell which is which."

Now I will give him a philosophically-loaded directive, "Tell me what you see." Suppose he starts, "I see six red rats. They are all about the same size. One is sniffing at the edge of the rug; another is climbing the lamp cord . . ." How will this do as a statement of immediate experience? In saying, "I see six red rats," he seems to be using a perceptual verb in the required neutral way, that is, he does not imply that there are red rats, and also does not imply that there are not. Does this meet the conditions? If there were two red rats there, he would expect to "see" at least two red rats. It seems to meet condition (4). "Were there any red rats there?" I might ask. He could reply, "I don't know for sure, but I 'saw' nine, and when I see more than six, there is a good chance some of them are real." So it seems to meet condition (5). What about the others? Here the difficulties begin. Suppose there are three rats in a line before him, and he says (using this presumed neutral sense of "see"), "I 'see' two rats." Now wouldn't I feel that I were in a position to say, "Look again, look carefully; you must see three"? Wouldn't I suspect that something was obscuring his vision? I might look over his shoulder to see whether one of the rats was hidden from his viewpoint. That is, I am questioning whether his report is

[6] Several of the lines pursued in this section were suggested to me by Mr. Ralph Davis.

"private," whether it meets condition (3). I tell him there are three rats there. Wouldn't he be disturbed? He has never before failed to see things clearly before his eyes. His visual world has at times been too rich, never too poor. When I inform him that there are three rats, would I destroy the possibility of his using "see" in the neutral sense? Would he now think that he was reporting on the rats on the rug, and be properly upset to find his report wrong?

If so, this presumed new verb "to see" has no life other than that given it by the mode of its introduction. I was fully informed of his hallucinations and his inability to distinguish real from delusive rats; and it was I who asked him to tell what he saw. It was to me that he replied, "I see six rats . . ." Perhaps I was the only person who could understand him; I was the only person to whom he could have spoken in this abbreviated way. I knew how to take his "see." When I am asking philosophical questions about his remarks, I must not forget that all this background is necessary to make his remarks understandable to me. If he tried to explain to someone else, it would take a long time. He would have to spell out everything I now take for granted. He would have to say, "I often hallucinate red rats, and I can't tell those rats I hallucinate from real ones. So there may be six rats there and I see them. I may be hallucinating the six rats. Or I may see some and hallucinate the others."

So what Ellis says comes to, "Either I see . . . or I am seeing . . ." I said that this would not meet condition (2) because it "implies something about the material world." Sometimes Ellis says, "I see red rats," implying that there are rats. Sometimes he says, "I am seeing red rats," implying that there are no red rats, implying that they are produced by his visual disorder. And sometimes he says, "Either I see . . . or I am seeing . . . : I don't know which." Each of the alternatives implies something about the existence of objects in the material world and hence the alternative as a whole implies something about the existence of objects in the material world.

I think that what I said is simply and obviously correct, but at the same time I feel discomfited, I feel a need to explain it. One alternative implies something definite about the existence of a physical object. The other alternative implies something else definite about the existence of that physical object. Hence the disjunction as a whole implies something definite about the existence of that physical object. Isn't that clear? But one alternative implies there are rats, the other implies there are no rats. So the implication of the disjunction is "Either there are rats or there are no rats." I am a bit uneasy about saying that this disjunction tells something definite about the existence of rats. Isn't it the sort of thing, a "tautology," which gives no information at all?

I think I am uneasy about this point because I am inclined here to misapply a partially-digested logic lesson. Logicians imagine that certain things can be said in pairs and that one of these things completely cancels the other: the result is nothing said at all. They symbolize the members of the pair as p and -p. If saying p is like drawing a cat on paper, then saying -p is like erasing it cleanly and completely—so that no sign of it remains. This way of talking logic and logical theory is easy to misunderstand. Logicians often say that p or -p " says nothing at all," or "tells nothing about the world, nothing about experience." This is not so of someone's saying, "Either there is a cat on the paper or it has been erased." I learn from him that either there is a cat there, or there once was—in any case, if I am really looking for a cat on paper, I ought to look *there*. Logicians do not want anything of that kind. They aren't talking about what is said, but about something else called a "proposition" which can be written in place of p and q, etc. (but it never is).

When we understand the logic lesson we give up the metaphor. If we misunderstand it, a better metaphor might help. Suppose I wire a complex machine to respond to a certain number of things I say to it. I say, "Mt. Whitney is less than 10,000 feet." The machine responds, "No. No." I say, "Mt. Rushmore is less than 10,000 feet." The machine says, "Yes.Yes." The "Yes.Yes." reply is like the logician's p; "No.No." is like the logician's -p. The machine can respond correctly to statements about the height of any mountain in North America. The machine can also answer arithmetic questions which involve no more than two numbers. Thus: "$x^2 = 4$. What is x?" The machine's reply: "$+2$ or -2." Now I say one of the things to which the machine can respond. "Mt. Shasta is over 10,000 feet." The machine replies "Yes.Yes. *or* No.No."

Someone who does not know the height of North American mountains can learn many things from the machine. But he can learn nothing from the "Yes. Yes. *or* No.No." reply. With those words the machine tells him nothing. The machine's designer would know that the machine had burnt out a transistor; but that is of no relevance in illustrating the logical point. Except perhaps that it bears some distant analogy with human communication. If a person could succeed in saying something "tautologous," he might be suspected of having burnt out some vital area in the brain's communication center.

Suppose I am trying to design a game in which a ball rolls into enclosures of many colors. There are difficulties with the design and an engineer tells me, "If you put an obstruction here, the ball will always go in the red. If you leave the obstruction out, the ball will always go in one of the other colors." This much is background to the example. Now I am about to play one ball, and I consider what will happen to it. I must have the obstruction in or I must have it out. Therefore, the ball will either go in the red or it will not go in the red. Either alternative is objectionable, so the alternation implies something objectionable. If I misapply my logic lesson here, I might become a pessimist. "Either alternative is bad, and I must live with one." But this is silly. I am not inclined to take "Either it will go in the red or not" as a "tautology." I am not inclined to think that "It will go in the red" can be torn out of context and become a "proposition" for the logic machine. I shall simply disqualify the game, tear it up, and design a new one. The same, I think, with the implication of Ellis's remark: "Either there are certainly rats, or there are certainly no rats." It simply disqualifies Ellis' remark as a statement of immediate experience, and I had better look for another one.

In fact, if the implication of Ellis' remark was, "Rats? Yes. Yes. *or* No. No." then his remark would have to be disqualified as a statement of immediate experience for that reason. For then it could never meet condition (5): it could never be evidence for a claim to see a physical object. I have already shown how Ellis's statement could provide some evidence that escaped rats were to be found in the living room. The sense-datum philosopher, if he thought of Ellis's remark as a sense-datum statement, would not be wrong in that way. He would not be wrong because it could not be taken as evidence for rats.

Suppose a man lost in the desert, tired and sick with thirst. He is aware that under such conditions people sometimes have hallucinations. He "sees" a small tree with a little puddle of water underneath. He says to himself, "Either I see water there or I am hallucinating." He would be silly, indeed, if he did not go to investigate. Unless he had gone mad he would not sit calmly saying, "Either there is water there or there is not. That's what I know, and so I know nothing at all. I shall waste no energy over it." He will rush to investigate because he knows the place to investigate, right there where he "sees" the water. And he has a little reason to think there is water at that spot. The same with Ellis, surely. He "sees" too many rats. When he picks out one of the rates and talks about it, he does not know whether that rat is real or hallucinatory. He must say, "Either I see it or I am seeing it." In saying, "Either there is a rat there or there is not," he has narrowed things down to *there*. His reason is poor, but he has some reason to believe there is a rat right there on the edge of the rug, starting now to climb the lamp cord. Along these lines, the only remarks Ellis could make which might "tell nothing about the world" would be remarks to the effect that there were rats everywhere, doing all sorts of things, and alligators and ferrets and flying fish. But then he would know that he was hallucinating, and so, in what he said, he would imply there were no such things. So Ellis's remark does imply that there may be a red rat *there*. This will not disqualify what he says as a statement of immediate experience.

There is another way of getting at the thing which disqualifies Ellis's remark. "I am seeing rats" implies there are no rats. But that is not all that it implies. "I am seeing rats" means I am hallucinating. It has the force it gains from the circumstances in which Ellis learned about his perceptual abnormalities. It implies, if you like, that there is something radically wrong with him in a visual way; though always a little upsetting, it is no longer misleading. Nothing in his visual field sets it off. He is not seeing something distorted or in a strange way. He sees things where there is nothing. Etc.

If we stick with the logical model and say now that "I see rats" implies c, then "I am seeing rats" does not imply not-c. If the model remains a source of confusion, one appropriate thing to say might be this: "I am seeing rats" does not imply not-c because it does not imply just that; it implies that and much more. Therefore it is wrong to represent the totality of its implications as not-c. So a or b does not imply c or not-c; a or b implies c or d, where d is the implicate of b; c and d together do not by any means exhaust the alternatives. And of course they do not. Ellis might see rats. He might hallucinate rats. Also he might see illusory rats. I shall project a moving picture of red rats in circumstances where Ellis will take the image for real rats. I arrange everything so that it is a genuine optical illusion. Now I show Ellis how it is done. He now knows the circumstances in which the illusion is apt to be produced. If I am not very careful, he will detect that I am producing an illusion. When he does, he will say "I see illusory rats" or "I see the rat illusion." Now I shall carefully arrange things so that he suspects, but cannot find out, whether or not I am producing the illusion. At the same time, and in the right place, I shall put some real rats. He will thus come to say, "I see rats or illusory rats; I can't tell." At last I shall produce the illusion and mix in some real rats while he is having his hallucination. He will not be able to tell whether a certain rat is real, an illusion, or an hallucination. He would have to say, "Either I see a rat, or I see a rat-illusion, or I am seeing a rat." Each of these disjuncts "implies something about the material world." The first implies there are rats. The second there are no rats, and no external stimula. The third implies there are pictures, perhaps, cleverly devised to look just like rats. There is no point in going on with this. We might be able to exhaust the possibilities: see, hallucinate, suffer illusion, and others. Even so, the implications of these taken disjunctively do not approach zero information "about the material world."

When he says "I 'see' six red rats: I don't know how many are real—maybe none," I have represented him as saying, in effect, "I am hallucinating one to six rats, or I see one to six, or both." (The understood condition here is that if one is seen it is not hallucinated and vice versa.) The implication of the disjunction is not "There are rats or there are no rats." It is "There are no rats or one to six rats." Ellis has some reason, admittedly very poor, for expecting one to six rats. He has very good reason for thinking there are no more than six. Because his comments imply something about the maximum number of rats, he was disturbed when he said, "I see two rats," and I told him there were three. He thought he was making a mistake.

It is easy to construct a new example in which Ellis makes comments which do not imply a maximum number. Suppose that when three rats are there he sometimes "sees" only two. Suppose that sometimes when several rats are there he "sees" none at all. Imagine that he adjusts also to this very different visual abnormality, that is, he knows that sometimes his vision for rats goes blank. Now, of course, when he sees two rats and there are three, he may actually see none at all and be hallucinating the two he "sees." Now I shall try to get a neutral report from him. In some situation where he is full of all these doubts, I ask him just to tell me what he sees—no matter whether real or delusive. So he says, "I see six red rats" and he tells the rest of the story.

Poor Ellis is now in a position where he cannot determine whether he actually sees rats before him—even when someone else tells him that there are rats there. He cannot tell whether he sees them even when everyone else sees them, and he has absolutely no doubts they are there. He may see none of those present and be hallucinating the ones he "sees." Clearly, now his comments will not satisfy condition (4). From the fact that rats are before him, one can say absolutely nothing about whether Ellis may or may not "see" rats.

Have I avoided the important question—or begged it? The real question is, "Can Ellis ever detach his report from any disjunctions and simply tell what he 'sees,' just give a report of his visual experience?" What am I to imagine? Ellis talks about the rats in his visual field, tells where they are and what they are doing. He does not bother himself over whether they are hallucinatory, illusory, or real. He raises no questions about whether or not he is confronted with rats or an optical illusion, or whether or not he is hallucinating. Of course he needs to know the alternatives and the likelihood of each in various situations. Otherwise conditions (4) and (5) could not be satisfied. But he must hold this knowledge in reserve; it must not flavor or enter into the reports of what he "sees." He must not think of what it is to see, or to suffer hallucination, or to be fooled by an illusion. He must just tell what he "sees." Can I imagine that? My inclination is to say "no." I do not understand how the verb "to see" could acquire a new life, one that is not to be accounted for by its genesis. That genesis begins with the "see" of childhood as in "See the big white dog." In the case of one as unfortunate as Ellis, it then gets a modification into "see" as in "I see (hallucinate)." My inclination is to say that it can acquire no new use which is more than a modification of the original "see" and an understanding of how illusions and hallucinations occur. But in truth I do not know what to say. The example has become almost too fantastic to be manageable. If Ellis were to become a philosopher and assure me that he could give "statements of immediate experience," I would think he had confused himself.

Even if I were to come to believe that I could make something out of this claim of Ellis to be able to give a "statement of immediate experience," there is still one more condition it must meet before it would fulfill the requirements of the epistemologist for a "sense-datum statement," or what. I did not list this requirement in the beginning because I did not know quite how to put it, and it is not relevant to the main part of the inquiry. The requirement is something like this: one who is properly trained could make such statements anytime. When we see anything, we also "see" it. With proper training one could report "seeing" it.[7] After someone has had the training Ellis has, could he then say what he "sees" when he sees a pelican catching fish or when he sees a fly on the porkchop? He has never hallucinated anything but rats, and only under certain circumstances. He is not in a situation where he has any reason to suspect hallucination. Now when he tells me what he sees I agree and enlarge in a way that agrees with what he sees. Can he tell what he "sees"? He says he can, and he starts talking. Now I cannot agree or disagree: he ignores entirely what I say. Can he do that? I don't know what to say.

AFTER-IMAGES

I have supposed that a "statement of immediate experience" was the thing writers on the theory of knowledge have been interested in. I have supposed that after getting "statements of immediate experience," they could then ask important questions about the connection of these with "physical-object statements." (Perhaps show how the physical world was "constructed" out of sense-data.) So I assumed that (4) and (5) were minimal conditions of what was wanted.

Some philosophers have had a great theoretical interest in kinds of statements which do not satisfy conditions (4) and (5), that is, kinds of statements which would not enter into an "analysis" of the perception of "physical ob-

---

[7] Here, for example, is Ayer's version of this requirement: " . . . glancing at the table in front of me, I now see a number of objects which I have no difficulty in identifying. I can say what properties they have . . . But if I am asked how these things look to me, I may well be at a loss for an answer. It takes skill to observe the looks of things, as opposed to the things themselves . . . One can describe what one sees, without perhaps being able to say exactly how it looks. But from the fact that I am not trained to make accurate judgments about the way things look, it does not follow that I can see them without their displaying any look to me at all . . . And this means that it is not possible for anyone to see a physical object, without it seeming to him that he sees it. The fact that he may not notice how it looks to him is irrelevant." (A. J. Ayer, *Problems of Knowledge,* pp. 103-104.)

jects." Whereas these statements are not the ones they want, they are interested in them because they seem so simply and obviously to meet conditions (1), (2), and (3). They are taken to provide simple examples of statements meeting the first three conditions. G. E. Moore goes further:[8] he takes citation of these statements as sufficient to make clear what is involved in "direct perception" and "sense-data" (what I have been calling a statement of immediate experience). One kind is "I have a pain," "I have a toothache." Such statements cannot be called in question on the basis of later experiences. They do not imply anything about the "material world," or any "physical object." No one is in a position to disprove or to corroborate that another is in pain or has a toothache. Of course no such statement is implied by any claim to perceive a "physical object." And such statements do not provide evidence for any claim to perceive a "physical object."

Another kind of statement used in this way is illustrated by "I see a pink after-image" or "I see a square grey after-image." G. E. Moore says that "see" in "I see an after-image" means "directly see" and hence such seeing is a case of "directly seeing" or of "direct apprehension." He says that what is directly apprehended is always a "sense-datum." Moore says "x is seeing a physical object" entails "x is seeing a sense-datum"—that is, he is ultimately concerned with statements which meet condition (4). But clearly he does not think "x is seeing a physical object" entails "x is seeing an after-image." After-images are one of the *sort* of objects directly seen. Philosophically more important examples would be visual sense-data in situations where one sees a house or tree, or auditory sense-data when one hears a trumpet. Moore obviously believes that seeing an after-image illustrates very clearly a part, but only a part, of what he wants.

Moore reflects very carefully on whether the meaning of "sense-datum" is such that it is self-contradictory to say of an object that it is "both a physical reality and also a sense-datum."[9] The only relevant "physical reality" here, he remarks, is the "surface of a physical object." He decides that it is contradictory.[10] It is impossible that a sense-datum be identical with the surface of a phys-

[8] G. E. Moore, *The Philosophy of G. E. Moore,* pp. 627-660.
[9] *Ibid.*
[10] G. E. Moore, "Visual Sense Data," *British Philosophy in the Mid-Century,* (London, Geo. Allen & Unwin Ltd., 1957), p. 211.

ical object. No physical surface and hence no physical object can be directly seen. Seeing and directly seeing are two entirely different things. Seeing necessarily involves directly seeing, but directly seeing is related in no simple way to seeing. Thus he seems clearly to have in mind statements which meet condition (5) as well as (4).

That he has in mind the other three conditions is made tolerably clear by the fact that he takes "I am in pain" as a paradigm; and he says his "directly see" is meant as the visual variety of what Berkeley called "direct perception." (*Sic*: he meant "immediate perception.") Berkeley characterizes "immediate perception" as necessarily free from possibility of error. " . . . his mistake lies not in what he perceives immediately, and at present (it being a manifest contradiction to suppose he should err in respect of that) but in the wrong judgment he makes concerning the ideas he apprehends to be connected with those he immediately perceived . . . "[11] Moore evidently thinks "sense-datum statements" must meet conditions (1), (2), and (3).

I want to raise a question about whether "I see a . . . after-image" can be regarded as meeting conditions (1), (2), and (3). Moore used this example to show what is meant by "directly see" and "sense-datum." I wonder whether this was not a mistake. In characterizing a class of statements as free from possibility of error, "indubitable," or "incorrigible," philosophers have not meant to rule out the possibility of any kind of mistake whatever.

(1) All have been willing to agree that statements of immediate experience may involve word mistakes. One kind is illustrated by this: "I saw a blue jay building a nest in the mail box." "That's very odd. Will you show me the bird here in my bird book?" "That is the one I saw." "That's a blue bird." "I thought that bird was called a blue jay." A similar mistake presumably could be made in a statement of immediate experience. "I saw a vermilion patch." Show me on the color chart." It is "cardinal." "I thought that color was called 'vermilion.' " Here, one doesn't know the right name.

(2) A similar mistake is possible where one does not have to be told the right name by another. He remembers. A student, Walton, has been taking an advanced course in bird-taxonomy. He has been working with the collection of skins in the museum, reading descriptions and poring over the color charts.

---

[11] Berkeley, *Three Dialogues Between Hylas and Philonous*, III.

His instructor asks, "Have you seen the new bird we got in from South America?" "Yes. I looked at it today." "What is the breast color?" "Chestnut . . . No. I mean 'rufous' . . . I remember the color clearly enough. I just didn't remember the name of it. The breasts are *rufous*. There is very little variation in the specimens we got."

(3) The right words are known; but a person might slip, and say the wrong thing. "I've been thinking about the report you dictated on the suspect's room. You said there was a telescope on the table." "Did I say 'telescope'? I meant 'telephone.' How could I have made a slip like that?" Philosophers have not wanted to deny the possibility of slips of speech in reporting sense-data or in giving statements of immediate experience.

(4) The former examples are word mistakes or language mistakes (I don't know why a label is needed). Here is a somewhat different example. Singer has made an elaborate description of the Christmas decoration on the town green. The decoration contains hundreds of red and green lights. Later he learns that he is red-green color-blind. Could he have just become color-blind? Say the evidence is conclusive that he has always been color-blind: he has just now found it out. What will he say of his description? He said all of the angels were green and white. Now he knows he cannot distinguish red from green. He now learns that some of the angels were red, some green. This example is hard to think about, but I want only to illustrate kinds of mistakes. This kind of mistake is surely possible for statements of immediate experience. "I see a patch, red in the middle, green at the edge": statements of immediate experience must go something like that. Later the person who said that could discover he was red-green color-blind. Some kind of emendation is now in order. I suppose one could call this a language mistake if he liked, but it would be a question of what he liked. Would he want to say a color-blind person does not know what the words "red" and "green" mean? Does he not know what colors "red" and "green" are names of? He can't, at least sometimes, distinguish between the colors of which "red" and "green" are names.

(5) There is another type of mistake which seems compatible with the idea of a statement of immediate experience. No one would want to call this a "language mistake." Salvo is an amateur ornithologist who spent part of every day in the field years ago and became a real expert. But that was years ago, and

he has now become rusty. While lazily lying in his yard he catches a glimpse of a bird flying between two trees across the street. He gets just a glimpse, and quickly says to himself, "There goes a crow." Then he thinks it over: he recalls the silhouette and the wing beat. Now he corrects himself. "No. That was a raven." This is not a case where he did not know the right name. It is not a slip of speech. He does not say, "I didn't mean 'crow,' " or "I didn't mean to say 'crow'." If one can imagine what statements of immediate experience are to be like, then I imagine they can be subject to such errors.

These are the main types of error of which statements of immediate experience are subject. None of these are possible with "I have a pain." (I wince and buckle over. A friend asks, "What's wrong," I say, "I have a pain.") For that reason, perhaps, Moore thought "I see an after-image" more representative. That is, reporting an after-image is more like reporting on a visual sense-datum. All of these types of error would be possible with reports on an after-image. Perhaps the last, (3), needs discussion. An experiment could be devised to illustrate it. Silhouettes of birds will be cut out of sheets of glossy white paper. They will be brightly illuminated and placed before the eyes of our rusty ornithologist, Salvo. We shall teach him to stare thoughtlessly at these. Now we shall turn him toward a white wall and ask, "Do you see a grey after-image?" "Yes." "What bird-outline is it?" Suppose now he quickly says, "Crow." Isn't it possible that he will reflect—perhaps after the after-image has gone—and say, "No. It was a raven outline"?

But other kinds of mistakes are possible in talk about after-images. (a) We determine that a subject sees a green after-image after he has stared at a light of certain brightness. He describes what he sees as a round, dark-green patch, uniformly colored. We determine that when the light is not quite so bright he does not see an after-image. Now we arrange a ground glass, softly lighted with white light. From behind we shine a green spotlight making on the ground glass a dark-green uniformly-colored circle. We have our subject stare at a light, one not quite bright enough to produce an after-image. Then we have him look at the ground glass. I suppose he will say, "I see a green after-image." Of course I shall now say to him, "You are wrong. Actually, you see this green circle of light. Come here, I'll show you." He agrees: he saw the green circle of light on the glass.

(b) I can report a kind of mistake here which I twice made. I used to shave with a bare light bulb reflected in the mirror before me. After shaving, of course, I rinsed the white porcelain wash basin. On two occasions, I tried to wipe off a circular red stain—which turned out to be an after-image.

Here are two mistakes one can make about after-images. In the language of philosophy of perception, the first is a case where a "physical object" is reported to be an after-image, the second is a case where an after-image is taken to be a "physical object." Moore says that seeing an after-image is a case of "direct perception." Presumably, then, when one says "I see an after-image" he is reporting on his immediate perception. Such statements are not to be subject to error, except for the kinds already illustrated. Here is a kind of error one can find himself in as the result of examining "physical objects." It is a kind of error another person can show me I have made, by showing me the relevant "physical objects." Surely Berkeley did not allow for such a possibility in his "immediate perception." I doubt whether any sense-datum philosopher has.

Perhaps this is the way out. Pursue the analogy Moore suggests. Statements of immediate experience are like reports on after-images. Reports on after-images can involve these mistakes. Sometimes when we think we are describing an after-image we are describing a physical object. Therefore sometimes when we think we are reporting on immediate experience, what is "directly seen," we are really reporting on a physical object. Why not simply disqualify these reports? We thought they were statements of immediate experience, but they were not. They are not, therefore, statements of immediate experience. Statements of immediate experience will remain incorrigible.

I think this will satisfy no one. It has now turned out that sometimes when we think we are reporting on what is "immediately perceived"—or what—we are not so reporting at all. I cannot believe that any philosopher has entertained this possibility: when we try our hardest and are quite convinced that we are talking, not about physical objects, but about what we immediately perceive, we go wrong. We go wrong because we are not after all talking about what we immediately perceive, but rather about a physical object. I believe Moore was mistaken in thinking that "I see an after-image" could illustrate the features of the kind of statement he was interested in.

Moore may have sensed this difficulty. This *may* be what led him to appeal always to seeing an after-image "with eyes closed." Still, isn't the same error possible with eyes closed? Suitably change example (a). The eye-lids now become the ground glass. Our subject will stare at a light. Then close his eyes. We shine a narrow beam of green light on the eyelid. Can't he say seriously, "I see a green after-image"? And then we shall point out to him that in reality he was seeing the little circle of green light. So, consider seeing after-images only when the eyes are covered with absolutely opaque blinders. Still, if his eyes were closed, he might not know we had put blinders on him; and so he might think that he was seeing a light on his eyelid when he was seeing an after-image. Suppose then that he has blinders on and knows that he has blinders on. Undoubtedly there are other ways of producing visual "objects" which might be mistaken for after-images; perhaps they can be produced by drugs. But, in the ways I have been suggesting, it would be impossible to cause a person to mistake an after-image for anything else, provided he had opaque blinders on and knew it. Even so, the impossibility is not of the right kind.

If I were in the next room and overheard someone report on his after-image I might have reason to think he was mistaken. I might think one of those silly experiments was going on. I would not know the subject had opaque blinders over his eyes. I could say and think that he might be mistaken because I did not know all the circumstances under which he was making the report which I overheard. Surely a report of immediate experience is not to be like that. I cannot think the reporter of his direct perceptions might be making a mistake because I do not know about his blinders, or eye-patches, or nose-stuffers, or ear plugs. If he is reporting on immediate experience he cannot make a mistake under any conditions, with any kind of paraphernalia. Except, of course, for the kinds of mistakes I first illustrated. In this respect "I have a pain" is closer to the paradigm we want.

We thought we knew what was wanted in a statement of immediate experience and we thought that reports of after-images gave a certain part of it. We could not have thought this because we looked carefully at talk about after-images. I suspect we did not consider that an after-image could be confused with a light-spot on a ground glass or a pin of light on our eyelid because we were thinking of an after-image as "private," as "inside." Not inside by being on the back of the eyelid or even on the back of the eyeball, but inside the mind perhaps; inside, that is, in an altogether different and wildly metaphorical way.

There is another respect in which after-image talk does not behave quite right for a statement of immediate experience. Statements of immediate experiences are not directed toward any of the furniture or drygoods of the physical world. Hence they are not subject to correction in any of the ways statements about physical things are. They are directed to the "private" and the "immemediate." A large part of this is presumably reflected in their "incorrigibility." But "incorrigibility" here is not, without complication, just freedom from possibility of error. Specifically, such statements are not subject to the kinds of mistakes possible in statements about people and trees and stones. The older way of trying to hit this off was to talk about the "objects" of immediate perception. Unlike physical objects, immediate objects are "seen" in their entirety. They have no insides, backsides, or hidden parts. When you see a direct perceptual object you see it all. The object is just what you see. (When you have a pain you have it all. There is no part of the pain unfelt.)

Consider this possibility with after-images. We shine a light in the eyes of Simon and he sees a circular green after-image against a white wall. We repeat the experiment and each time he sees the green circular after-image. Now we try green walls, and one by one we shall go through all shades of green. Is it possible that we should find a wall the same color as his after-image? Suppose we do. Is it possible that against this background he will not see an after-image? Suppose when he turns toward another background he sees an after-image; when he turns again to the green wall he sees none. Suppose this can be done repeatedly. In reporting after-images we have two idioms, "I see an after-image," and "I have an after-image." For the most part, they seem interchangeable. Would Simon, when facing the green wall, have any inclination to say, "I have a green after-image, but I can't see it now. I can see it when I turn my head to the other wall"?

Complicate the experiment just a little. Draw a straight vertical line on the wall. Paint the surface on one side of the line white, on the other side the right shade of green. Now shine the light in Simon's eyes and turn him toward the wall. Have him turn his head slowly back and forth. Suppose when turned toward the white he seen an after-image; when turned toward the green he sees none. Now ask him to turn so that the after-image is "on" the straight line between areas. Is it possible that he will now say, "I see an after-image, a green semi-circle against the white. The straight line side of the semi-circle is the vertical line in the wall"? If so, will he have any tendency to also say, "I have a circular green after-image, but I can only see half of it"? I imagine that as he moves his head back and forth he will see more or less of a circle.

My point is this. I do not know quite what it is to be in Simon's position. I do not know quite what I would say. But I do not think speaking of having an after-image which I cannot see or speaking of seeing part of an after-image are flatly wrong things to say. Yet if talk about after-images were to be the same as talk about what is immediately perceived, they should be flatly wrong things to say. There are no items in an immediate sense-field which are not perceived, and nothing perceived which is not perceived in its entirety. As Simon faces the wall divided into two color areas, he can say, "I see a semi-circular after-image." Perhaps also he can say, "I have a circular after-image. It's green, and I can only see the part of it which is against the white background." Should we count the first as a report on immediate perception, the second not? We could direct him to tell just what he saw, no more. Then maybe he would say, "I see a semi-circular green patch." Wouldn't he be thinking all the time, "If only it weren't for that green part of the wall, I could make it all out, the circle I mean. When I move my head a little I can see more of it"? I do not know whether things can be arranged so that one will have after-images of the kind I have imagined Simon to have. I have experimented just enough with this to think that they can.

In conversation (Spring 1963), Elizabeth Anscombe told me a story about a lipstick factory. Workers were required to look at lipsticks all day under bright lights. They were bothered by seeing green after-images. The management corrected the situation by painting the walls green. The workers saw the after-images no more.

III

HOW PHILOSOPHERS SEE STARS

The stars are astounding distances from the Earth, distances which astronomers express in immense units of light-years. Even these units are too small
for convenience, since some stars are known to be trillions of light-years distant.
Light takes over four years to reach the Earth from the nearest star, Alpha-
Centauri. This fact used to be cited by philosophers as part of an argument for
sense-data. The star we "see" might well not exist: it might have exploded
many years ago—between the time these light rays left, and now, when they are
stimulating the receptive tissues of my eyes. What we "see" would be the
same whether there is a physical object seen or not. It is possible, therefore,
that there are no stars, no such physical things. Our visual data do not imply
that stars exist. Physical stars must be one thing, our visual data quite another.
These data are the immediate objects of awareness, "sense-data."

More recently, the same fact, the vast distances of the stars, has been cited
in support of quite a different philosophical conclusion, namely, that we have
direct perceptual contact with the past.[1] We literally see the past states of the
stars: in some cases, we see trillions of years into the past. Ayer thinks this
conclusion lends some plausibility to the theory that in memory, also, we have
direct contact with the past. This direct-contact theory of memory is an effort
to allay our philosophical feelings that the past is gone, to counter doubts about
the possibility of memory with the blunt assertion that we have in memory
direct access to the past. When we wonder at the possibility of memory, we
are supposed to get some help by looking at the stars and saying, "The past
is not gone; it is right here." Ayer does not explain himself, but apparently he
wants us to think that seeing stars literally gives us a chunk of the past, the

[1] A. J. Ayer, *Problems of Knowledge,* (Baltimore,, Penguin Books, 1956), pp. 94-95; R.
Chisholm, *Perceiving,* (Ithaca, Cornell Univ. Press, 1957), p. 153.

same kind of stuff we can remember. Whitehead too accepts the conclusion that our only direct contact is with the past. In addition, he attaches great significance to the corollary: that there is a "barrier" separating us from the contemporary world. It is in this isolation that there is a place in the universe for freedom, "irresponsibility," "independent activities."[2]

With a little philosophical ingenuity, I suppose one could accept both arguments. With proper terminological modifications, I suppose Russell[3] and Whitehead do accept them both. Yet the arguments seem to pull in different —if not opposite—directions. The first cuts us off from the physical world; the second cuts us off from the present. The first works because it involves the assumption that what we directly see is present. The second depends on the assumption that we unquestionably see the stars. If one thought our vision of stars was quite indirect, involving sense-data and perhaps inference, some of the philosophical sting would be taken out of the second argument.

The first has far less life now than the second. Apparently there are several reasons for this. Sense-data are currently out of favor. Furthermore, I think the argument for sense-data from star light was always a kind of subordinate, almost parenthetical, argument. It was just one among many, and for this reason was never greatly elaborated in its own right. However there is a more significant reason than either of these: the second argument is simply more straightforward and compelling. It has a more direct philosophical pull. This may come from our philosophical attitudes about time. From a philosophical point of view, the word "present" may seem too vague and variable. We want to tighten it, make it strict; then we promptly reach the conclusion that we *never* see the present. This is too paradoxical; so we set the line between "past" and "present" to allow vision of the "present"—"for all practical purposes." We want stricter, clearer words, but we also want practical application; in making concessions to practice, we seem to gain the welcome support of "ordinary" usage.

"Past" and "present" are sometimes used to contrast the present moment with that just before; at other times, the present hour, week, year, with hours,

[2] A. N. Whitehead, *Adventures of Ideas,* (New York, Macmillan, 1933), pp. 251, 317.
[3] B. Russell, *Human Knowledge, Its Scope and Limits,* (New York, Simon and Schuster), 1948, p. 205.

weeks, years passed by. For laboratory purposes, the present moment may be a millionth of a second. The present presidential administration may last four (or eight) years. The present epoch may be a million years. What does the philosophical argument (no working context or situation) demand? Nerve currents take time. So we may be limited by the sense of touch to the past states of our own skin. Perhaps the only real present things we know are the denizens of our mind. No. If we give up guidance of situations where talk works or plays, we must at least have "common-sense." It may lead us to say that for all practical purposes we see the present of the chair we are about to sit in. In "ordinary" usage, the near past is what we call the "present."

Both arguments alike yield bewildering conclusions. Why should thinking about light from the stars produce these disturbing results? I want to see whether I can gain any insight into this matter. I shall begin with the first argument. It has never, I think, been stated very completely or examined very thoroughly. It is now quite lifeless. It might be useful to try to give it life. Perhaps it could be reformulated to more closely parallel the second; perhaps it could be given the same kind of philosophical "pull."

The second argument, if I have understood its mode, moves in this way: from "Stars are past" to "All is past." This being too paradoxical, we soften it to "Some things are present—for practical purposes." Then we return to "Stars are past." Let us try to modify the first argument so that it moves from "Stars are not physical" to "Nothing is physical." Then, perhaps, we can make it move back to "Stars are not physical." We need some uses of "physical thing" which will foster the classification of the nonphysical into the simply nonphysical and the practically physical. The stars are simply nonphysical, therefore nothing is physical. At the end we want to conclude bread and beans are practically physical. We might try dreams (the things we dream are certainly nonphysical), and if sufficiently orderly our dream-things will be practically physical, otherwise simply nonphysical. But how, then, could light from the stars show that stars are dream things. And if everything is a dream, we cannot classify into merely dreams and practically physical, because if everything is a dream, we classify in a dream. So we dream we classify, which is not at all the same thing as classifying.

At one end of the series we want sense-data. How can one put in linear order such diverse things as physical object and sense-datum? At this point we must notice an obvious feature of the argument. It contains a great gap which the "see-the-past" version does not. How, after all, did we get from stars to sense-data? The argument by itself will not take us. One would draw the conclusion "sense-data" only if he thought he had independent reasons for believing in sense-data. Because light takes time, we never see physical things. Ergo, sense-data. But we do see twinkling things in the sky and these things lack the most important characteristics of sense-data. They are public. My judgments about them can be, and are, often wrong. They can be corrected by other observers. I often discover my mistakes in observation myself, and correct them at a much later date. The members of the astronomy club can spend a pleasant evening watching an occultation of Aldebaran. At various times they will point to the star. They may differ in their recorded times of disappearance, and one member may discover that his error was caused by a defect in his telescope eyepiece. Let us not have to lean on anything outside the argument. Let us draw only the conclusions which the argument supports. Then what are the members of the astronomy club supposed to be seeing? The purely negative conclusion is, they do not see a physical thing. But what is their visual object?

We say "I hear a sound," and also "I hear a flute." Sometimes we may take a sound to be the sound of a flute where it is not. Then at any rate we heard a sound, a sound which others heard also. When we look at the stars, maybe we are supposed to see something related to seeing a physical thing, the way hearing a sound is related to hearing a flute. But the seen star cannot be like that. I took the sound to be the sound of a flute, and it was not. How did I find out I was wrong? Because someone else with a keener ear told me it was no flute sound. Or because I discovered it was the sound of something else, an antique toy whistle. In the case of the seen star, there is no one with a keen eye who can recognize a star right off as not a physical thing. Also, the star is not a star-thing of something else, which is not a physical thing. What is it to be the star-thing of a nonphysical thing?

How does the argument leave the star we see? As something like cosmic ectoplasm, a heavenly will-o-the-wisp, perhaps? Something adrift in a dark night like the intrinsic illumination we all see in a very dark room. It would have to be a mixture of these: like intrinsic illumination in involving no external thing as source of stimulation, like the will-o-the-wisp in that it can be pointed to. Suppose we call it "sky-ghost." Now at any rate we can form a series: ghost, shadow, sky-ghost, will-o-the-wisp, smoke, cloud, super-saturated cloud, jelly, rock. Of course this is not like past-present: it does not suggest quantification, or even comparisons, like more or less a physical thing. Still, the argument to seeing the past did not depend upon comparatives "more or less remote past," or quantities "two or three days ago." We need only to give plausibility to the distinction "practically—" as opposed to "strictly a sky-ghost." In the see-the-past version we were led to teeter between "never see the present" and "see the present on the face of the Earth" or "see the present about up to the moon." In the argument which is to replace the sense-datum one, we should be led to teeter between "Everything is a sky-ghost" and "The stars are sky-ghosts." Our first conclusion will be pure but terrifying. Finally we shall trade it for the tamer, hybrid one.

Let us put the sky-ghost argument together. When we look at what we think are stars, we see sky-ghosts. Why is that? Because light takes a long time to travel from the stars to our eyes. How does that prove the point? Because the physical things which we think of as the stars may be extinct, and still we look and see something. Stop! Here, surely, is a defect. It does not follow that because something *might* be extinct that we cannot see it. The ivory-billed woodpecker might very well be extinct. At the last estimate, there were only half a dozen or so in existence. One bad storm could wipe them out. If an ornithologist were to report seeing one, we would not promptly conclude that he did not, could not, have seen one. The Audubon Society would be delighted, perhaps send a warden to protect it. Because the stars might not now exist, it clearly does not follow that an astronomer cannot see them.

We can easily revise the argument and eliminate this flaw. It is only true of some of the stars that we have reason to say they might not exist (the old, very red ones). Some, perhaps, we have good reason to think do not now exist. Those, therefore, we cannot see. We cannot be sure which do and which do not exist. So, for any given star, we cannot be sure whether it exists or not. Therefore we cannot see any star at all. The last step? If we see something, we must be sure it exists. If we are not sure it exists, we cannot see it. Maybe this patches the argument. Unfortunately at the cost of using a false premise. The premise "For any given star we cannot be sure whether it exists or not" is simply wrong. Of many, many stars we know their ages, their likely lives, and their distances from the Earth—which adds up to knowledge that they exist. With regard to closer, younger stars there could not be a shadow of doubt that they exist.

Let us suppose we do not know this: we do not positively know that some stars exist.[4] Therefore, of any star whatever, we cannot be sure whether it exists or not. Of any star we see, we cannot be sure that it exists. Therefore, we cannot see a star. Why? Because we cannot see something whose existence we doubt. Of the ivory-billed woodpecker, I may have doubted its existence until I saw one. But having seen it, I cannot doubt its existence. If I still doubt its existence I must doubt whether I had seen it or am seeing it. In the case of stars, I not only doubt their existence before I see them, but also when I see them, and after I have seen them. Therefore I cannot see them: I cannot see stars. I do see something. Therefore the things I see are not stars.

What is involved in doubting that what I see exists? I suppose wondering whether I am having an hallucination. But that is not in question here because everybody else sees what I see. Mass hallucination? No. Not mass hallucination involving absolutely everybody over centuries and centuries. I omitted the last step in the argument. Perhaps if I put it in, it will help. I do not see stars. Therefore I see sky-ghosts. It was precisely to allow for this step that I created the category of sky-ghosts. The conclusion then is not such as to admit of anything like hallucinations. The point is not that I see what does not exist. It is rather that I take what I see to be one thing when in reality it is another. The step in the argument is this: if I see something and doubt that it exists, then that something which I see is not a physical thing (but a sky-ghost).

Crumley doubts that there is any such animal as a giraffe. I have told him stories about giraffes, shown him drawings and photographs. He still thinks I was pulling his leg, telling him yarns; he thinks I concocted drawings and faked photographs. So I take him to the zoo and confront him with a giraffe. He says, "I see it, but I still don't believe it." What is he saying? "I see some-

---

[4] From this point on the argument, I believe, takes the same steps as the more familiar arguments from hallucination. I think the following observations, therefore, apply to other, perhaps more important arguments than the "starlight" one.

thing all right which looks as if it were the fantastic animal you told me about, but I'm still not convinced you haven't faked this, too."

When I look at the sky I would see the same thing whether there was a star there or not. So what I see must not be a star. Crumley would see the same thing whether there was a giraffe there or not. Does it follow that he does not see a giraffe? If finally I convinced him, he would say, "Yes, what I saw was a giraffe." I have the first and third person accounts mixed up. Of course, if Crumley had any doubts that what he was seeing was a giraffe, he would not say (first person), "I see a giraffe"; but if what he sees is a giraffe, we, the observers, would say (third person), "What he sees is a giraffe."

If, when I look at the sky, I doubt that what I see is a star, I will not say "I see a star," but others who have no doubts will say, "What he sees is a star." This is certainly not the kind of conclusion intended in the argument, something which is relative to doubt. Anybody at all who says that what I see is a star or who says that he sees a star is supposed to be wrong. I need the conclusion that if he is not in doubt he ought to be; or rather he would be if he knew the facts about light and vision.

I said that Crumley would see the same thing whether or not there was a giraffe there. Should I have said that? If there were a giraffe there, we should say that what he saw was a giraffe; and if it were not a giraffe we should say that what he saw was a fake giraffe, an imitation giraffe, or something of that sort. But even if there is a star there, I am supposed to conclude that I do not see a star, or that what I see is not a star. And that is because I should supposedly see the same thing whether there were a star there or not. The argument has become preposterous. If I see the same thing regardless of what is there, why should I conclude I always see sky-ghosts, never stars? Why not always stars, never sky-ghosts? The argument can just as well run: whether there are stars or not, I see the same thing. Therefore I see stars. In truth, if there are stars there, I see stars. The strongest relevant conclusion I can draw is that if there are not stars to be seen, then I do not see stars but sky-ghosts.

If, when I look at the sky and see those bright twinkling dots, there are no stars in the sky, it follows that the things I see are not stars. But if I see things in the sky and there are things there just where I and others always see them, surely these are the things I see. I see stars. The argument needs the statement,

"What you see is the same whether there are stars or not." Could this mean simply, "I look at the night-sky and I cannot tell whether I see stars or sky-ghosts"?

Suppose we have a box of chocolates. Some have pink centers, some white. They look exactly the same: same chocolate covering, same dip-marks. Now when you look at a certain piece you do not know whether you see a pink-center chocolate or a white-center chocolate. Therefore you see a pink-center chocolate. No? Therefore you see a white-center one. Absurd. I should not have got the argument into this difficulty, because if two things appear exactly alike, we would not say we saw one or the other. How do I see a pink-center chocolate? "Look carefully at this chocolate. What do you see?" "I see a pink-center chocolate." "Why did you say that?" "Because the chocolate is thin on one side and I saw the color of the filling showing through." No one, by looking at a star, can see a sky-ghost peeking through. No: the chocolates, like the dots in the sky, are to be indistinguishable. I look again, carefully, among the identical chocolates, and pick one. "What did you see?" "I don't understand. I didn't see anything in particular. I just picked one." "Which kind is it?" I do not know, of course; so I break it and it is pink. "Which kind did you see before you broke it?" How could I answer such a question? I would not say that I saw a pink one. But was the one I saw a pink one? Here I have made another mistake. I have mixed "I saw a pink one with "What I saw is a pink one." They are not the same, and the argument for sky-ghosts needs only, "What I saw was a sky-ghost." Was what I saw a pink chocolate? What am I to answer? "No, I guess what I saw was a layer of identical chocolates." "You saw the one you picked?" "Yes, of course." "Well, when you saw that one, was what you saw a pink chocolate?" I do not know what to say. I guess what I saw was neither a pink-center chocolate nor a white-center chocolate. I guess when I look at the night sky what I see is neither a star nor a sky-ghost. Assuming, that is, that "what I see is the same in either case," a mixture of indistinguishable stars and sky-ghosts.

I am afraid this argument just cannot be brought around to the required conclusion, even by using what we know to be a false premise.

The first argument (for sense-data, or sky-ghosts) I am afraid cannot be salvaged. Let us turn to the other (to sight of the past). I do not know how to improve the statement: it is wonderfully simple and can exert a great pull. But the conclusion is ridiculous. It certainly can be disturbing in a way that a scientific conclusion ought not to be. We not only see the distant past but we often point to it; we point to the distant past, it being right now before us. What can one do to straighten things out? I shall try something old. I shall ask a question which has sometimes led to helpful results.

(1) What has a scientific description or explanation to do with a philosophical thesis? Consider these two cases, and ask, do the scientific explanations bear identically on the philosophical theses? (a) White light is a mixture of all colors. Hence we do not really see the color of white paper. (b) Light takes some time to get from a physical thing to our eye. Hence we do not see physical things. Or, hence, we do not see the present states of things. We can say that in (a) we have given a partial explanation of color vision. But nothing along these lines would explain what we *mean* when we say, "I see white paper." Likewise, we might describe (b) as giving a partial explanation of the vision of physical things. Surely this cannot explain what we *mean* when we say, "I see the star there, now." It has become a philosophical commonplace that we can clear things up by concentrating on meaning.[5] Ayer and Chisholm who accept the conclusion that we see the past of the stars, reject the conclusion that we do not really see physical things. Their rejection is doubtless based on an understandable reluctance to disturb our linguistic dealings with trees, birds, people, and buildings. They seem to have no similar misgivings about disturbing our linguistic dealings with stars. When we look at the stars, our eyes are reaching out directly into the distant past. That is quite strange. Surely that cannot be involved in the meaning of "see," "sight," "vision?"

---

[5] From this point on I go along with a certain philosophical myth, namely, the idea that there is some one, universally applicable question about what we say or mean. And I take it as obvious that scientific explanation has no part in an answer to this question. We are misled by our desire to give a scientifico-philosophical answer. I assume that we can counter this by giving another kind of answer which, of course, is confusing in other ways. But I take it that this other answer is more benign in that, at the end, it can easily be taken away. This remains a promise. I do not succeed in taking it away; I do not even try. That would require writing on and on. In an effort to shrug responsibility here, I call my line of inquiry "something old," "a philosophical commonplace." Later (p. 62), I make an unnamed philosophical friend partly responsible for it.

Do these two conversations ring right? And are they parallel? (a) Willard: "The table is mostly empty space." Rupert: "What?" Willard: "I'm sorry, I shouldn't say such things. You ought to study physics." (b) Gibson: "When we look into the sky we see into the distant past. If we choose the right constellation, we can see simultaneously what is going on in many different centuries." Lowell: "What?" Gibson: "I'm sorry . . . you should study astrophysics." Isn't the second as right as the first? Perhaps it all depends on what follows. No very deep apology would be needed for these jarring remarks if they were proper parts of introductions to science. If the story of Cepheid variables and their periods and magnitudes follows the shocker about seeing the past, then maybe all would be put right. This sort of thing might be all right as a push-off onto a successful adventure in astronomy. (But I doubt it.)

However, Ayer says things of this sort in order to lend a kind of scientific respectability to the naive realist theory of memory. Because we see the past, it is not wild to think we have immediate memory contact with the past. Whitehead, too, says this sort of thing and takes it as showing that there is room in the world for freedom and spontaneity. Everything is cut off from the present of everything else, and in this isolation lies independence and freedom. The observation that the star-past statement might excite interest in science does not, of itself, shed much light on the statement. It remains worrisome. We cannot clear up the difficulty by turning away from it and learning science. (We could, of course, forget it.) The fact that a puzzling expression can play a part in learning science does not show that it is not troublesome on its own. We have simply to look up there, at *Beta* Centauri, say, and we do not see what is there now, but what was there many years ago. This is profound, true, and philosophically disturbing. We may want to say that it is disturbing only because science shows a commonsense belief wrong. It has done so before. Why not again? The adjustment to new truth takes time, but we do not have to get upset about it.

What commonsense beliefs has science shown wrong? (1) "We naturally believe the moon is just a little way beyond the tree tops." "Well, and then we learn that we are wrong." We make many mistakes, and I suppose some of them are "commonsense," that is, we all make them or are inclined to make them, and in the right circumstances would make them. Likewise, we are supposed naturally to believe we see the present of the stars. These cases are not at all similar. In the moon case we learn the truth, and by that are turned against our simple mistake. It is not easy in the star case to see what our mistake is, what belief we are supposed to give up. (2) Consider the classic example. We wonder why Venus can be seen only in the morning and evening, and we notice the retrograde motion of Jupiter. Then we learn the Copernician model and all this is explained. Before, we said the sun rose and set, the moon and planets moved across the sky. Now, perhaps in premature enthusiasm, we are tempted to say these were primitive beliefs shown wrong. We may say, "The sun does not rise in the east; it does not move across the sky." Others will point and make observations and say the sun has moved east to west, five hours and thirteen minutes. And of course it has. One can look to the east and watch the sun rise, Venus rising just ahead perhaps. Copernicus, Kepler, and Newton together showed earlier astronomers wrong. Did they show commonsense wrong? Well, they did not show that the sun does not rise in the east and set in the west, and move across the sky between its rising and setting.

See the column of smoke rising, the balloon rising there in the east. The sun too can be seen rising—more slowly—in the east. This is the way we talk about such things and motions. This is the way mothers, fathers, and school teachers throughout the English-speaking world have spoken to us. If the sun does not rise in the east, what does? This is a language-involving issue in a way that the distance-of-the-moon is not. If it were needed, a calculation of the distance of the moon by triangulation showed our childhood fancies wrong. It is proved that we cannot reach the moon—not with the tallest ladder. Even if we did once believe the moon was just a few feet from the treetops, our language habits are not disturbed by learning the moon's true distance.

But isn't it useful, with a Copernician model before us, to say, "You see the sun does not really rise in the east: the Earth turns slowly to face the sun. That is why the sun appears to rise in the east"? We imagine ourselves to be situated just outside the solar system looking in and talking to someone who has made a mistake about what is in motion: like someone on a train who thinks the platform and station are being moved away from him. Do we ever, even in our most theoretical moments, make such a mistake? Surely not. Anyway, it is easy to remind ourselves that English is a language of the face of the earth, spoken by and for people on the face of the earth. Let us suppose the sun appears to rise in the east. What would that be? It might be a pleasant evening with the sun setting behind a mountain of clouds. Because of some queer, reflective, thin vapor high in the eastern sky, the image of the sun is reflected clearly upon it, and appears to be rising there. "Look at that, 6 P.M. and the sun appears to be rising in the east."

If we had made some theoretical mistake, and this language holiday helps correct it, fine. Providing, in turn, we return quite sober from the holiday. Now say, "You do not see the present of the stars but only their distant pasts." Does this counter an error, a "commonsense" mistake, one that all of us make? I do not know what it could be. Chisholm seems confident that it does: " . . . we tend to assume, until we are taught otherwise, that any event or state of affairs we perceive must exist or occur simultaneously with our perception of it."[6] How did he find this out? Do we *all* tend to assume this? Could we ask and learn? "Do you, sir, assume or tend to assume that any event or state of affairs you perceive exists or occurs simultaneously with your perception of it?" How would we interpret the answer?

"See that peculiar bird over there. Which one? The one with the yellow rump. I can't see very well It's the one singing *now*. Which? Wait and listen: the one singing . . . *now*."

"See that star flicker. No. it's not doing it now. Wait. There, see, *now*. I will drop my arm when it flickers. Now!"

This is the sort of thing we say. I suppose it expresses what we tend to believe about the times of goings-on which we perceive. Does it express what Chisholm attributes to us? I am quite sure I do not believe what he says I do. I am certainly not tempted to believe it now. I say that something is going on now, because it *is* going on now, and I can see that it is. You can see that it is too. And if you do not know how to use the word "now" in this way—an absurd assumption—I suppose I can teach you. (It is also absurd to have to say, "I say it is now because it is now.")

It is many years after I learn to talk about the stars that I become apprized of the facts of physiological optics. Thereafter, when against the summer sky

<hr>

6 R. Chisholm, *op. cit.,* p. 153.

I point out the stars, is there some reason why I should feel apologetic? I shall continue to say, "See that star flickering now," and, "That star flickered just a moment ago." Just as I continue to say, "The sun rises over there between the mountain peaks," even after I have learned the Copernician explanation of the solar system.

(2) In a hushed voice, a friend once gave me some philosophical advice. He said that language is not a filing system with a proper place marked out for recording everything that is learned. Puzzles arise from a crossing of pictures. Put the troubling phrases back in the language game of which they are a part. We must learn to leave everything just as it is. Learning a language is learning a way of life. These are dark sayings. I do not know exactly what my friend meant by them, but I see a way of putting them to some uses of my own.

We cannot see without light. And light, we know, takes many years to reach us from a star. Therefore we must see the star as it was many years ago. We do most certainly see into the past. What could be simpler than that little argument. Now that you look at it this is not puzzling at all. Not as long as it tickles the mind a little, not as long as it is an interestingly funny way of bringing home the idea of the great distance of the stars, not as long as we do not bear down theoretically upon it. We might say it is a dramatic way of bringing a scientific discovery up next to, beside, our language. Do not try to force it in, or again, it becomes silly: "See into the past? Not see what is going on in the heavens now?" "Point a finger into the past and I shall show you many, many centuries ago."

Perhaps language has no prepared place for this fact and we fit it into the wrong place. Where are we trying to fit it? Is there a picture possessing us? Aren't we thinking of something like a letter from a long distance which came by slow carrier? "Uncle Mills has just finished the addition to his house." No. He finished it over eight months ago—when he wrote this. See the date." I could make such a mistake. What was I thinking? Perhaps that the letter came by jet plane. I am "forgetting" the language we use in pointing out the stars, and I am trying to fit a scientific discovery into the way we talk of communication by letter, telegraph, signal. Here my most direct communication tells me what is past; here is the room for freedom, freedom from the orders and demands that come by mail.

I point to the star and say, "Now it's dimming"; I am not making a theoretical mistake. I am not thinking that information came from the star faster than it does. I am not thinking of information at all. What information do I get from a star? "What's the news?" But the signal takes a long, long time to reach us from a star. A signal? A light signal. What is a light signal? Flash the light twice if you see them coming tonight. Surely we must be able to see or hear or touch or feel a signal: a smoke signal, stones in a pile, a red lantern, two short rings, a pinch on the arm. We see, hear, touch no signal from the stars. We must learn the meaning of a signal. What does light from the stars mean? Where do we learn the meaning?

Part of the picture that grips us is the idea that we see what is at the far end of a light ray. I have travelled on my eyes into the distant past, retracing in my mind the long trip of a light ray. Doesn't that fit? What we learn about is the one who sent the letter. What a dull letter that must be, perhaps from an egotistical lover, tells only about himself, his own feelings. People write letters about all sorts of things. We see what is at the other end of a light ray. How can science teach us what we see? We see what is around us, and above us. Why could we not just as well see what is at this end of a light ray? The insides of our heads, a cross-section of the optic nerve, the back of the eye. But when we receive a letter we are not informed of the workings of the post office or told about the construction of our mail box. Yes, but we might be, in a letter from the postal inspectors checking an insurance claim. The star is the origin of the light rays. We see what is at the point of origin. What is the point of origin of a letter? The author's pen, the surface of the paper, the author's hand, arm, thoughts? A light ray begins in a star. A letter, like philosophy, can begin in wonder.

In moments when my mind is not completely occupied by picture-thinking the modern optical, physiological story, I can see how natural it was for the ancients to have had a very different picture of vision. Forget light rays. Then isn't it natural and easy to think that seeing is a reaching out instead of a coming in? When you set yourself to talk about seeing, without any special point or problem (as in philosophizing), don't you move your head forward a little to show how the eyes reach out, or something reaches out from the eyes and contacts the object seen? Something darts out like a lizard's tongue and grasps its object. Consider this picture and our problem about seeing the stars. Something is sent forth from the eyes. Surely it takes time to get where it is going. By the time it gets there, the excitement may be over. I may arrive too late for the celebration, but then I do not claim to see the banners and the bonfires of years gone by. I see only today's abandoned streets. Seeing is consummated upon my arrival. This picture has plenty of troubles, but it does not lead me to think I see the past.

Now think of the vast distances of the stars. These distances are so great that my eye will never be able to reach them before I die. Again, the conclusion we cannot see the stars. And how are we to talk of the time between the starting out from my eyes and seeing? Is this looking? Then I look a lifetime through for the stars and never see them. And if no one ever sees them, how would I know what to look for? This picture will not do. No, but it is not wrong either. I do reach out with my eyes. Some people have more roving eyes than others. If I strain my eyes, I can sometimes pierce the darkness or the fog. I look *through* the dusty window. Can't we sometimes feel a pair of eyes upon us? The picture is not wrong, but some of the conclusions I drew from it, if I had taken them with philosophic seriousness, would be puzzling indeed. This old picture does not lead us much astray, because we do not expect to satisfy by it any theoretical craving.

The trouble with the belief that we see what is contemporary with our seeing is that it is understood as the contrary of the belief that we directly see the past. So it is just as puzzling and as little at peace with our usual talk. I suppose that if one were dominated in his thinking by the picture of the eye reaching its tongue out into the world, he might indeed think that "a state of affairs he perceives exists simultaneously with his perception of it." That is, if we were asked the philosophical question, "Do you, sir, believe that what you see is simultaneous with your seeing?" he would be inclined as Chisholm says we all are, to answer "Yes." I suppose also that if that picture seemed to him to determine and to be determined by all the idioms and phrase-uses involved when we talk of seeing, his answer would be described by him as "common-sense." Would such a person be disturbed by learning about light rays, the scientific explanation of vision involving photo-chemical stimulation of the retina, and the discovery that light takes years to reach the eye from stars? He most certainly would not be shocked and bewildered by an *announcement* of all this. He could not be informed of the scientific account of vision as he could be informed of the death of a close friend. Such things cannot be learned in a moment or an afternoon.

If "commonsense" in such a case amounts to being ruled by a picture, it is not a superficial thing. It is, rather, the outcome of life among people who have such a way of thought, a way which has some definite basis in commonly used metaphors and styles of talking. Then against all this there would not be just a moment of discovery, but a slow mastery of new techniques and modes of explanation. In the process, I suppose that one would learn that he had to fight against and overcome some deep-set resistance. He might find his "commonsense" steering him wrong. He would not discover that "commonsense" was giving him the wrong answer to some definite question, because the new questions would arise as suggestions of a new and very different picture. It is most unlikely that he would ever have been confronted by a question torn out of this new context, like the one Chisholm imagines we would all answer wrongly. Suppose we knew such a man, from a nonscientific society. And suppose we, people from a culture of science, were to ask him Chisholm's question, and suppose he answered "Yes"; he did believe that the object seen was simultaneous with the seeing of it. What would we make of that? It would certainly be grossly misleading to say that he had a strong tendency to answer a factual question in the wrong way, that is, that he was inclined to get some fact wrong.

His picture is a very pretty thing. It is fun to consider, but I do not know what to say about it—seriously. The modern picture, of light travelling, stimulating the eye, starting a current in the optic nerve, is another matter. It can grip some of us, and lead us wrong, not to get our facts wrong but to get things wrong in other more roundabout ways. One of the ways in which it leads us astray is one in which our nonscientific man will not, I suppose, be misled by his picture-thoughts. His picture presents seeing as something done by the seer, reaching out and getting hold of an object. The light-ray story, if we are not very careful, leads us to represent seeing as something which happens: and, moreover, something which happens because something else happens. Light starting from a star, after its long, long trip, is focused by the lens on the retina, a nerve current travels along the optic nerve, and then—and then we see.

It is in part this way of thinking about seeing, I suspect, which gives us the misleading idea that the velocity of light has something to do with what we say when we talk of seeing stars. We think of seeing as something which light rays bring about. But what does this physico-optical story have to do with the way we see? Let us look at some examples. First, consider how we see a pattern. There is a group of stars which I cannot see. Someone points, traces the outline by shining a light; I cannot find it. Then he describes the pattern: a flattened dipper, a box kite, a squat tea-kettle. He talks and I look, trying to visualize the pattern, trying to find it. I relax my effort a little, and suddenly I see it. It is not quite what I was looking for. But I see that his description was appropriate, and I understand why I could not at first find the pattern. Can I think here of a series of happenings which begin at the star, proceed through my eye, then in the optic nerve, and finally I see a pattern. Where does my understanding of familiar patterns, my knowing what to look for fit into the series of happenings? What about my concentrated, attentive looking, the relaxation of slightly mistaken anticipation, the surprising emergence of that pattern out of the thick spattering of stars over the sky? The light-ray and nerve-current account is just the wrong kind of story.

Think of another example. One night there was an important meeting at the Boar's Heart Lodge Hall, and only a select few of the oldest members were allowed to attend. A very young and very ardent member who was not among those invited watched through a window. He watched, and shook with fear as he watched because he could not keep himself from violating the sacred law against uninvited eyes. He said he saw the white-haired, old exalted master pass over his hat and his powers to the new exalted ruler. The janitor, waiting to clean up the hall, said that he saw two silly-looking men with gold stripes on their sleeves mumbling to each other, and one of them removed a hat with horns and put it on the other's head. Did the two see the same thing? Is what they saw the outcome of light rays? If the janitor should later join the lodge, even years later, and he learned its rituals and respected its rules, he would give a different report of what he saw. Then he would say, perhaps, "I saw what few are allowed to see, the ritual of the passing of powers of the exalted master." This does not conflict with his former report; it is not a correction. What he sees in this case depends upon changes which take place in him over many years, and may become effective long after the original occurrences at the back of his eyes. As children, when we begin to talk of seeing stars in the sky, we know nothing of light rays and optic nerves. Later we learn. Is our position, then, something like that of the converted janitor? Do we now say we saw something different? Do we say, "I saw the distant past of a source of light in space"? It is most unlikely that learning the theory of light could bring about a conversion which would make one see the sky so differently.

Simpler things can change what one saw. You walk through a room where two people are playing a game. You catch a glimpse, say you saw someone hopping a little black horse. Later you learn chess. You may learn about the game you saw that day and come to say, "I saw Ninsky making that odd knight's move in his variation of the Indian defense." You see a stranger standing beside the clothes rack, hanging up a coat. Later you learn that he was stealing a valuable gift from the pocket. You then say you saw the thief in the act of stealing. Here you come to understand what was going on. We do not come to see anything like a ritual or a pocket-rifling going on in the heavens. There are other related cases. At the beginning of a biology course, you say you saw a queer-looking machine with a crank like a coffee grinder. Later you learn its use and its construction. You say you saw a microtome. Or, you saw a curiously-marked rock. Later you say you saw a fossilized Devonian shark's tail.[7] In these cases we tell, after the fact, what we saw as a result of a new understanding of the object. We tell truthfully what we did see. The philosophical thesis about seeing the past is not illustrated by examples like these. The thesis is not a prediction that after a study of astrophysics we shall say we saw something different in the night sky. It is not a report of what astronomers say they saw. It is not advice to acquire the educated eye of the astronomer.

These examples suggest that "seeing the past" might be like "thief," "microtome," or "Devonian fossil." Of course, it is not: maybe this is one of the reasons it is so disturbing. The phrase refuses to behave as a technical one ought. The phrase is disturbing because from a very definite scientific discovery, I

---

[7] Compare these cases with that of the pink-center chocolate, which works out differently. The question there, too, was what one saw before he knew. But what one learns in that case does not effect what one saw because, I suppose, it cannot effect what one can see in future cases.

get such puzzling, and such indefinite, results. Shall I say I look into the past? point to the past? or into the past? Do I hear the past? directly with my ears? listen for sounds from the past? direct my hearing into the past? I do not say such things. And I want to know whether anything might justify me in saying them. And which of them I should say, and why these and not others. Does the idea that I see the past of stars help me to understand philosophical theories of memory, or the nature of human freedom? So I have tried to remind myself of how I talk about seeing, and especially about seeing stars. And I have become aware of the obvious, namely, that looking at a star even while thinking or talking about its distance is not the sort of situation in which we say we are looking at the distant past. A dramatic archeology professor might say, "We are looking at the distant past," while displaying some unusually realistic paintings of prehistoric man. I needed only a general, but pointed, reminder of how we talk, how we learned to talk, too, perhaps. The light-ray and nerve-current consideration has nothing to do with that. It tends to misrepresent the facts, of which I need reminding: one of these facts is that the verb "to see" is not used to announce something which happens, that is, not in the way the physico-physiological picture leads me to think. "I saw the stone" does not tell of something that happened to me as does, "I was struck by the stone," or, "I stumbled over the stone."

If seeing is something which happens, perhaps I can be surprised when it happens. Maybe it could happen without my being aware of it. What would that be like? Suppose we build a narrow room with powerful electromagnets in the walls. Then by creating a strong magnetic field in the room we can induce hallucination in a person standing there. When the magnets are turned off, the hallucination ceases. Now we have a subject, Dreyfuss, standing at one end of the room. The magnets are turned on and Dreyfuss says he sees an orange ball floating in the air near the farther wall. He walks toward it, reaches out, cannot touch it; it seems to pass through his hand. Then we turn off the magnets and the ball disappears before his eyes. He learns what to expect, and in later experiments he will say, "It seems as if I am seeing an orange ball."

At last we shall make all preparations for an experiment, and instead of turning on the magnets we shall swing an orange ball about on a thin transparent string. Suppose again Dreyfuss says, "It seems just as if I were seeing a ball." Now we let him feel the ball. We show him the string. We tell him what happened. He might say, "I was not aware that I was really seeing a ball." This, I suppose, is the sort of thing which we would say was "a person seeing without being aware of it," or "a person surprised to discover that he was seeing." However it is not what the light-ray picture suggests. It is not a case where someone becomes aware of something which happens as a result of light rays. Dreyfuss did not finally notice that something was taking place in him. He was shown that the orange ball was real. He could touch it, put it in his pocket. What he noticed, what he became aware of, was the reality of the ball. His attention was not called to something going on in himself. He noticed nothing in his nervous system, nothing in his mind.

The picture leads us to believe that we could invent an electronic device which could correctly use the word "see." It would be like a camera with an electronic scanner which classifies images on the ground glass. It types the names of each. Let us call it "George." When it receives reflected light from a buffalo, it types "buffalo," from a bandicoot, it types "bandicoot." We say, "George sees a bandicoot," "George sees a buffalo," and things like that. Now let us examine some other cases of seeing.

You might not recognize a man you see, but you remember that he is an airforce colonel you once met. You might say, "I saw that airforce colonel." Will the machine be able to see an airforce colonel, even when he is not in uniform? Can we rig the machine to see a pattern in the sky? Will it be able to see a polar bear or a spouting whale in the cumulus clouds? Compare George's performance with our having seen a thief at the clothes rack, a microtome, a Devonian fossil. Just as there is a great difference often between present tense and past tense reports of what is seen, there is an analogous difference between first and third person accounts. Someone says he saw a man at the clothes rack. We, quite correctly, say he saw a thief at his crime. Suppose the machine types, "Man standing near round object on stick." Would we feel right in saying, "George saw President Roosevelt reading to the nation a declaration of war against Japan?" If the machine is to represent the role of the verb "to see" in our language, it will have to be vastly complicated.

Compare the machine with the behavior of Crumley. Crumley doubts giraffes deeply. A friend takes him to the zoo, and shows him one. Crumley sees but does not believe. What will his friend say to him about his seeing? Perhaps he would ask a question, "Now, surely you see a giraffe?" Or he would say, "Now you can see a giraffe. Right there it is." Crumley still doubts. What will his friend say then? "You really do see a giraffe"? "You really do see a giraffe, there"? "What you see is a giraffe"? "What you see is really a giraffe"? "You ought to realize that you see a giraffe"? "You will come to realize that today you did see a giraffe"? He could even say simply, "You see a giraffe," or "You *do* see a giraffe," without being misunderstool. There would have to be a certain tone of voice, and this would depend a lot upon what had come before, and upon what he thought was likely to follow. Well, does Crumley see a giraffe? He will not say he does: he will deny that he does. We can say he does or we can say he does not. I suppose if we pursued some philosophical interest in the "concept of seeing," the answer would be "Yes and no, but mostly no." Mostly no, he does not see even when his eyes are pointed right, and the proper assortment of light rays are stimulating his receptors, and I presume, also, the right nerve currents and the rest. Still, mostly he does not see. But what would one want with such a question or such an answer after he had seen the facts. If our machine is to keep pace, it will have to learn to doubt, and to refrain from typing when it doubts.

What are we to do with our machine in the light of these observations of Crumley? I suspect, in this case as in others, we can imagine more and more complex machines until we had one about which we should be inclined to talk as we talk about Crumley. We would address the machine in a kindly tone, in an effort to help resolve its doubts. "George," we would say, "you really do see a giraffe, there." Then we would have imagined a man with Crumley's doubt about giraffes. But the picture of light rays and nerve currents is much too little with which to do a man's job.

For philosophical purposes, we must not think of seeing as something which happens at a certain time, or has anything to do with the time light travels. We need to be reminded that it involves matters which precede and follow by years; learning the patterns recognized by the eyes of a culture, learning to live the rules and ideals of a lodge or club and to perceive the sights which its attitudes determine, to know the illusions and tricks, when to doubt, and how to correct mistaken reports, how to modify past tense reports in view of what we learn, of law, of science, of almost anything. Learning to say, "I see . . . ," "I saw . . . ," and "You can see . . . ," "He saw . . . ," is learning a way of life. Part of this way of life is to talk of seeing stars from smoky back yards and clear mountaintops, to know what shepherds might see as they watch over their flocks by night, to test one's vision on Alcor, the little companion of Mizar.

At any rate, I think I can understand why it is an ideal just to get everything set before us: the things we say about the stars, the metaphors we use, to what uses we put them, and the ways they bedevil us when we do not watch out.

IV

AND THEN I SEE

I have not really come to grips with the "causal" picture of vision. Perhaps one can't: it takes so many forms, and it leads one astray in so many different directions. I only wanted to say (in Essay III, "How Philosophers See Stars") that if we don't watch out, it will lead us to think of seeing as something which happens at the end of a sequence of things, things which begin in the reflection of light-rays from some object seen. It is quite apparent that vision will not fit the place assigned to it in this representation: so the causal picture will not mislead us for long. At least it will not mislead us in this way for long. But we do not promptly put the picture out of mind: it has a firm hold on our thinking.

The picture gets a hold on us and we become mystified by vision; out of the mystification, we ask questions; and the picture *seems* to give us answers to the questions. For one thing, vision can seem mystifying because of the distances involved. "How *can* I see that—over there—over a block away?" What are some answers? "I can see it by squinting: otherwise the light is blinding." "I can see it by using my minus-5 glasses: otherwise I am too nearsighted." These do not answer my question. What is my question? My colleague Morton, a physiologist, seems to answer it for me in a popular lecture. He asks, "How can I see that over there?" Then he goes on, "Light is reflected from the surface, focused by the lens of my eyes. An image is formed on the retina which causes chemical changes there. These chemical changes generate electro-magnetic impulses which travel the optic nerve to the brain. The structures and processes involved are now understood in considerable detail."

Ah, yes. That's the explanation I wanted. So I think at first. But then perhaps Morton's question is not my question after all. He is perfectly satisfied with his answer, and he is not a stupid fellow. I soon discover the answer will not do for me at all. I think of a series of things that happen, beginning with the reflection of light rays at the object. They effect electro-chemical changes in my nervous system. And at the end of this sequence of events, I see. I confront this with the facts, and of course it will not do. How does the picture fit the fact that sometimes I see, sometimes I do not see, and sometimes I think I see but I'm not sure? I am lost with a friend, and I go up on the hilltop to look around. My friend calls, "What do you see?" "I think I see a barn in the distance." How could I think I see? Does the sequence of electro-chemical changes in my nerves and brain sometimes produce something between seeing and not-seeing? Perhaps the causal picture will lead me to say that I do not doubt *that* I see: my doubts are about *what* I see. Yet when I see, I see something. Seeing is closely tied to its object.

Doing a jigsaw puzzle becomes inexplicable in terms of the "purely causal" picture of vision. I look over the pieces carefully many times. I know exactly what shape piece will fit. I conclude the piece must be missing. And then I see it. It was right before my eyes all the time. I examined it several times before and did not recognize it. How could I not have seen it before? It was in good light. My eyes were pointed right at it: they were focused clearly upon it. Was there some chemical or electromagnetic failure in my retina or in my optic nerve? When at last I see the piece, I may say, "I see it," or, "That's it," or more likely, "My good God, that's it right there." I announce success, I register achievement, and I am often right, but I may be wrong. There is no room in the causal story for achievement, success, right and wrong. There is no room for what precedes and leads up to the success—if success comes. If success does not come, there is no room for what makes the failure a failure. There is no room for educated and refined searching: the very thing which makes the jigsaw piece so hard to see.

What one sees depends in so many ways upon who he is, what he knows, what business he is engaged in, and many other things. Often what one sees depends on something he learns later, sometimes many years later. I say that I saw my father playing Santa Claus, although I only learned later that it was not really Santa Claus and that it was really my father. There is no place in the causal picture for dependent variableness in the *object* of seeing. Depending on how far my lessons in plane-spotting have gone, I may see a small plane, a small jet plane, a single-engine jet plane, an F104. Yet, after surveying these things and many more, I do not simply put away the causal picture. It keeps a strong fascination. Something about the picture fits or seems to fit. "Seeing," I think, "results from this." "Seeing is produced by this." And sometimes something does result in seeing. "What happens when you press inward against your closed eyes?" "I see blue patches." "What happens when you are hit on the head?" "I see stars." "What happens when we turn the bright light in your face and then turn it off?" "I see a green after-image." These are cases where we speak of "causes." "A blow on the head frequently causes one to see stars."

While exercised by the so-called causal picture I am not interested in causes in that way. "What caused the accident?" "Faulty brakes." If "faulty brakes" is the answer, then "the wheels turned" is not the answer—although the faulty brakes caused the accident by grabbing in such a way that the wheels turned. This, in turn, led to one car's fender coming in contact with the fender of another car. Still less does "One fender came in contact with another" give the answer to the question, "What caused the accident?" Yet one fender coming in contact with another is what happened just a very very short time before the accident. Also, the cause is not the whole sequence of events leading to the accident. The answer to the question is not, "Everything up to and including one fender coming in contact with another." When I try to explain seeing to myself in terms of the causal picture, there is not one thing—say, light refracting in the lens of the eyes, or a chemical change taking place on the retina— which I call "the cause" of seeing. The explanation I want is given only by the whole pictured sequence of occurrences.

There are other times, too, when I speak of the cause of seeing. "What caused the blind man to suddenly see?" "A pressure on the optic nerve was relieved by a fall." This seems to be the home of the physiologist's explanation. It enables us to find causes in cases like this. We can discover the causes of blindness and of visual defects. I do not ask, "What caused the blind man to see the cheetah in the zoo?" even though he regained his sight at the zoo, and the first thing he saw was the cheetah. The cause in question is the cause of the blind man's recovery of vision. It seems we ask for causes of untoward, unexpected, unusual, out-of-the-way occurrences, or for wanted or unwanted occurrences. And for a variety of reasons, we identify the cause as one thing: an unusual thing, a thing we can change, a thing in which we have some other special interest. I am not, in these ways, interested in "the causes of vision." The explanation which keeps hold of me is the picture of a long sequence of events leading up to vision. And it is the whole "act" of seeing with its complete detailed object that I expect to be explained.

Sometimes we point out one thing which explains how we see something, although we do not speak of that thing as the cause. "How did you happen to see that?" "The wind blew the curtain aside at just the moment." "Someone flashed a light at just the right moment." Unlike the explanations of the blind man's recovery, these are things which explain my seeing some particular thing. Although they seem to fit the "causal" picture, they are not explanations of the kind I want. Such explanations will work for only very special occurrences, and I imagine an explanation which will fit anyone at any time seeing anything at all. I think I see that no such explanation is to be found. There is no relevant question to be asked. Also, my examples show that seeing involves features which fall completely outside the scope of any such explanation-outline. And still I do not simply put away the causal picture. The fascination of the picture remains.

I hang on to the picture, and I think of a way I can save it. Right and wrong, success and failure, what I know or find out—all these things apply to the interpretative element involved in seeing. Something is produced by the action of light rays and nerve currents, and that something must then be recognized, classified, interpreted. I say, "I see an immature golden eagle soaring over the hilltop." Something is produced in my mind by light rays and nerve currents. Having that in my mind, I take it to be the product of or to somehow represent a soaring, immature golden eagle. If the something in my mind were not so complete or distinct, or if I had less experience in identifying birds, I might say, "I see a large, soaring bird," or, " . . . large, broad-winged, hawk-like bird." I might make different interpretations of the same mental something.

Although the word "interpretation" comes to mind when I try to express this philosophical theory, it does not seem the right word. I think that there is something given, and I "interpret it." I am thinking of the thing given as like an object, a stone, a bird, a tree. It is less than an object, an "inner" object, but it must be something like an object. What else could I be thinking of?

When do we "interpret" an object? "I interpret that stone on the walk as some-one's deliberate effort to make me stumble." Interpretations of objects, it would seem, are in terms of human (or divine) purposes or plans. "Interpretation" goes easier with actions. "He interpreted my movement as a threat. I intended it as a friendly gesture."

Still I am impelled to use the word "interpretation" in trying to speak of an element in perception. The word "interpretation" sticks in my mind. And there is more trouble, too, in making "interpretation" do the job. I can look long and hard at a drawing and not see the animal hidden there. Later I can return and find the animal immediately. In both cases, there are light rays and nerve-cur-rents. In one there is seeing and success, in the other not-seeing and failure. How does this fit the idea that there is something produced by light rays and nerve-currents, and then also an "interpretation?" I must say that the role of interpretation is not simple. Of course I must be familiar with the animal and its outline representation. Also, I must not be looking for the wrong sort of animal or the wrong sort of representation. I must not anticipate too definitely that the animal will be in one position rather than another. I must blame "pre-mature interpretation" for keeping me from seeing what I am intended to see, what otherwise I am capable of seeing. But when I fail to see the hidden animal in the painting, I have placed no interpretation on the painting. Unless, of course, I interpret it as someone's effort to make me look a fool. And when I see the animal I do not say, "I interpret the lines as an animal."

Yet I want to save the picture: I want to say that something like interpreta-tion must be involved. Something is given to me and "I make it out to be ... ," "I recognize it as ... ," "I identify it as ... ," "I see it as ... ," "I take it to be ... " I'm afraid none of these expressions fare better than "I interpret it as ... " With blinders on my eyes, I handle an object. "I make the object out to be a magnifying glass." "Although repaired and repainted, I recognize the chest of drawers as the one I carried to the dump last summer." "Although it was in winter plumage, I was able to identify the bird as a Myrtle Warbler." The trouble here is that the thing confronted and the thing it is made out to be or the thing it is recognized as being or identified as being, are the same thing. My theory of vision requires that the thing given, the "inner" thing, be different from the thing seen, the "outer" thing. They must be two distinct entities. I think I see a man on the hill. It turns out not to be a man. What I see is a dead bush. I do not say, "I saw the dead bush as a man." I might see a stone on my walk as a deliberate effort of someone to do me harm. "See as" is more like "interpret as." At least these two idioms are appropriate in one respect: each is used to refer to two different objects. The first object, a stone is different from the second object, a plan to do me harm. But a plan to do me harm is not the kind of "object" my theory requires. I might say, "I took the dead bush on the hill to be a man," but I would say this only when I had made a mistake. I cannot use the phrase, "take to be . . . ," in stating my theory of vision, because my theory must cover getting things right as well as getting them wrong. This two-part theory of vision leads me astray at every step. And still I want to cast the causal picture over perception. I shall have to borrow a little from one word, a little from another, and try to get on. Can one do that? At least, when I think the theory and these words come to mind, I will always imagine the words in quotes.

(1) I am trying to read a short message written in code. I try various simple tricks and fail. By this time I am so familiar with the coded message that I can carry it about in my head, the letters and spaces exactly as they are on the paper. I can try to crack the code while waiting in bus stations and while having lunch. Then one time I say, "I've got it. I see it. The words are broken into their syllables and each syllable is spelled backwards." (2) Harley has eidetic imagery. We show him the drawing with the hidden animal, and he cannot see the animal. Later, while sitting in the park, whittling a stick, he has the drawing clearly before his mind's eye. And suddenly he sees the animal in the drawing.

Here are cases where one sees, but not with his eyes. An object is before the mind's eye (a mental object) and one can consider it this way and that, one can recognize or fail to recognize what is there. To make a place for causation, I imagine seeing with the eyes as like these cases. Something is produced by light-rays and nerve currents, something mental. It is the mental counterpart of the lines and spaces in the drawing. This is the first part of seeing. The rest of seeing comes after, the rest comes as a result of recognizing, identifying, interpreting, that mental object. Right and wrong, success and failure come with this second part. Seeing the animal comes in here.

What is the something which is produced by electro-chemical changes in my brain? What is this something which I interpret? I have already noted that some occurrences can produce seeing: seeing stars or after-images or blue patches. Perhaps the object produced by light rays and nerve currents is like the objects of these seeings: like stars or after-images. In these cases, what is produced is "seeing an after-image" or "seeing stars." If by analogy, some object is produced by nerve currents, then the nerve currents ought to produce my seeing that object. Yet that does not seem to be right. When I see a strange bird pecking at the suet-ball on my fence I do not see another kind of thing which I interpret. I may or may not recognize the bird. I may take it for a winter Audubon's Warbler when it is really a winter Myrtle Warbler. Always, it's the bird I recognize or fail to recognize, not some other inner, mental object.

I may have the object present and not see it. I have the object. Then something like interpreting it takes place, and so I see the bird. Seeing the bird must consist in that. Likewise I may have an after-image and not see it. I stare at a bright red circle (about two inches in diameter) and then when I turn my head upward, I see a green after-image. However, when I turn toward the green wall, I do not see the after-image; and then when I turn toward the white wall I see it again. "I must have the after-image all the time. I just can't see it against the green wall. It's the same color as the wall." In this case, I could say that I have an after-image at a time when I can't see it, and this would be understood by anyone knowing the details of the case. I would not say this, however, unless I could turn toward the green wall and then the white wall, that is, I must be able to have the green wall and the white wall in my field of vision. Neither the green wall nor the white wall is one of those somethings produced by light rays and nerve currents. They are what philosophers call "physical objects."

Well, suppose I did not see the walls. Instead, when I turn my head one way I see a circular green after-image against a white background and when I turn the other, my whole field of vision is a uniform green. There are now no walls in my field of vision. Rather, the whole field is just as if it were produced by staring at the bright red circle. Now, I think I will not say that I have an after-image which I cannot see. I may say that the after-image changes when I turn my head. First it is a small circle; then it fills my whole visual field. More likely, I will not know what to say or think. Perhaps some new phenomenon is at work here, one I know nothing about. At any rate, this seems to show that my saying that I have an after-image which I do not see depends on my seeing a "physical object." And, of course, I wanted it to be the other way around. My seeing a physical object is supposed to depend on my having something like an after-image which I do not see. Then my interpretation of that something should amount to seeing a physical object.

Perhaps I do see the something, but I am not aware that I see it. "Did you ever see the changing of the guard?" 'No. I've always wanted to. I've gone to the tomb, and all I've seen is several men in uniform marching up and down." "How many men?" "Sometimes four, sometimes eight." "When there are eight men, that *is* the changing of the guard." "I saw the changing of the guard, then. I was not aware of it." This does not give what I want at all. I saw eight men. I did not know that four of them were the new guard and four the old. I did not properly interpret what I saw. I am trying to imagine that I see something which I interpret, and I am not aware that I see that something. I am trying to imagine something like this: I see the changing of the guard but I am not aware that I see some men in uniform.

I have the idea that beneath each interpretation there is a simpler object, until at last I arrive at the simplest, a something which is completely uninterpreted. I see it, but I am not aware that I see it. "Are you sure it was a man you saw on the dark street? Didn't you think it was a man because of the clothing?" "Well, I saw somebody." "Are you quite sure it was a person?" "It was something." "Couldn't it have been an after-image you saw when you turned your head from the lighted paper to the dark window?" If I saw an after-image, I was certainly not aware that I did. Perhaps it is possible to think an after-image is something moving on the street. The trouble is this: if I admit that I saw an after-image, I deny that I saw a person or even the shadow of a person. In seeing a simple something, I must not deny that I see a physical object. In seeing a physical object, I must *always* see a simple something—and yet be unaware that I do.

I am trying to think of a case in which a person really sees a thing, and in seeing that thing he also sees a simpler thing of which he is unaware. Since once reading about it, Hadley has wanted to see a Meta-Sequoia tree. One winter day, while walking across the campus, Hadley mentions this to a botanist. The botanist says, "Why that's one there, right in front of your office building. See the queer shape. Didn't you notice that the needles dropped in the Fall?" "Why, I've seen that tree a thousand times. I guess I'm not very observant on my way to and from the office."

Later, to a friend, Hadley says, "You remember I told you I wanted to see a Meta-Sequoia?" "Of course." "I learned that I've seen one every day for years." Hadley saw the Meta-Sequoia many times and was not aware of it. I suppose he also saw an evergreen which loses its needles in winter, and he was unaware of that, too, a simpler object. In seeing the more complex object, a Meta-Sequoia, he saw a simpler object, a deciduous evergreen. And he was unaware that he saw the simpler object. This is not the example I want, because Hadley was also unaware that he saw the more complex object. He did not interpret what he saw as a Meta-Sequoia tree. I want an example in which someone correctly interprets what he sees; and in seeing that, he also sees something simpler of which he is unaware.

I have been a bird watcher for many years. I have seen many ravens and I have never had difficulty in identifying them. One cannot always tell them by size from the crow; but the profile is different and they fly quite differently. Mostly it is a matter of the way they hold their wings when they glide, I think. One day I am on a field trip with a friend who is new at bird watching. I raise my binoculars to my eyes, and he asks, "What do you see?" I say, "I see a raven." He asks, "When you see a raven do you see a bird with a wedge-shaped tail?" What am I to say? I ask what he means. "I mean do you recognize it as a raven by it wedge-shaped tail?" Then the answer is, "No." In fact, I have never thought about the tail. I have never noticed the shape of the tail. If you had asked me about the shape of the tail I could not have told you it had a wedge shape.

I want an example where in seeing one thing, I see another simpler thing of which I am not aware. I supposed that in seeing a raven I might see a bird with a wedge-shaped tail and be unaware of it. So far, it seems that I do not. Suppose two other new bird students are along on the trip. They are bringing up the rear. The first raises his binoculars when he sees me raise mine. He hears me speak. The second asks, "What does F. E. see?" The first replies, "I didn't quite hear what he said, but I'm sure it was that large black bird with a wedge-shaped tail." So, I do see a bird with a wedge-shaped tail although I am unaware of it.

My philosophical quest leads on. Now, I want to say that behind the bird I saw a feathered blob and behind the blob the simplest thing of all, an inner something; and I am unaware of any of the characteristics of the something, unaware even of its presence. I was unaware of the shape of the raven's tail and in that sense unaware that I saw a bird with a wedge-shaped tail. The rest of it will not do. When I see the raven I could not be unaware that I see a bird, or a black flying object, or anything at all. My picture has led me on a ridiculous hunt and I should not be surprised, because the quarry has been that queer, elusive entity, the sense-datum.

Ridiculous as it now seems, it is still not easy to be free of the confusing influence of the causal picture. Something is produced, and I interpret that something when I see. The something is inner, mental. Isn't this shown in cases where I am extremely cautious about what I see? Usually I retreat to another, simpler object when my interpretation is wrong, or at least not certain. And in unusual circumstances I may retreat again and again. In the most extreme of cases I may mistake an after-image or a product of the heat-oppressed brain for something or some person.

Philosophers who labor under the influence of this causal picture usually urge security, and they think that security demands complete retreat. They have become suspicious of any visual object beyond the very simplest, the bare something. I imagined that we were first mystified by the distances involved in vision. Perhaps ontogeny recapitulates phylogeny. The first philosophers may have been puzzled by the distances over which we see. I see a blue coffee can on the table across the room. How can I be sensitively aware of something way over there? My sentience does not extend beyond my body: as I reach, it ends at my finger tips. Then comes the explanation: light rays, chemical changes, electro-magnetic currents and finally the inner object. At my end of the causal transactions I have something produced by electromagnetic changes in my brain. The coffee can cannot be transmitted to my brain, yet I take the object to be, or to represent, a blue coffee can. It is perhaps easiest to become suspicious of the color. How could anything corresponding to color be in the coffee can? Color is the product of chemical and electrical changes in me. Colors are not in the visible objects, but in me the viewer. The distinction between primary and secondary qualities comes early in the history of philosophy.

Soon, I find myself saying, "We could not really see color." "Things only appear to be colored." I look at a drinking glass. I see an amber colored drinking glass. Then I say, "Things are not really colored"; I say, "It only appears to be amber." A thing often appears to be one color, when it really is another. Perhaps it's really brown, and a yellow light is shining on it. Then it may appear to be amber; but it is really brown. I want to say, "It appears to be amber, but it is not: I mean it is not any color. The color you see is not in it." What could that mean? It's clear glass, and it's lighted by an amber light. The color is really in the light. It has no color at all: it's clear, transparent glass. That's not at all what I want to say. A clear transparent surface is not part of the thing either. "It only appears to have clear transparent surfaces. In reality it's nothing like that." Then perhaps it's a mirror. I may think I am looking through the mirror: I may think it's transparent. Really it's not. But a thing can't have a surface like a mirror either. It can't have any surface-characteristic discernible by sight, except perhaps size and shape. What sort of thing could that be? Nothing with which I am familiar. Yet the philosophical theory purports to talk about all the most familiar things: birds, flowers, teapots, candy boxes, and coffee cans.

In the case of color, I want to say that everyone gives the wrong interpretation and everyone learns to do this at a very early age. The propensity to be wrong becomes so strong that later lessons in physiological optics are of no avail. Even epistemologists are strongly inclined to say they see colors, and they usually do say they see colors—except when they remind themselves of the error.

There is a special difficulty with the idea of interpretation when the interpretation is always, or nearly always, wrong. Can I suppose for a moment that in vision there is a something which I interpret? I don't know how, but I shall pretend that I can. I shall give the causal picture free rein, and think as it leads me. In the skull, at the end of the optic nerve is a little theater. The optic nerve produces pictures on the screen of the theater, and there I can examine them. When I have a certain picture there, I say, "I see a stone fence." How do I know that is the right interpretation? How do I—except that others, under similar circumstances, say that they see a stone fence and the proper related things? They say, "There is an old stone fence," "The stone fence is made of granite," and things like that. While looking at what others call a stone fence, if I say, "I see a dead boa constrictor," then I know I have it wrong. I am giving the wrong interpretation of the picture on the screen of my little theater. I say, "I see a small bird with a hooked beak and pointed wings. It has a red back and its wings are blue." When I say that I am making a mistake. No bird's back is really red, no wings are blue, because nothing is really colored. (I know I must not say, "The back *appears* to be red, the wings *appear* to be blue.") Why do I say, "The bird has a red back; its wings are blue"? That is what everybody or nearly everybody, says under the right circumstances. If everybody, or nearly everybody, says the bird is red and blue, isn't it red and blue? Nearly everybody calls it a sparrow hawk, and it is a sparrow hawk.

A zoologist might say that although everybody calls the bird a sparrow hawk, it is really not a hawk. It is a falcon. He might say the name "hawk" is a misnomer; people would better see the relations among birds if they did not use that name for it. In time he might succeed in a new-name campaign, and people will come to call the bird "sparrow falcon," or "blue-winged falcon." The names of the colors, too, we learn in childhood, and from the people around us. But there the similarity between bird names and color names ends. When I think that things are not really colored, I am not registering any complaint that our color words obscure the relations among things. I have no new color words to propose, no new color distinctions to make. New color words would be no better than old; for no color distinctions can really be made.

"I *see* the colors of the hawk, I see them clearly with my eyes." I say that now only because I have not learned my philosophical lesson. I could not really see colors. To say I see something is to say it is the way I see it. I cannot see something which is not there, and colors are not there. There are no colors on the wing or on the back of the sparrow hawk. Hence I cannot see the red of the back, the blue of the wing. What explains such a big mistake? I must realize that vision is most unreliable. It is very indirect: between a visual object and the brain the causal chain is long, and it has many kinds of links. (It was the distances involved in vision that first provoked wonder.) By contrast, touch is direct. The real features of a thing are registered directly by bumping, poking, jabbing the body. Hence I must expect misjudgments of vision, and I must correct them by the more reliable judgments of touch. As before, these conclusions seem to fit some things, but they do not fit others. I do often correct visual judgments by touch. "It looks rough, but it is really smooth." Just as often, however, the correction is the other way around. I correct judgments of touch by vision. "It feels curved, but it is really straight, as I can tell by sighting along the edge." "It feels as though an insect were walking on the back of my hand, but I can see that none is there."

I did not mean that judgments of color are wrong in the sense that they need correction. I meant they are wrongly applied: they have no application at all. That's what I meant by saying, "Things are not really colored." The causal picture leads me to think that I learned a great mistake in childhood. What exactly was it? To make all kinds of color judgments when, in fact, there are none to be made. How could this be? It must be like this. In childhood we learn the meaning of color words. We also learn the meaning of shape words. And we learn that color words and shape words are applied to things in the same way. Each is intended to name a real feature of things, and each is correctly applied only when it does refer to the real feature of a thing. The shape of a thing can be determined by touch in the dark. The color cannot be determined by touch. Ergo, the thing is not really colored.

Isn't it strange that I never came to realize that color words are all a big mistake, that is, I never came to realize it until I began to study philosophy. How could I have learned that color words are like shape words when that means they would have no use at all? Somehow in the carefree years of childhood, I learned to live a beautiful, coherent delusion. This conclusion requires a certain very old story about meaning. We learn to use a word, but the real meaning of the word may not be reflected in its use. Everyone might always use a word in a way which runs against its true meaning. After having learned the real meaning, one may "forget" it. It may become buried in the depths of the mind, and only philosophical analysis or dialectic can bring the hidden meaning back into the open. When at last it is revealed, it may turn out to be contradictory. This is the case with color words: they refer to real features, but they also refer to unreal visual features.

It is little wonder that we "forget" the meaning of a color word, or at least, forget part of it. How could we ever have learned it? We must have learned it by analogy, the way we might learn to carry a gun by carrying a broom-stick. Or perhaps it would be more like learning to ice-skate by practicing on roller-skates. When we finally turn to the ice-skates, we must unlearn a great deal. It would be even more like learning to fly in the style of superman by running and diving, arms out, into the water. When we try it in the air, we sadly discover that it cannot be done at all. How we could have learned the color words, whose use hides a contradiction, is, in fact, a mystery.

Colors are out, and lady-bugs do not have characteristics other than those we can learn by touch. I cannot drive out of my mind the wrong idea that lady-bugs and many other beetles, too, are brightly colored. I got this idea by incorporating into my own speech the way everyone else talks of the color of beetles: some are red, some blue, some irridescent green. The colors change with age, and they often vary geographically within one species. All of this orderly array of distinctions, all of this way of speaking has no application. It is all a grand delusion. Well, since everyone speaks this way and find its useful, is there any harm in it? Yes, I must suppose there is, because it leads us to think that we can learn how things really are by looking at them. And how do we learn how things really are? By touch alone. Has the phrase "really are" now come to mean "determinable by touch"? Then to say a thing is not colored is to say that we cannot speak of the color of a thing if we rely only on the sense of touch. And to say that color words have no application is to say that we cannot use color words to report what we learn by touch. After going round and round, the hunt now seems to be heading toward home.

I want to turn from the philosophical hunt for awhile and reflect on the question with which I began. Why did the causal explanation send me on a fantastic search? Why did it not send Morton too? Isn't it that same old thing? I was looking for the "essence" of seeing. First I thought that Morton gave me the answer, but I found he did not—rather, he did not give me the complete answer. Then I thought of seeing itself as something which could be analyzed into parts: the causal part and the interpretative part. I thought Morton's explanation gave me the causal part of what I wanted. My question was "What does seeing (always and everywhere) really consist in?" That was never Morton's question.

Isn't it like this? We want to know what "telling time" consists of. We use time-keeping mechanisms, and we think that if we understood a time-keeping mechanism we would know what "telling time" is. So we learn about the workings of the cuckoo-clock. The outcome of the sequence of movements in the clock is this: the clock tells the time. The cuckoo tells you what time it is. The cuckoo cuckoos five times, and it is five o'clock. But then I think. Suppose a child asks me how the cuckoo clock tells time. I find myself saying, "The cuckoo clock doesn't *really* tell the time, you know." The clock maker adjusts the gears and springs, then he sets the clock, and later when the time is one, the cuckoo cuckoos once. The bird doesn't know what he is doing; neither does the clock-works. Neither the bird nor the clock *really* knows what time it is.

If you understand the machinery and watch the clock, you can tell what time it is. You must know when it was set; you must figure out whether it is losing or gaining. The clock will give data; if you know how to interpret the data, you can tell the time. We started with the question, "What is 'telling time'?" We thought we could find the answer in the clock mechanism. We conclude that it only gives part of the answer. And it *does* give part of the answer. What does seeing consist in? My head is a mechanism (like a cuckoo clock). Emanations strike the eyes, and then there are nerve-currents and electromagnetic waves and so on. And what is the outcome? Well, not seeing. Just the mental something. We still must interpret the something—and that finally comes to seeing. Yet we think that an understanding of the machinery gives part of the answer.

It may suddenly strike me that I am in a most unfavorable position. I was taught to tell time by looking at the clock. And now I am trying to find out what "telling time" is when I have nothing to go on except what I have been taught, and the cuckoo-clock. I can only say, "It must have something to do with the machinery." How could I ask a question whose answer is expected to go far beyond what I know? I was taught to tell time by the clock, but I soon begin to suspect there is more to it. I learn about checking and setting the clock. Later I see a big book about the movements of the sun and stars, the astronomers and their instruments, the clockmakers and how they adjust the clocks. I ask the question, "What does telling time consist of?" because I realize there is far more to telling time than I know.

Now I am inclined to say that when I was taught to tell time by looking at the clock I was not taught to really tell time. The astronomers do that. Looking at the clock is only a small part of telling time. And unless we know something about the machinery (whether it runs slow or fast) and unless we understand what telling time really is (the standard and how the clocks are set by it), we are very apt to be wrong when we tell what time it is by looking at the clock.

When we see we have a something in our heads; it is the outcome of the machinery of perception. We could not understand what seeing is through a survey of the something and the machinery which produces it. Because like "telling time," "seeing" is a claim to know something. It is a claim to know something about the world of things and objects. Fortunately, there is a way we can learn about that world without mediation of the machinery involved in seeing. We can reach out and touch it. And we can read the books by physiologists which confirm what we learn by touch. Thus we learn about the machinery and we understand how it will mislead us. Things are not really colored. Hence we do not really see colors, although we think we do. Observing the stars is the real way of telling time. When we see with the eyes we are like little children who tell time by the clock. I am almost led to say, "We cannot really see with the eyes. We really see with the fingertips."

We look at the clock and see that both hands are at twelve. We note the date and we read in a book that we shall be on daylight savings time on that date. We read the tag on the clock: the clockmaker noted that the clock gains five minutes a day. We remember it was set three days ago. Hence the time is one-fifteen. I say I see a red coffee can. This is a pronouncement from within my head. I feel a smooth cylinder. Next I apply what I read in a book on physiological optics. I really see a something which I take to be a red coffee can. In reality I see a smooth cylinder. The cylinder has no color. Perhaps I should say that I cannot see a coffee can: "coffee can" may be an incorrect interpretation of the visual something given to me. I cannot really see what is not there. What is there is a smooth, hard cylinder, five and one-half inches high and four inches in diameter. That is all that is *really* there.

Isn't something like this behind the philosopher's distinction between primary and secondary qualities? When that distinction is made, vision becomes suspect; and touch, reading, and reason are the ways to reality. The philosopher starts with the causal story, but his theory is not completely causal. He takes into account the fact that seeing is not passive: it is not just a result of occurrences in the air, the eye, and the brain. It is a claim to know an object, the thing seen. Also seeing is removed from its object by a long, long sequence of events, and so it becomes suspect. If we can learn the truth from vision, we must learn how to learn the truth from it. We can learn how only by finding what seeing really consists in: the machinery and the something, and all the rest.

Haven't I asked, "What is involved in seeing?" the way I might ask, "What is involved in telling time?" I think there is some big idea or conception, "seeing," which I know only a little about—just as there is "telling time" which I know only a little about. We might observe some primitive people and as a result of our study conclude that they have only the crudest idea of telling time. I have almost put myself in the position where I think that I and others have only the crudest idea of seeing.

I might counter the misleading presumptions of my question with some misleading denials. There is something we do when we tell the time, although it is not always the same thing: we may look at the clock, perhaps check it with a phone call or with the sunset chart in the almanac. There is *nothing* we do when we see. An explanation of the clock's workings can help us understand what is involved in telling time. The physiological explanation does not help us understand what is involved in seeing, because nothing is involved in seeing.

V

THE OBJECTS OF PERCEPTION AND DREAMS

Philosophers have long felt that even when they are the most trustworthy, our senses deceive us still. Maybe I should say it is our perceptions that they think deceive us. It is hard to get the right words. When we "perceive" the familiar items in the inventory of the world, the trees, houses, birds, and butterflies, we are blind to the complexity of what we do or of what happens to us or in us. It seems so simple; it is really very mysterious. All of us have grossly erroneous ideas about perception and what it is that we perceive. Our errors may have little practical consequence, but they are philosophically ruinous. The truth is that our direct perceptual object, what we see, for example, is not what we think it is. It is a private thing, peculiar to our own present seeing. From all we can tell by direct inspection of that object there might be no "physical" or "material" world. The things we think we see might not exist at all. I might see and have no eye with which to see; I might have no head, no arms or legs. By considering carefully the object I see, I can determine nothing about the "physical" or "material" world.

In an effort to make this clear, to help us concentrate on the perceptual object, private and peculiar, philosophers have frequently compared perception with dreaming. That dream things are not "physical" or "material" is presumably quite plain. Socrates, in elaborating with Theaetetus some such account of perception, asks:

SOCRATES: . . . what evidence could be appealed to, supposing we were asked at this very moment whether we are asleep or awake—dreaming all that passes through our minds or talking to one another in the waking state.

THEAETETUS: . . . the two conditions correspond in every circumstance like exact counterparts. The conversation we have just had might equally well be one that we merely think we are carrying on in our sleep; and when it comes to thinking in a dream that we are telling our dreams, the two states are extraordinarily alike.[1]

On the pages where modern philosophy is sired we find the same story. Descartes does not think the appeal to dreams is a clincher, but he obviously attaches first importance to it. By noting that we might now be dreaming we can come to realize that the objects of our direct awareness are things which figure only on our own private inventory.

> So let us suppose now that we are asleep and that all these details, such as opening the eyes, shaking the head, extending the hands, and similar things, are merely illusions; and let us think that perhaps our hands and our whole body are not such as we see them.[2]

The clincher is the possibility of the arch-deceiver, the evil genius. An evil genius might take away the whole world including my own body; and this need not alter my perception. The appeal to dreams is still basic: the evil genius turns things into illusions and dreams.

> I will suppose that the sky, the air, the earth, colors, shapes, sounds, and all other objective things that we see are nothing but illusions and dreams that he has used to trick my credulity.[3]

If I am to understand, then, the nature of perception, I must see that the things perceived are the same as the things in dreams. I am perceiving now. I see the walls of my room, my desk, the paper before me. While in the midst of perceiving, I must set myself the exercise of imagining that I might now be dreaming.

Do I understand what I am to do? I am to suppose or imagine that I am now dreaming—not merely to exercise my powers of imagination, but in order to see that I might be deceived about everything (or almost everything) as I have been deceived about everything while dreaming.

How do dreams deceive me? Well, when am I deceived? I have often been deceived by *people,* but no one is involved now except myself. I have also been

---

[1] *Plato's Theaetetus* tr. F. M. Cornford (Liberal Arts Press, Bobbs-Merrill Co., Inc., 1959), pp. 52-53.
[2] René Descartes, *Meditations,* tr. Laurence J. Lafleur (Liberal Arts Press, Bobbs-Merrill, 1951), p. 17.
[3] *Ibid.,* p. 20.

deceived by *appearances*. "I am amazed," I say, "Your house gives the appearance of being very small. I would have sworn you couldn't have more than three rooms this size. As I was coming up the walk, the appearance was deceiving. It looked so small. I thought it was much smaller than it is." This is the way I am deceived by appearances. Instead, suppose I dreamt that I visited your house, and while walking up to it I thought, "My, this house is made of gingerbread with white frosting. It's very small." How was I deceived then? I was deceived when I thought your house was small; I found it to be much larger than it appeared to be. What I thought was shown wrong. I revise my belief. In my dream, too, I thought your house was small. Do I need to revise my dream-belief?

What sort of question is this? I think of two circumstances where questions like this might be asked. First, if I were telling my dreams and said, "I thought it was small . . . , " a listener might well expect me to add, "but I went in and found I was wrong." If I did not say what I found upon going in, he might ask, "Did you have to revise your belief?"—requesting me to tell some detail of my dream which he thinks I left out. Secondly, suppose I were telling my dream to some friends, and someone joined my audience as I was midway through my story. He listened while I said, "I thought your house was very small." Now he asks, "Weren't you wrong? Didn't you have to revise your belief?" I shall tell him he misunderstands. He arrived late and missed my prefatory remarks: I was telling a dream. I dreamt I thought the house very small. Both these are questions which others may ask of me when I have described a dream, but what question can I ask myself? I know the dream I had, and whether in the dream I did or did not have to revise my beliefs. If I dreamt that I walked on into the house, and said, "My, how spacious, but no difference; I thought it was small and it is," I should not be surprised. Things go like that in dreams. I shall not now, while thinking back on the dream, say, "That was wrong of me. I should have revised my belief." While telling the dream I might say, "I knew that was wrong of me. I ought to have changed my belief, yet I didn't," but I should say this only if it were telling part of the dream. When I ask, "Should I revise the belief I had in the dream?" I am not asking myself whether I have forgotten some detail of the dream.

I must try to construe my question as like the second. It is almost as if I were a man who had walked in on a dream story in the middle—only the dream story is my own. Almost as if I had forgotten I was telling of a dream, and now I ask, "Did I make a mistake? Ought I to revise my belief?" Well, I shall say the question is like that, and so I shall answer that it is a misunderstanding. I dreamt I thought it was small. I made a mistake the day I walked to your house, and thought from the appearance it was small. But when I dreamt it was small I made no mistake. In the waking-life case, there was a clash between my belief and what I discovered when I looked inside. There is no clash between what I dreamt and the facts, because what I dreamt was just a dream. I feel uneasy about answering in this way, because there is no such question I can ask myself about being wrong.

I seem to be floundering over the very first step in the exercise. If there is no question, I cannot go on. If I accept my answer, where did I go wrong? I find no incompatibility between dreaming that I believed your house is small, and the fact that it is quite large. Oh yes, but I found out I was dreaming only after I was awake. While I was asleep, I thought your house was small. I am back at the same misunderstanding. While I was asleep, I did not think your house was small. Sleepers are not thinking about things at all. When I was asleep I was dreaming. I did not think it; I dreamt I thought it. But of course when I was asleep, I did not know I was dreaming. All the same, I *was* dreaming. People who do not know they are watching the tricks of a magician may have mistaken beliefs about what is going on. But people who do not know they are dreaming when they are dreaming, are not making any mistakes. When I am deceived, I may refuse to recognize it. I may even argue for the truth of what I thought I saw. In such a situation I argue for a falsehood. That may be so, but how many falsehoods can one maintain when he is sound asleep? The question is based on a misunderstanding—if I can imagine myself having such a misunderstanding. So I cannot be deceived while dreaming about your house. Perhaps this is because, while dreaming, I can not cognitively get at your house. But I can get at my own dream. Suppose I had a dream of myself in a very queer and frightening room. There was a sickening purple light everywhere. I said to myself, "I mustn't be afraid, because this is a dream." Then an old friend appeared and said, "No, you are wide awake and your fears are right, for we are all about to be hanged." Then I knew it was not a dream; I knew I was awake. At this point, I woke up, bewildered to find myself not in a strange, purplish room but in my own bedroom.

Here I feel I was deceived in a dream. But was I? I said, "I know I am awake," and I was asleep. No. I did not say it. I dreamt I said it. What I dreamt I said is not the important thing; I believed I was awake. Even when I dream about whether I dream or not, I am dreaming the question and the answer; I am not asking the question or giving an answer. I cannot see how one can make a mistake in a dream at all. The idea of it is more and more ridiculous. Suppose someone said, "I missed three questions on the exam: two while writing in the classroom, and then I dreamt I missed another." How many questions *did* he get wrong? In order to carry out the Cartesian exercise, it seems I am required to act the part of a late listener to my own dream story, one who does not know that what is described is a dream. I have to try to underwrite his misunderstandings in my own name. But then I have to reject them. I am not making much progress, certainly. Where have I gone wrong? For I certainly am sometimes deceived by a dream. Oh yes, I know how that happens. I hurry to get my appointment book out of a desk drawer. It is not there, and then I remember: I did not put it there; I dreamt I put it there. How stupid, but that *was* a very vivid dream. Could I not be deceived like this right now—because I am dreaming? I do not see how from the example, because in it I was not deceived *while* dreaming. I was deceived because I was led to look in my drawer for my appointment book. While I was dreaming I was lying on the couch. While dreaming I did not think my appointment book was there; I dreamt I put it there. Even if I had dreamt I wanted it, and in my dream I remembered putting it there, I should not have gone to the drawer looking. I should have stayed right there on the couch, sleeping.

Am I not deceived only because I do not walk in my sleep? I am not certain what sleepwalkers do, except walk in their sleep. Suppose, anyway, that they dream while they are walking. I am watching a sleepwalker who wakes with a shock, finding himself with his hand in a desk drawer. Suppose he says sheepishly, "I dreamt I was looking for my appointment book." I say to him, "It isn't in your desk drawer." He might reply, "Oh, I know it isn't, but I just dreamt it was." In the proper philosophical tone, I point out, "Well! Then I caught you being deceived." He might say, "Er—yes, I was certainly mixed-up." The trouble is, he could just as well say, "Oh no, I didn't want the damn book. I certainly didn't need it—don't need it now. I wasn't even looking for it; I was dreaming I was looking for it." Or again, he might say, "I guess I thought my book was there." Where any of these would do, no *one* of them is *the* right description. Perhaps his inability to tell what he thought, and whether he was deceived is because of his confused state of mind. I, the observer, am not in this befuddled state. I have been coolly watching and listening. What should I say? Did he believe his book was in the drawer? Was he looking for it? Was he wrong in his belief? I certainly know what happened: he walked as if drugged, he shuffled through the drawer, then he awoke puzzled and astonished. This is something *like* what one does when he wants something, has a wrong idea about where it is, and is surprised not to find it there. However, when a person is wide awake and searching for something, I can ask him what he is doing, what he wants, and his answer will usually settle any questions I have about what he is after and what he thought. The sleepwalker who wakes with his hand in a drawer cannot give clear answers to my questions. When a person who is awake and sane looks confidently for something—right where he remembers putting it—and finds it is not there, he does not wake up at that point, terminating abruptly all familiar developments. What the sleepwalker did was something *like* acting on a false assumption all right, but also something very unlike. Does it belong under "false opinion" or does it not? Well, how like does it have to be to belong? There is no criterion, no way of deciding, and it is easy to see why there is none. Usually it would make no difference which way we put it: no misconceptions would arise. When one can say any of several different things and accomplish the same purpose, they come to the same thing, perhaps "they mean the same thing," that is, we should say they mean the same thing in the circumstances in which they would be said. In circumstances in which they are not said, then they are just not said. If there were any reason for it, I could make a decision. I could decide to say that sleepwalkers who have dreams that correspond in the proper ways to their waking behavior have false beliefs. But my decision to say they have false beliefs would not settle anything about whether they have false beliefs or not.

Of course this decision-making is bewitching business. Once one is committed to it, he is required to make more and more decisions, each a new challenge to one's ingenuity, because we want them made in an orderly and consistent way. What of the man who wakes up in the nightmarish dream that a spider as big as a Great Dane is sitting on his chest? His heart thumps, he sweats, and screams. Does he believe there is a spider on his chest? For how long? While he is screaming? His heart races for five minutes after awaking. Shall we decide he believes for five minutes? It may color his behavior for an hour: he may get up and be fearful of going back to bed. He may return to bed but be afraid of the dark room and keep a light on. Shall we decide that he believes for an hour or two? Until he turns off the light? Regardless of how these questions may be decided, for those who sit and sympathize with him in his fear, it makes no difference whether they say he believes in a chest-riding spider or not. For those who want to settle some point of theory, the *truth* is he does not either believe or not believe.

I understand well enough how one might be deceived by a dream, but I am supposed to imagine how one might be deceived *in* a dream. Since my hypothetical sleepwalker does not provide a case, I am beginning to despair of finding one. Of course there is the great range of hypnagogic states, of experiences of half-sleep, of times when one is not quite but almost dreaming, and so forth. I might wake slowly to an overcast and gloomy day, and lie suspended between sleep and waking. I might feel as if I were floating on a magic carpet. I wonder where I am. I feel alarmed. I feel I am moving, but yet I see—now— I am lying on my bed.

The trouble with such cases is that everything is "mid-way" and "as-if" and "as-it-were." One can say, "I believed I was floating, then I discovered I was not." And one can also say, "It was as if I were floating, then I discovered I was not." And one can also say, "It was as if I were floating; it was almost as if I believed it, not quite a dream, not quite awake. Then it seemed as if I made a discovery—much as if I found out I was wrong." Here again the background and the cues would make all this clear.

I cannot now see how any such examples can give me a case which I should unhesitatingly describe as "being deceived in a dream." I am almost convinced that it is impossible to be deceived in a dream. I almost want to say that even if I were dreaming now, I cannot see how I should be deceived. I should not be operating on any false beliefs, because it is not clear that I should be operating ony any beliefs at all. I should be dreaming that I was operating on certain be-liefs. Yet this is a queer thing for me to want to say, because when I am dream-ing, I do not know what I am doing. I cannot say anything about what it would be like to be dreaming now, because while dreaming I am not in any position to say what it is like. Anyway, this would be to despair of success in the Car-tesian exercise.

I must try to imagine myself in a position to say what it is like while I am dreaming. Maybe it is not necessary first to understand about being deceived in dreams. If I could come to see the possibility that I might be dreaming now, then perhaps I could see how I might be deceived. Although it sounds as if I must crawl into a dream while still awake—a most unlikely occurrence—I shall keep trying. I shall try to imagine that I am now dreaming. Is it not easy enough to imagine almost anything I want to imagine? Yes, when the occasion is right. It is the proper occasion that I cannot imagine. Someone just says, "Everything you know—everything you have—is a dream. Even now you are dreaming." Can I imagine that? I begin to feel a weariness come over me. I think that one by one the things I love are taken away. The old times are gone, all the brave and fine things. Once the springs came, moist; and the nights were warm; so deep the solitude; tears, too, and now no child's tears. All this is gone, and I am waking ever from a dream; yet the dream goes on. Here am I, then, now dreaming—feeling sorry for myself. Is this a philosophical exercise? My philosophy has dissolved into sentiment, or worse.

At the very end of *Through the Looking-Glass* Alice says to her kitten, " . . . let's consider who it was that dreamed it all. This is a serious question, my dear . . . You see, Kitty, it *must* have been either me or the Red King. He was part of my dream, of course—but then I was part of his dream, too." Finally, I, the reader am asked, "Which do *you* think it was?" Well, *I* think it was I dreaming and they were all in my dream, and I am dreaming still; for I can turn back the pages and lo! the adventures go over again, but I know how they are going to turn out as I sometimes do in dreams. Now my philosophy has turned into nonsense. I do not want nonsense or senimentality; I do not want soft or silly, I want hard imagination.

The trouble is, I cannot think of the right occasion; I cannot think of anyone asking, "Can't you imagine you are now dreaming?" when he does not want to moralize or sentimentalize, or just have a little verbal fun. I want a situation which will call on my logical and analytical powers. For the time being, I guess I shall just have to forget about the situation. A philosophical directive is given to me, "Imagine you are now dreaming!" I shall just repeat to myself, "Be hardhearted, do *hard* imagining!" All right, I shall try some logico-philosophical steps. If I am now dreaming I must now be asleep. I must imagine I am asleep. How can I do that? To imagine I am asleep, I must imagine, and to imagine I must be awake. That is no good; that is like saying, "I can't imagine what it will be like in the middle of the next century, because by then I shall be dead, and dead men don't imagine." Or suppose that an astronomer is lecturing on the solar system. He says, "Let's imagine we are on the sun." I shall not say, "I can't do that because I couldn't survive on the sun to imagine." Of course I shall not say that. He only wants me to think how the planets and stars would look from the sun, if I could be there.

But the Cartesian philosopher does not ask me to imagine how things would be at a different place, or in a different time. He does not want me to imagine myself at a different place or time; but to imagine myself, right here and now in a different state—dreaming. In that state I could not be imagining, I should be dreaming. That is all I have shown. All right, I imagine myself in that state; I just cannot put too much of myself in, for I must remain in this state, imagining. I imagine I am now asleep, and dreaming. What more is required? Now I must imagine I am dreaming *all this*. I see all this, my desk, my pen, and other things. *No*, I do *not* see it; I dream I see it. Only, when I am dreaming I do not know that I am dreaming. Of course not; but I do not see things either. This line of thought merely takes me back to all my difficulties about deception, and the queerness of talking about dreams in the present tense.

When asked astronomically to imagine myself on the sun, it was not important that I imagine myself there in some super-insulated, air-conditioned cell. The question was to consider what the planets would look like from thereabouts. Perhaps the philosophical question is what would all this that I now see look like in a dream. But I neither look nor see in dreams; I dream I look and see. There is my mistake again: I have brought dreaming back in. That is as irrelevant as my insulated shell on the sun. I am just to imagine what it would look like. From where? When? Here, now. Silly. It looks like this; only in a dream. No, I must forget the dream part; but how can I? In order to imagine myself philosophically dreaming, I must make sure not to imagine myself dreaming.

Surely I can do better. I have assumed that saying, "Do philosophy; be rational; hard work, now!" would enable me to escape from imaginatively constructing the circumstances in which one might say, "I am dreaming." At the great risk of not knowing what I am talking about at all, I have tried to get inside a dream. Still it is impossible to escape from where I am. I cannot say "dream" without being reminded of dreams. I cannot talk about dreams, without talking at least indirectly about dreams. I seem to be held down from the required flight of imagination by the dead weight of my words. There seems to be something to say, but language prevents me from saying it. So I must go back, and begin again. I must imagine the circumstances where one would say, "I am now dreaming," and this context must not be such as will lead to sentimentalizing or nonsense, or anything like that. I need to imagine someone talking in his sleep, saying, "I am dreaming." Then I need to imagine myself in his place. That looks fearfully hard to do. Maybe I can get inside a dream more easily if I take it in two jumps. First I shall just get access to the dream, then later I shall get inside. How to get access to a dream? That is easy. I shall just imagine someone, say Jason, describing a dream. He tells what happened in his dream. Suppose he says that he dreamt there was a street fight and that he stood at a window watching as if history depended upon his remembering the details of that scene. He describes all this, in the past tense of course, as one does when he recounts a dream. Now I shall imagine myself doing something like that while awake; I simply describe a street fight which I saw some time ago from my window. If I can now imagine that my description and his description are the same sort of thing, I shall have access to a dream while awake. They are both "describing," but beyond that I cannot see how I am going to construe them as the same thing at all. I am telling what people did on the street. Insurance companies might have an interest in my account. They would have no interest in Jason's story, even though he dreamt that his watching was important. My listeners might want to check up on my story, for my prejudices may distort my report. What I say may easily be checked by interviewing people who were on the scene—or better by watching a movie made at the time of the fight. My description may be doubted for all sorts of reasons, checked in all sorts of ways. But what of Jason's description of his dream—or for that matter any description of a dream? When it is honestly told, given in considerable detail and with confidence, it makes no sense to doubt anything. Nothing anyone could do or say would ever count as "checking up on the description of a dream." Describing a dream and describing what has been observed while awake are clearly very different. Then what I am doing can by no stretch of the imagination be what Jason is doing.

So I cannot make it inside a dream from that jumping-off place after all. All right, I shall try to make it in one big jump. I imagine someone (call him Grant) lying on a couch. His eyes are closed; he breathes slowly, the rhythm of sound sleep. He says, "I am dreaming." What should I make of this? First off, I might think he was awake: he's making a philosophical joke. No. This interpretation is ruled out because I must imagine him asleep. He is asleep, and he says, "I am now dreaming." What do I say? Well, he is talking in his sleep all right. How do we take what people say in their sleep? It all depends: it depends on what they say, what we know about them, the purpose for our listening to what they say, and other things. If a sleeptalker insults me, I am sure I cannot sue him for slander, even if I have a tape recording of his words. Suppose that a man while talking in his sleep describes an invention. I realize its importance and have it patented. He is not an inventor, does not know anything about it, does not remember talking in his sleep. Have I stolen the idea from him? I think I should feel uneasy about it. Suppose a man in deep sleep says, "I promise to meet you for lunch tomorrow." If he does not show up for lunch, he has not gone back on a promise. He made no promise. Suppose he said, "You will find a hundred dollar bill in your middle desk drawer." I look in my desk drawer and find no money. Was his assertion false? No. He can no more assert than he can promise. While talking in sleep, one cannot make claims or assertions. If Grant, my hypothetical sleep-talker, is not asserting that he is dreaming, how can this case help me?

Maybe these questions will be clearer if I fill in the example with more details. While sleeping, Grant says, "I am dreaming," and then he goes on like this: "And I am dreaming of a large, very large Siamese cat, larger than a lion, and he leaps at me now out of the bushes. I am running . . . " Suppose, also, that when he awakes he relates a dream. He says, "I dreamt of a gigantic Siamese cat which leapt at me out of the bushes . . . ," and he goes on like that, telling the details of a dream which perfectly corresponds to what he said he was dreaming while asleep. Suppose, moreover, that Grant's performance is regular : whenever he talks this way in his sleep, he has the corresponding dream which he relates when he wakes. When he does not talk in his sleep, he claims to have no dream. All this is what Grant can do. Now I imagine him asleep on his couch talking. He says, "I see a street fight from my window . . . ," and he goes on telling about it.

I want to imagine myself in his place. I imagine a news reporter calls me on the phone, asks me to describe what is going on below my window. I tell him as accurately as I can the details of a street fight. While I am describing what I see, I ask myself, "May I not be doing the same thing as Grant there, talking in his sleep? Could I now be dreaming?"

When I am giving a running commentary of what takes place on the street below me, I am describing what I see. Is that what Grant is doing? He does not see anything. His eyes are closed and he is sound asleep. That is good ; that brings out the philosophical point, because I must imagine that I do not see anything either. I dream that I see this fight in the street. Then I must dream that I describe it. Does Grant dream that he describes his dream? A trumpery detail. We shall say that he does. When he tells his dream he says, "And I was standing by, describing all this." He dreams he describes what he dreams ; still, the question is, does he describe his dream? He talks in his sleep clearly enough and what he says has this amazing point-by-point correspondence with what later he describes as a dream.

In one important matter, the case of Grant sleep-talking is more like reporting on events in the present tense than Jason's describing his dream is like my describing past events. They are more alike in this matter of doubt and subsequent checking. Suppose discrepancies occur between Grant's sleep-talk and his later description of a dream. Surely, then, the later, normal account is definitive. This is something like correcting what was first said. Only it is just *something* like it, and not *very* much, at that. It would not really be correcting what he had said, or finding he had made a mistake, because while sound asleep he had not made any assertions or put forth any claims. The question remains, was he "describing" his dream while he slept? I do not see that it would make any difference what I say to this. I have already noticed how very different describing a dream is from describing a street scene. They are made no more alike than they are by being counted two cases of describing. Likewise, Grant's sleep-talk and my present-tense reporting of a street fight are either the same or different, quite without regard to what I should call or decide to call Grant's peculiar kind of sleep-talking. Which are they, same or different? Am I sure what I am asking? What do I mean here by "same"? What is same or different depends on the circumstances. If Xavier lights up his pipe, and it is suggested that I do the same thing, I shall take out my pipe and light up. This would be doing exactly what was suggested, namely, doing the same thing as Xavier. Suppose I am invited to a Cheyenne Indian Council. The chief is smoking a pipe and he suggests I do the same thing. Then I should not be doing what he suggested if I pulled out my pipe and lit up. I should have to wait until he passed me the peace pipe in order to do the same thing he was doing.

In the case of Grant's sleep-talking, and my describing a street fight, the circumstances do not seem to be important. I want to be able to imagine that I am now, while describing a street fight, really sleep-talking as Grant is doing. I may be doing what Grant is doing; I may really be in Grant's place. For this I can say *everything* must be the same, *everything*—except, of course, Grant is dreaming.

I say "everything," but I cannot make it work out the way I want. As soon as I put myself in Grant's place, *almost* everything seems different. What he is doing, talking in his sleep, and what I am doing, describing what goes on around me, are very different. The first and most obvious difference is that I am aware of what I am doing. Grant is not; he is asleep. This is one of the reasons why I am making assertions and he is not. I can be held accountable for what I say; he cannot. Next, and this strains any likeness almost to the breaking point, I know perfectly well what I am doing. I do not know at all what he is doing— beyond talking in his sleep in the strange way that I have imagined him to do. No, I should not say that: it is very misleading. Rather I *do* know exactly what he is doing, but I do not know what to say about it. The point is, I know all there is to know. In this respect what Grant is doing is like describing a dream, because when someone tells me his dream, I know all there is to be known about his dream and his dreaming it. I know well enough what Grant is doing, lying there, talking away. I know he will soon awake and tell me his dream. What I am doing is describing something. I do not know whether to say he is describing anything or not. Even if he is, he is describing what he dreams he sees, not what he sees. The logic of talking about dreams is just stubbornly different from that of talking about things and events.

Even so, are the differences enough or of the right kind to be sure that these two occurrences are not the same? I assumed that saying, "everything—everything the same" would make it plain whether Grant's sleep-talking and my describing were the same or different. I found differences and concluded that Grant and I were doing different things. I should not have done that: in general, the presence of differences does not prove "everything is not the same." Suppose I am taking a cowhand to dinner and he is uneasy about his manners. I tell him, "Just do everything the same as I." If he uses the right spoon in the right hand, and so forth, he carries out my suggestion. "Fine. You did everything exactly the same," I'll say. This does not mean that he coughed when I coughed, smiled when I smiled, and dropped his napkin when I dropped mine. Perhaps with all the differences I noted between my describing the street fight and Grant's sleep-talk, they are still exactly the same. Perhaps they are, but how can I tell? And if they are exactly the same, is he doing what I am doing —describing?

A child may ask me to show him how to sweep floors. I hand him an old broomstick and say, "Watch, and do exactly what I do." Then I take the broom and sweep, and he does exactly what I do. I was sweeping. Does it follow that he is sweeping, too—because he did exactly what I did? How could he sweep without a broom? But if I had given him a broom in the first place, then his doing exactly what I was doing would mean that he and I were both sweeping. It does not follow from some general rule that if Grant and I are doing exactly the same thing, we are both describing. Nor does it follow from some general rule that what Grant is doing and what I am doing are cases of doing exactly the same thing. These matters depend upon special circumstances. What must I do now? Give a description of the conditions under which my questions arise?

I can imagine an insurance investigator who has heard tape recordings of

Grant's sleep-talk and my report. He says, "I don't see that it makes any difference which recording we use in court because the two of you seem to be doing the same thing." I should certainly reply, "No. We weren't doing the same thing at all. You don't seem to understand. I was watching the fight. Grant was asleep at the time." I can imagine a teacher of journalism who wants to give his class an exercise in analyzing a present-tense description of a street-fight. He is about to concoct one himself when he runs across the two tape recordings. He says, "I won't need to make one up. We'll use one of these. No matter which. Both are doing the same thing."

I am not interested in any such conditions. I want the situation right here and now, in which I am asking this question: were Grant and I doing exactly the same thing? Could we both be describing dreams? I ought not to need a description of these conditions because I am in them. If there are any conditions which are complete and which I understand, these must be the ones. Right here they are—now. I can see why I was inclined to say Grant and I are not doing the same thing, because most of the situations which come quickly to mind where the question might be asked are such that the answer would be unequivocally, "No, they aren't doing the same thing at all." I feel inclined to say my situation is more like these which come easily to mind than it is like the others. But what I am inclined to say is not what I do say, and I ought not to have to discuss how like to others and how different from others my situation is. Here is my situation and I want the answer. The answer is, "I can't tell what to say. The situation is not such that I can give an answer."

If I were standing in a classroom with chalk in hand before a blackboard, I should accuse myself of the "classroom and blackboard fallacy." This fallacy is the assumption that the special conditions which make it possible to answer a question can miraculously be produced by writing an interrogative sentence on a blackboard. I am very familiar with it by being often guilty of it. I am now beginning to think there is a counterpart fallacy, the fallacy of philosophical meditation, which is subtler because it calls for no classroom, no blackboard, no chalk. I was guilty of it. I can also see that I am getting tired and hasty, because I am strongly inclined to think that Descartes somewhere along the line must have been guilty of it too.

I thought it would be possible for me to imagine myself dreaming if I thought of something one did while dreaming which was the same thing I sometimes did while awake. Then all I should need to do was imagine myself doing the same thing. I thought of Grant's peculiar kind of sleep-talking, and my reporting of a street fight. First I thought Grant and I were not doing the same thing at all—so that I could not imagine myself now dreaming by pretending I could be in Grant's place while everything remained the same. I discovered a mistake in that conclusion. Finally, I have come to the conclusion that I cannot even tell whether Grant and I were doing the same thing or not. I cannot even get the question asked in such a way that I can see how it could be answered. And I now suspect that something is wrong with the question and not with me. If I cannot even ask the question, then I cannot possibly imagine by such means that I am in Grant's position now. I simply am unable to imagine that I might now be dreaming. I cannot see how one could say, and mean, the *philosophical* statement, "I might now be dreaming."

I must go slowly. Before I become too presumptuous, I had better lay aside this exercise and continue when I am fresh and have recovered from my first frustrations. I know this is an arduous undertaking, and I must be suspicious of fatigue, like that "indolence which leads me back to my ordinary course of life."

VI

FEELING EGGS AND PAINS

We may think something like this. If I feel a pain, there is something there to feel. A pain is something there to feel. So maybe one of the reasons we think of pains as though they were entities or objects or beings, is that we think they are among the things we feel. The things we feel are things. We think this way because we have a certain picture of feeling. We think of feeling as a mental reaching across or through the body. I feel a stone in my right shoe. It is as though I reached down through my body, through the right leg and into the foot. I am here in the head, behind the eyes, and I feel from here the various parts of my body. I suspect this idea of reaching through the body derives from the frequent action of reaching out with the hand to touch something. I reach out and feel something with my fingers. I feel it is smooth, or cold. The things I feel are at the tips of my fingers, at the far end of my arm. Or, they may be at the far end of a leg—or almost anywhere in the body. Just as I can feel a stone in a shoe, or a cold, metallic cylinder with my fingers—so I can feel a pain in the shoulder, an ache in the calf.

We have the idea that we feel some things outside the skin and we feel other things within the body: there is no important difference except in the location of the object. I feel a heavy pressure on my leg: it is painful. I feel a pain in my leg. The pain is on the near side of my skin. (That is why I think that only I can feel it: no one else can. It is in my body and no one else can feel within my body because no one can mentally penetrate it.)

Then we are surprised and puzzled by many things this picture makes us think. Or we can be tickled by some of the funny things it makes us think. Feeling involves my having to reach out, to sense something at a place removed. So I must be someplace other than the toe which hurts, or the ear which itches. Where am I? I said I was behind the eyes. It is next to impossible to think hard about this picture of things without making a caricature of it. Where am I? Am I always there? Can I move to another place? Can I get closer so as to get a better feel? Suppose someone else said solemnly that he was just behind his navel. Should I believe him? Should I have any reason to doubt his location? Am I the only one who can feel a pain in *my* shoulder? Suppose someone else said he felt a pain my shoulder. Should I disbelieve him?

Thinking in this subject-object way of feeling pains leads into many confusions. Yet the picture is persistent: it is so natural, inevitable. My confusions about the subject, the one who feels, are wild: it is hard to take them seriously. My confusions about the object, the feeling, are subtler. I want to explore some of the ways this picture of feeling gets me into difficulties with the objects of feeling: eggs, pains, sensations. When I think of pain in terms of the picture, I naturally think of pain as a particular, specific object. (When I hear a robin in the evening, it is that particular robin I hear—the one sitting on that bare limb right over there.) Therefore I think of feeling *a* pain, or feeling *that* pain, or of having *a* pain or *that* pain. I do not, first off, think of feeling pain or of being in pain. Mostly, therefore, I want to examine the way the picture fits or misfits the idioms "a pain," "that pain."

I represent feeling a pain and feeling a drop of paint on my cheek in much the same way. The pain is an inner thing, the drop of paint an outer. Yet I can have a drop of paint on my skin and not feel it; I cannot have a pain in my arm and not feel it. The two are not alike in all ways my picture would lead me to think. Some have said that I might rid myself of the misrepresentation by taking note of the identity between having a pain and feeling a pain. Some have said that having a pain and feeling a pain are one and the same thing. Having a drop of paint and feeling a drop of paint are not the same at all.

Do "having a pain" and "feeling a pain" come to the same? (1) While hiking with a friend I limp to a halt and sit on a log holding my knee. "What's wrong?" "I have a terrible pain in the knee." (I certainly do not say, "I feel a terrible pain in the knee.") (2) A man has suffered paralysis of the legs and is slowly recovering. Every day the doctor touches, probes, moves his legs. He asks, "Do you feel anything?" One day the patient says, "Yes. I feel a deep pain in the ankle." In this example "I feel a pain" is a remark on the speaker's sensibility. When he says, "I feel a pain," the patient asserts he is no longer numb. (3) We say, "The principle of the counterirritant is this: when you have a pain, we shall make it so uncomfortable someplace else that you will not feel the pain so much." When the counterirritant is applied, I say, "It burns and itches so much, I scarcely feel the pain." "I do not feel the pain so much" or "scarcely feel the pain" means I do not have my normal sensibilities, they have been disturbed.

(4) I have injured a leg and am suffering from an unbearable pain in the knee. I am given a local anesthetic and gradually the pain subsides. My leg becomes completely numb. Later the doctor asks "How is it now?" "I can feel the pain again." Or "I can feel that pain again." My sensibilities are returning to normal.

I meet a man who is doing research on what he calls "the tactual sense." I do not know exactly what he is, a psychologist, physiologist, or something like that. His research is sponsored by an institution in Anaheim, California, and he wants to remain anonymous. I shall call him Allister. I volunteer as subject for some of his experiments. (5) Allister covers my leg with a device. I cannot see my leg. I cannot see what he is doing to my leg. He asks, "Do you feel anything now?" I say, "No." "Feel anything now?" "No." Then he sticks me with a pin. I yell, "Ouch. That hurt." He asks, "What did you feel?" "I felt a sharp point jab into my leg." Here I say, "I feel a sharp point jabbing my leg." I do not say, "I feel a pain."

(6) Now Allister places my leg in another device so that strong magnetic fields can be created around it, and high frequency currents can be passed over it. Without touching my leg, he changes the fields and currents. With each change he asks, "What do you feel?" "I feel a tingling sensation," I might say. Or maybe, "I feel a dull pain throughout the whole leg." Here I was asked, "What do you feel?" If I had been asked, "Do you notice anything?" I suppose I might naturally have replied, "Yes, I feel a dull pain." I might also have said, "I have a dull pain." (7) Suppose Allister had said, "I'm going to do various things. Tell me anything that happens to your leg. Tell me anything you can about your leg." I should now quite likely say, "I have a dull pain in my leg."

These last two examples give a situation where one would say, "I feel a pain" or "I have a pain," sometimes one, sometimes the other, sometimes either.

So there are times when they come to the same thing. If they only come to the same thing sometimes, should I say that they come to the same thing? In the other examples, "I feel a pain" is clearly tied to the question of sensibility or numbness. The point of the remark "I feel a pain" is so clear in those cases, that one is inclined to regard the case where "I have . . ." and "I feel . . ." are used indifferently as an anomoly. I suppose it might be explained as a kind of zero-case, where the normal distinction has cancelled out. There does seem to be something to this. When directed, "Tell me anything about your leg," I say, "I have a pain." The background for "I feel a pain" must be carefully prepared. I am put in a situation where I might be expected to say, "I feel a pin prick" or "I feel a cold draft." And then a pain. The question is put, "What do you *feel*?" I am led by indefinite expectations and by the question to reply, "I feel a pain." When the question is changed, I return to the more normal idiom, "I have a pain." Whatever there is to this, it is a dangerous and unnecessary explanation. The fact remains clear that "I feel a pain" and "I have a pain" are not everywhere the same.

If I try to quickly summarize, I might put the difference between them in this way: "I don't feel a pain everytime I have a pain." I suppose such a summary is all right as long as it is said in connection with the examples. I might even say, "Sometimes when I have a pain, I do not feel a pain." As long as I keep the examples clearly in mind I would not be inclined to say, "Sometimes when I have a pain, I do not feel it." When the desire to theorize comes on me after I have lost track of the details, that is precisely what I am inclined to say. I am likely to think that I am here and a pain is there, and I feel the pain —there where it is. When I think this way I am even tempted to think I could have a pain and not notice it.

We sometimes want to combat the picture of feeling by saying that having a pain and feeling a pain are one and the same thing. The trouble is, we may think this in terms of the picture it is intended to combat. When I sit philosophizing, without thinking in terms of examples, I can say to myself, "Now I shall imagine having a pain in my foot." And then I say, "If I had a pain in my foot, I should feel it." "Having a pain in my foot and feeling a pain in my foot amount to the same thing." "Of course I should feel it." This is so clear and simple I may want to say it in the face of the examples. The examples, I may argue, do not show that having a pain and feeling a pain are different. They show that there are not many occasions on which I would *say,* "I feel a pain." Whenever I have a pain, I do in fact feel the pain: I just should not say so. Whether I should say so or not does not change the fact. The difference between "I have a pain" and "I feel a pain" is in the superficial circumstances surrounding communication: who is present, what questions have been asked, and other contextual things. It is not a difference in *meaning.* "I have a pain" and "I feel a pain" mean the same thing.

What am I thinking of? Something like this? There is a large maple tree in my front yard. The walk goes around it. I pass it many times every day. I follow the walk as it detours around the tree. The question is, "Do I see the tree as I pass by?" Of course I do not say, "I see the maple tree" as I walk past it. I do not talk to myself and I do not talk to maple trees. I might mutter to myself, "I see that tree," if there were any reason for it, but there is no reason. I meet a friend on the walk. I say, "Hello, Harvey." I do not go on to say, "Harvey, I see that maple tree." As I think about this philosophically, I think that the truth remains: I do see the tree. If I should not say it, why do I think it true? Someone points to it and, as a preliminary to some conversation, says "You see that tree? (I want to tell you something about it)." I shall reply, "Of course." Later in the day, I meet a botanist who is making a survey of old trees in the town. He asks me, "Did you ever see the maple tree in front of 84 Emery Lane?" I reply, "Of course I have. That's my house. I see the tree every day." So I have seen the tree; but only when the occasion arises will I say so. Whether or not the occasion arises has nothing to do with the fact that I have many times seen the tree. The reason I think I see the tree when I would not say so seems to be this: with a suitable change in situation, I say, "Of course." "Of course": it is obvious, simple, clear.

The same, I want to say, with feeling pain. Is it the same? I have a terrible pain in my hip, and I am on my way to see a doctor. Someone says, "You're limping a little. What's wrong?" I say, "I have a pain in my hip." He now knows I have a pain in my hip. Later, can he say, "Do you feel that pain in your hip?" Can anyone ask, "Did you feel that pain in your hip?" Is anyone making a survey of hip pains? Someone may think my tree very unusual. As we are standing on the walk, he says, "Do you *see* that tree?" I reply, "Yes, of course," thinking, "What about it?" Suppose someone thought my pain unusual. Would he say, "Do you *feel* that pain?" All this is silly.

On the way to the doctor's office my leg becomes completely numb. In alarm I tell my doctor the whole story. He prods my upper leg. "Can you feel that?" "No," I say. "Less than an hour ago, you felt a pain there?" "Yes." Does that show that whenever I have a pain, I feel it? Does it show that with a suitable change in circumstances I shall say so? When I was asked, "Do you see the tree?" or, "Have you ever seen the tree?" I said, "Of course." That's what led me to think, "Of course I saw it. There was just no reason for saying so." I do not say to the doctor, "Of course I felt a pain." In reflecting on this example, I am not now inclined to say of it, "Of course I felt a pain. It's quite obvious that I felt a pain. There was just no occasion to say so."

As I go down my walk, I become blind. Later I say, "The last thing I saw was the maple tree by the walk." I wasn't thinking of this when I thought that of course I saw the tree: there was just no reason for saying so. Now I am telling someone at what time I lost my vision. I am telling someone who is pressing me for symptoms. In the case of feeling pain I was telling when I became numb. I'm sure now that "I felt a pain" had best be left in its natural setting together with what came before and what came after. In order to combat the analogy which leads me to say "I had a pain" and "I felt a pain" mean the same thing, I might say "I felt a pain" means "I was not numb" just as "I saw a tree" means "I was not blind."

Feeling an egg in my hand is not the same as having an egg in my hand. And in that respect, feeling a pain and having a pain are similar to feeling an egg and having an egg, that is, they are different. The confusions of this comparison can be dispelled because feeling a pain in the hand and feeling an egg in the hand are not parallel. Consider some more examples. (1) I go to a child with hands behind my back and say, "Which hand do you want?" He is skeptical. I say I have something in one hand. I do not usually say, "I feel something in one hand." Allister has some new experiments for me. He blindfolds me and has me out-stretch my hand. He puts things in my palm, sometimes lightly, sometimes pressing them firmly. Sometimes he leaves them in place, sometimes he removes them. Sometimes he closes my hand and squeezes it shut. He asks what I feel. I may say, "I feel something warm in my hand."

(2) Suppose I say to Allister, "I feel something like an egg in my hand." He takes off my blindfold and shows me there is nothing in my hand. "I thought I felt something—something like an egg. How did you do that?" Or, "It was exacly as if I felt an egg." Is there anything which will lead up to, "I thought I felt a pain in my hand" or "It was exactly as if I felt a pain in my hand"? (3) There is the phantom limb case, but in that case there is no one thing which is *the* clear and definite thing to say. I suppose one could say, "I thought I had a pain in my [amputated] leg." One could also say, "I had a pain in my [amputated] leg." In either case it calls for understanding of the details, and when the details are understood the amputee could say many different things and not be misunderstood. In this case, "I thought I had a pain in my leg," and "I had a pain in my leg" would come to the same thing. In the former example, "I thought I felt an egg," and "I felt an egg" do not come to the same thing. (4) Still, there is a situation where "I felt an egg in my hand," and "I thought I felt an egg in my hand" would be taken in the same way. A man has tactual hallucinations: he sometimes "feels" an egg in his hand. He becomes quite accustomed to this, and I know all about it. He says to me, "I felt an egg in my hand just a few minutes ago." He could also say, "I thought I felt an egg in my hand again a few minutes ago."

(5) Return to Allister and his experiments. He asks, "What do you feel now?" I say "Nothing." He shows me I have an egg in my hand. "I have an egg in my hand, but I didn't feel it. How did you do that?" Surely there is no parallel here for feeling pains. How could an experimenter induce a pain in my hand which I do not feel? The nearest thing I can think of is the effect of the counter-irritant. There I say, "I still have the pain, but I do not feel it so much." I do not say, "I have it, but I do not feel it at all." Here my picture of feeling leads me wildly astray. I can reach out, have an egg put in my hand: I can have the egg in my hand and not feel it. It is right there and yet I do not feel it at all. I shall try to accommodate this to the picture. I shall say that my whole body is sentient. My feeling reaches easily to all parts of my body. No pain anywhere in my body will go undetected. That misses the point. I can imagine a situation in which I have an egg in my hand and not feel it. I cannot imagine a situation where I should say, "I have a pain in my hand, yet I do not feel it." It's not just unlikely. I can't make sense of it. I can't think of any situation, regardless of how

unlikely, where I could say that—and where anyone could make sense of what I say. The picture has a strong hold. And the situations for "I feel a pain" are very special and hard to keep clearly in mind. It's not likely the picture's hold will be broken by this observation.

My picture leads to another surprise. If I reach out from my mental place and feel a pain, then I ought to be able to feel a pain anywhere in my body. Except perhaps for hair and nails, no part of my body is permanently numb. I mean that it is conceivable that I should feel a pain in any part of my body which is not numb. This is not right. Can I conceive of feeling a pain in my skin: in a patch of skin, say, on the back of my hand? The question here does not have anything to do with feeling. Can I *have* a pain in the skin on the back of my hand? A very irritating substance is rubbed on my hand. It feels like concentrated nettles. "That stuff hurts." "It smarts." "The back of my hand hurts." "The skin on the back of my hand hurts." The back of my hand is badly scraped. "The skin hurts." I do not say, "I have a pain in my hand," because I do not have a pain in my hand. I do not say, "I have a pain on the back of my hand," or, "I have a pain in the skin on the back of my hand," because these make no sense. I burn my lower arm: although it hurts badly, I may not have a pain. If the burn is deep and severe, I suppose I shall have a pain in my arm—maybe a pain clear up to the shoulder.[1] Nettles produce a painful sensation on the skin, but not a pain.

When thinking in terms of the subject-object model, this observation about pains comes as a surprise. It is not a great discovery: I already had all the data. I followed a misleading representation. Still this does not help me much to disentangle myself from it. The pictorial representation has such a strong hold, I am inclined now to ask, "Well, then what is a pain?" I am inclined to think it is an object too thick to be on the skin. Hurts and itches are thin and flat; pains are thick and solid. What is it to have a pain or feel a pain? The thing I feel can't be a pain unless it is some distance inside the body. I've got to be able

---

[1] Berkeley seems to have been confused about this. He says "...intense heat is nothing but a particular kind of painful sensation; and pain cannot exist but in a perceiving being; it follows that no intense heat can really exist in an unperceiving corporeal substance." Heat, painful sensation, and pain do not have the connections this argument requires. I suppose this is of no importance. His argument needs only "painful sensation" not "pain." *Three Dialogues between Hylas and Philonous,* I.

to feel all around a pain; I've got to be able to feel it on all sides. An itch can be on the surface of my skin. It is thin, but it has two sides. I scratch it on the outside; I feel it on the backside, the inside. I am still thinking of a pain as an inner thing, and I am still mystified that I cannot conceive of a pain which I do not feel.

I have been led to think that a pain cannot go undetected. A pain, I may now think, is an object of some size. I can't have a pain on the tip of my nose. Being of some size, there is all the more reason for thinking that a pain could not be there in the body without my feeling it. I can think that it is a peculiar feature of inner objects that they are right there within feeling's reach. It's only as I stretch my powers to the outside of the skin that I become subject to error. I am still ruled by the picture; but why? I am slowly reviewing the details. Where the picture has led me astray, I am putting things back right. Why can't I simply replace the picture with a review of the details? They are too numerous, too hard to keep in mind simultaneously. Why would one want to keep all those things in mind? And why, on the other hand, does one think a picture of things, which does not happily represent the details?

I may be misled in thinking that I could have a pain in or on my skin. I am not misled into thinking that I might have a pain in a piece of wood which I am holding in my hand or that I might have a pain in the floor on which my feet rest. I have the idea that feeling is reaching out within the body: it stops at the skin. Therefore I cannot feel a pain outside the body. I could not, for example, feel a pain in someone else's body. I feel my pains. He feels his pains. He cannot feel my pains; I cannot feel his. Again, this has nothing particularly to do with feeling pains, except that my picture of feeling is one of the things which leads me to it. I cannot *have* another's pains. No one else can have mine. I am quickly led to say, "No one can have the same pain as I. Two people cannot have the same pain."

I have lost track of the details once more. For, of course, I can have the same pain as you. You tell me about a peculiar pain you have in the hip. I say, "I've had that same pain." I'm not wrong in saying that; or, at least, not always wrong. I am inclined to say that "same" here means "same kind," "same sort." "Same pain" would always be short for "same kind of pain." But we distinguish between "same pain" and "same kind of pain." A doctor wants to know whether an injection of serum-X always has the same unwanted side effect. Does everyone get the same strange pain in the chest? "What about George Graham? Did he have the same pain?" "No. Not exactly. He had a pain of the same kind, but he declared it was not centered in the upper chest."

Even so, I want to say that "same" here comes to "same kind." If two are alike in all describable details they are "same," but still not the same, identical pains. There are still two pains, yours and mine. "I've read the same book" isn't the same as "I've read the same kind of book." You may think that we have read the same copy. I can show you that you are wrong by producing two copies, the one I read and the one you read. "This is my copy. That is yours. You couldn't have read my copy. It has never been out of my study. I always keep my study locked." The same, I think, with pains. You could not have my pain because it is never outside my body; and you cannot feel within my body.

Smog has descended on a village and people think it is causing a great many pains in the muscles and joints. The public health officials are making a study of the average number of such pains in villages with smog and villages without. In one high-school room something else is happening. During a certain class period many students have an intense pain in the right hand. It lasts only for a few seconds. A student may have it several times during the period. The teacher is asked by the health officials to report this phenomenon in terms of average number of pains, and in quadruplicate. When orders come for reports in quadruplicate, the teacher does not question orders. In order to get the total number of pains, the teacher adopts the following method. Every time a student has a pain, he goes to the board and writes a number. The first person who has a pain writes 1, the second writes 2, and so on. The person who had the first pain has another, and by this time the line of numbers may be up to 12. He writes 13. The teacher notices there are two 4's in the row of numbers. It goes 1, 2, 3, 4, 4, 5, 6, etc. She asks "Whose pain was this?" pointing to the second 4. Two hands go up. She says, "You can't both have had the same pain." "If it was your pain, Mary, it wasn't Marvin's. If it was Marvin's pain, then it wasn't yours, Mary."[2]

---

[2] I am indebted to my colleague, John Cook, for the outline of this example. It was included in a paper he presented to the University of Oregon Philosophy Club. I have developed (and distorted?) his example to suit my own purposes.

Is this what I was thinking of? I was thinking it would be more like the books. "You can't have read the same copy, because it has been locked in my study. No one can get in there except me." What did Mary think when the teacher said, "You can't have the same pain as Marvin"? "The second number 4 refers to the pain I had in my hand. Marvin has no access by feeling to my hand"? No. "I think it was I who made the mistake. I think I put the second 4. Marvin was right behind me, and I'm sure now that I saw him write 5." Of course this is the kind of reaction the teacher's remark would get. This is the way it would be understood: "Someone made a mistake. Each person was to write a different number, one higher in the series of cardinals." I thought of feeling the pains in my body. I thought my powers of feeling stopped short at my skin. I thought of others feeling within their bodies in the same way. They could not feel a pain beyond their skins. So I said, "Two people can't feel (or have) the same pain." I didn't mean that someone made a mistake in the way he reported a pain. I didn't think I was reminding anyone of rules we might agree upon for counting pains in quite unusual circumstances.

Is there no end to the ways I am misled? I think of a pain as an object. I feel a pain. When I feel the surface of a brick or paper, I can feel it plainly or not so plainly. I can feel it well or not so well. My fingers are cold, they are becoming numb. I say, "I cannot feel the surface very well. My fingers are numb. I can feel it, but I can't make out the exact texture." I have a pain in my leg. I am given a local anesthetic, and my leg is becoming numb. I do not say, "I cannot feel the pain very well." My picture tells me that this is exactly what I should say. I am alert, reaching out, feeling: the anaesthetic prevents me from getting a good grasp of the pain. As my leg becomes numb, are there details of the pain I can no longer make out? No, but I quickly say, "That is a peculiarity of inner objects and the way they are felt. I never meant that inner objects are just like outer objects."

I think a pain is something there to feel. I think there are other inner things I feel. This, too, is connected with the picture I have of feeling. I think there are things I feel on my skin, and there are other subtler things I feel *in* my skin or on the near side of my skin. These are the "feels" of things when I feel things on my skin.[3] I want to get a clear idea of these objects of feeling.

[3] "Sometimes when the same wind is blowing, one of us feels chilly, the other does not ...

When I said I felt an egg and there was no egg in my hand, I then said, "I thought I felt an egg in my hand." I could also say, "It felt as though an egg were in my hand" or "It felt as though there were an egg in my hand." Yet I shall not say that I feel something in my hand. Now surely there is something which I feel and it is not *on* my hand: it is not on or outside my skin. I think there must be an object of some kind here—an internal object which I feel. I say, "It feels as though . . . " or "My hand feels as though there were an egg in it." "It feels . . . " I say, and "My hand feels . . . , " but what do *I* feel? I want to say, "I feel a something there—as though an egg were in my hand."

Perhaps another example will help. Allister continues with his experiments. He blindfolds me again, and does many different things, asking me always, "What do you feel?" He touches me with a hot, flat piece of metal. I say, "I feel a hot flat smooth object." He brings the hot metal near my skin, but does not touch me. I say, "I feel heat on my hand." He rubs the back of my hand with an irritating liniment. "I feel something irritating on my hand. It makes my hand feel hot." (I do not feel a hot substance; I do not feel heat; I do not feel hot skin or a hot hand.) Suppose he can produce something like this sensation without putting anything on my skin, without rubbing my hand. "My hand feels hot—as if it were rubbed with liniment." Now Allister removes my blindfold, and tells me to notice my hand. He directs on my hands an invisible beam from a great distance. "I feel heat on my hand. Strange it is just my hand. I do not see where it is coming from." I feel one hand with the other, "My hand is hot." "Yes," he says, feeling my hand, "It is hot." Sometime later all this is repeated, but now when I feel my hand, it is not hot. "My hand feels hot, but it does not feel hot to my other hand. It does not feel hot when I hold it to my cheek." Allister feels my hand. "It isn't hot, I assure you." "Well, it feels hot. It feels as though it were near something radiating heat."

Out of these new examples, we get, "My hand feels hot—as though it were rubbed with liniment," and "My hand feels hot—as though it were near something hot." We do not get "I" as the subject of feeling. We do not get, "I feel

it is cold to the one who feels chilly, and not to the other . . . it . . . appears to each of us . . . And 'appears' means that he 'perceives' it so . . . 'Appearing', then, is the same thing as perceiving, in the case of what is hot or anything of that kind. They *are* to each man as he perceives them . . . Perception, then, is always of something that *is,* and, as being knowledge, it is infallible." *Theaetetus,* 152b,c (on Protagoras's theory of knowledge).

my hand as hot," or "I feel as though my hand were hot," or "I feel as though my hand were rubbed with liniment," or " . . . as though my hand were near something hot." The results are the same as in the experiments with the egg. There we had, "My hand feels as though there were an egg in it," "It feels as though an egg were in my hand." But not, "I feel as though an egg were in my hand."

I expect to find something, an inner object, which I feel. Why do I not get the result I expect? My picture has dictated the choice of situations in which I am searching for examples of objects of feeling. I think I must have my feeling power ready: I must be able to send the full force of it wherever an object appears. I think of cases where I am required to notice what happens—as if I were to reach out mentally through my arm and into my hand. When do we say, "I feel as though an egg were in my hand" or "I feel as though my hand were near something hot"? Not in the situations where I have been searching. Where then?

I may go to a doctor complaining that there is something wrong. "I feel as though my entire head were swollen." I may complain, "It's hard to walk; it's hard to do anything. When I am sitting I feel too heavy to stand up. I can hardly lift my arms or legs. I feel as though I had gained a great amount of weight." Can we imagine the same kind of concern over a hand that feels hot or one that feels as though it held an egg? "I feel as though my hand were hot. There is nothing else wrong, but I can't get it out of my mind. I hesitate to shake hands or to touch anyone; but, of course, my hand isn't really hot. I find it difficult to do anything using that hand." It's farfetched; but if there is a place for feeling as though an egg were in my hand, it must be something like this. "Doctor, I know it sounds silly, but I feel as though I had an egg in my hand. I find myself trying to drop it out or throw it away, but I know there is really no egg there. I feel as though I had something which keeps me from closing my hand. I feel as though I must close it gently so that I don't break the egg."

I have been looking for an inner object of feeling. I started with situations where someone asks, "What do you feel?" and I reply, "I feel . . ." I report that I feel such things as eggs and marbles, cat fur and soft spaghetti. Then I tried to find answers to the question in which I reported an inward, private object.

Any possible report, it seems, would take the form, "I feel as though . . . " These words fit in a context entirely different from that of the experimenter and his theoretical-sounding question, "What do you feel?" These words might be addressed to a doctor by a man who often suffers minor but disturbing psychogenic symptoms. They might come in reply to a question asked by the doctor —asked as he hides a smile—"How do you feel today, George?" They go with answers like "Dizzy," " . . . as though my head were spinning," "Very tired." And not with answers like "A piece of warm metal," "A cold breeze," or "A coarse rope." In these reports to the doctor one does not speak of feeling an object—a thing.

Yet having reported my tactual hallucination to the doctor, I can go on and describe the object to him. My doctor may say, "Tell me in detail exactly what you feel." And I could go on: "I feel a medium-sized egg. It has a very smooth shell. I seem to be able to turn it in my hand and feel every part of it. That's why I know it's shaped like an egg: and there are no rough places on it." Here is an object of feeling, but it is the wrong kind of object. I want something located on the near side of the skin. The as-it-were egg is on the far side. Also I have been imagining the inner object to be of an entirely different kind, subtler, mental, akin to the mind's powers of feeling. The object I think I must feel would not be beyond the skin. It will be like a pain, but thinner, and nearer the surface. Such an object being inside the body would be in a most favorable position for feeling. It is next to impossible that such an object should be there and I not feel it. It is also as unimaginable that I should misidentify such an object as that I should misidentify a pain. The as-it-were egg is not like that: I might mistake an as-it-were egg for a real egg. My doctor asks me to close my eyes while I describe the egg. He slips an egg in my hand. I go on with the description. Now he asks, "What exactly is this you are describing?" I say, "I'm talking about that unreal egg, the thing I feel I have in my hand." He directs me to open my eyes, and I see that I have been talking about a smooth, white, large egg. I drop it and it breaks.

The same is true of "I feel as though my hand were hot." "It feels as though my hand were near something hot." I can tell exactly what I feel. "I feel heat —a little more on the back than on the palm." While my eyes were closed, my doctor could place a large heated tube around my hand. "My hand really is hot," I should say when I knew what had been done. I have been thinking of a more inner, more mental object—more like a pain. Sometimes I feel an egg, a real egg. Sometimes I feel an unreal egg. An experiment could easily be arranged so that I could not tell whether I felt a real or an unreal egg. After the doctor has placed an egg in my hand, he asks me to close my eyes again. He says that he may remove the egg, also that he may not. I cannot tell whether he removes it or not. He wants me to tell what I feel. I do not know whether there is an egg in my hand or not. Of course, I do not now say, "I feel as though an egg were in my hand." That's what I say with concern when I know there is no egg there.

I want to say, "There must be something I feel. I can't tell whether it's an egg or not." When I felt as though an egg were in my hand, I must have felt something, something somehow connected with an egg. It must be neither a real egg nor an unreal egg, but something else entirely—something I can take as the sign or representation of a real egg or of an unreal egg. When I tell what I feel and then open my eyes, I discover that I was feeling an egg or I discover that I was feeling an unreal egg. I don't think that I was feeling something else, some third thing.[4]

I *must* be feeling something else—something nearer than the real or unreal eggs. They are outside the skin. I must feel something which I have to interpret. The presence of an egg must normally bring it about that I feel the inner object. I must take this inner object normally to mean the presence of an egg. I am thinking of feeling as following a route from where I am to where the egg is. And that place just at the end of the route is a critical place, the place just under the egg. I am even inclined to think that I can't really feel beyond that place, beyond the extremity of my body. I must infer an egg from the inner feel. The egg itself I do not feel. Here is another thing about which I am misled. I am surprised and mystified that I can feel eggs, cat fur, and ball-bearings. It can't be pressure on the skin that I feel. I may feel no pressure on the skin. Even if I do, pressure on the skin is like heat on the skin. It is either real

[4] If one were searching for a "tactual sense-datum"—which is a more elaborate object than the "inner object" I am looking for here—he would come to the same impasse. This is important, I think, because we are inclined to think that tactual sense is the stronghold of the sense-datum theory: the "feels" of things are sense-data. I examine a parallel attempt to turn up a visual sense-datum in Essay II, page 29ff.

or not; it's outside and needs a mediator. Would it help if I invented a name for what I want? What shall I call it? "The feel of an egg"?

"The feel of an egg." A piece of unglazed pottery can have the feel of an egg. I might say to a potter, "I want some small cups. It's mainly the surface I'm concerned about. Can you make me some which have the feel of an egg?" He could try and he might succeed. Well, I didn't mean to call what I want "the feel of an egg." At any rate I didn't mean anything which can be a feature of a ceramic surface.

"Sensation" is the word I want. I have the sensation of an egg in my hand. Or it would be the sensation of having an unreal egg in my hand. Either would do—because these would be one and the same sensation. I say, "I have the sensation one has when he has an egg in his hand." When I say that one cannot tell whether I think I have an egg in my hand or whether I think I do not. "I have a sensation of heat in my hand. Either my hand is hot or not; I don't know." Of course these words would come to the right thing only in this very special circumstance. I have the tactual hallucination of an egg in my hand or of heat on my hand. And I have been fooled because a real egg has been put in my hand, or my hand has been surrounded by a hot object. I say, "I have the sensation of an egg," or, "I have the sensation of heat nearby." I do not know whether I am suffering hallucination or not.

Normally, with my eyes open, and my hand in clear view to all, these words would come to something quite different. "I have a sensation of an egg in my hand," might be announcement of this odd hallucination. If Allister has me blindfolded and asks what I feel, I might use these words in reply. I should be making a hesitant identification of an object, an egg. "I think I feel an egg; I'm not sure." This is not the outcome I want. I ought to be able to talk about a sensation any time, anywhere. No object of feeling should be any clearer. Yet I am now unable to fasten my attention clearly upon any such object.

I have a sensation. I do not *feel* a sensation. Even in the experimental situation, when asked what I feel, I should say, "I have the sensation . . . "; "I feel the sensation . . . " would be a solecism. I am led to think that the sensation is what I ought to feel. I ought to feel it more clearly than anything else. It is nearer: it is inside my body. It is the proper object of feeling, more certainly there than the eggs which sometime produce it.

No doubt the verb "to have" is misrepresented here by yet another picture. The things I have are objects, just as much as the things I feel. Undoubtedly I think that having a pain is like having a pig. Having a pig is having it in a pig-pen; having a pain is having it in the body. The pig and the pain are enclosed, surrounded. I am trying to worry here only about the problems created by the picture of feeling. That is what leads me to puzzle over the fact that I *have* a sensation and I do not *feel* a sensation. If I have a pig in the pen, I ought to see it. If I have a sensation, I ought to be able to feel it. It's not just that I always miss or overlook the sensation. The idea of feeling the sensation does not make sense.[5]

How have I focused on an object, the sensation? I have not brought any new element of the situation into view. I say, "I have the sensation one has when an egg is in his hand." If I am asked to explain, I shall say, "My hand feels as though an egg were in it." Or, "I feel as though an egg were in my hand." Is there some object referred to in the first which is not mentioned in the others? With "My hand feels as though . . ." and "I feel as though . . ." I do not think of any object other than an egg or an unreal, hallucinated egg. How then can a new object suddenly come into focus when I say, "I have the sensation one has when an egg is in his hand"? The words do not conjure it into being. If not "sensation" what shall I call the object I want? How do I know what to call something I cannot fasten attention on, something I cannot point out to myself, even to my mind's eye?

I think of feeling a pain as feeling an inner object. I think of it as analogous to feeling an egg. Only the object differs. In connection with feeling an egg there should be an object like a pain—in being inner, inside the body, beneath or near the egg. I seek such an object and it is not to be found. It might be better to say that in the search for such an object the sense of "feel" changes. "I feel an egg in my hand" leads to "I feel as though I had an egg in my hand."

---

[5] Here I am thinking only of "sensation" as it comes up in connection with feeling an object, i.e., the sensation of an egg in the hand. I am not thinking of "a tickling sensation," "a pleasant tingling sensation," or anything of that kind. In an experimental situation, perhaps I would report that I feel a tingling sensation on my leg, but that does not sound right. My doctor is rubbing my paralyzed arm, and asking, "Don't you feel anything yet?" I might say, "I feel a tingling sensation." We talk of feeling these sensations in much the same way we talk of feeling pains.

I begin with a situation in which I am asked to identify an object, "What do you feel?" I may be asked to consider the object carefully, "How does it feel?" "It feels like an egg: slightly round, ovoid." An altogether different background leads to "I feel as though an egg were in my hand." If it answers a question, the question is "How do you feel?" rather than "What do you feel?" The questioner is one who is concerned with my physical welfare. "My hand feels as though there were an egg in it" gives the same answer to the question. There are many other answers to the question, "How do you feel?" "I feel dizzy." "My head feels as though it were spinning."

There are two different kinds of feeling here—or two senses of the verb "to feel." I have been trying to interpret "I feel a pain" as like "I feel an egg." I seem to get my picture of feeling from the idea of reaching out and touching something or handling something. And I have been misled in all sorts of ways. It is hard to quickly review the ways without being overly crude. I can have an egg in my hand without feeling it. I can have a pain in the hand without feeling a pain in the hand. I am led to think I might have a pain in my hand without feeling it. And that is wrong. I can feel an egg anywhere I can think an egg might be: on my hand, my cheek, under my foot. I am led to think that I could feel a pain in my skin, that I might have a pain in my skin. That is wrong. I think that structly speaking I could not feel an egg. I should have to infer an egg. There is no such inference, and none is called for. I say, "Two people cannot have the same pain." I think that is a description of the limits of feeling. It is not: it is a call to correct a mistake in reporting pains.

The idea that pain is an object is forced on me by the picture of feeling. I am led constantly astray. Yet I can't break the hold of the picture. The picture also led me to think there would be an inner object or sensation underlying every outer object felt. The picture produces such wild expectations here that at least on this point I can shake its hold. I am led to think that "I have the sensation of . . . " ought to give me an object I feel. I should be able to say, "I feel the sensation of . . . ," but that is nonsense. "I have the sensation" is another way of saying "I feel as though . . . " With, "I feel as though an egg were in my hand," I can dispatch the temptation to locate some inner object. The only objects mentioned are real eggs and hallucinated eggs. I think that "I feel a pain" and "I feel an egg" are alike. Perhaps I could break the hold of the picture if I could think that "I feel a pain" is more like "I feel as though an egg were in my hand" or "I have the sensation of an egg in my hand."

I can describe the sensation of an egg in my hand, "As if it were an egg, a large egg, with rough places—and it's quite warm, as if it had just come from the nest." I can also describe a pain. It is intense, diffuse, sharp, stabbing, throbbing . . . as if I had been hit by a blunt instrument, as if my hand were in a vice. When am I called on to give a careful description of a pain or of the sensation of an egg? When I have a sympathetic listener and I expect sympathy. I may exchange symptoms. Or I give the description to someone, a doctor, a physiologist, who is trying to make a diagnosis. I give it to someone who wants to find the cause, someone who wants to help me. Only in very special circumstances is "I have a pain . . . " an answer to, "What do you feel?" It is more commonly an answer to "How do you feel?" The same with "I have the sensation of . . . " or "I feel as though an egg were in my hand."

I am not inclined to think of a sensation as an object except when I say, "I have the sensation . . . " The picture of the object is dispelled when I replace that with the synonymous "I feel as though . . . " or "My hand feels as though." "I have a pain . . . " can often be replaced with "My knee hurts," "My leg aches," "My leg feels as though it were being crushed."

I can see that "I feel dizzy" and "I feel as though I had an egg in my hand" are not reports from behind the eyes about an object somewhere else in the body. How about "I feel a pain"? It remains tied to "I feel an egg." Perhaps I could fasten it to "I feel as though I had an egg . . . " if I had some formula, some general description which fits both. If they are not reports of objects at another place in the body, what are they? They are reports on the state of the organism as a whole. Feeling does not involve just a small place in the body; it does not involve just two small places or a narrow pathway. It involves the body as a whole. And a report on feeling is about the body as a whole. I'll say that! But isn't that just as silly a thing to say as, "I am behind my eyes feeling a pain in my leg." Reply: "No, I am reporting on the state of my organism as a whole." When philosophizing on the beach, one cannot draw this on the sand. There are no tongues of feeling one can scratch out through the crude outline of the body. Saying this in the philosophy classroom, one cannot turn to the blackboard and make a sketch: a human body with causal lines following the path of the nervous system—all leading to the head. One cannot sit in silent solitude, wiggle his toe, think of feeling it wiggle, and then say, "I am reporting on my organism as a whole." Why not stick with the details? Why not? Can't I summarize the details? Can't I say that "I feel a pain" is both like and unlike "I feel an egg"? And also say "I feel a pain" is like and unlike "I feel as though I had an egg in my hand"? Immediately philosophical questions come. In what ways like and unlike? How many ways are there? What counts as a likeness or a difference? Aren't there important and unimportant likenesses and differences? And how to determine what is important and what not? Aren't the important ones the ones that strike me as important? Don't they stand out because of the picture in terms of which I see the thing? Why not stick with the details? Why not?

This picture I make so much of. I am sure that I think that way when I don't watch out. That is autobiographical. I'm also pretty sure that everyone thinks that way at times. The picture seems natural, it comes so easily to mind. In those relaxed, but highly intellectual moods, unrestrained but theoretical, when we ask questions like, "Why is there something, not nothing?" we can also ask, "How is it possible to feel anything?" Often these are playful child-like moods, and we ask such questions as, "How do birds identify birds? They have no bird guides." When we ask, "How can we feel?" I think the first thing that is apt to come to mind is the prehensile picture, the idea of the mind reaching out. More importantly, I think this picture remains in the background, as we become more persistently theoretical and ask further, more specific questions. I suspect it would have determined the first, most primitive theories of feeling. I would not be surprised to find such a theory held by Thales or Anaxagoras. In all likelihood, they did not think about it at all. Theophrastus complains that his predecessors say little about the tactual-sense. But the earliest theories of vision were based on prehensile models.

I further suppose that the reason it is not expressed or developed by later philosophers is that it early became apparent that the prehensile model would bear no scientific fruit. Philosophical and scientific speculation were closely tied together. The prehensile was displaced by the causal picture. I suspect, however, that it was not entirely displaced. I do not see how the causal picture could work, unless it were grafted on the prehensile one, unless some remnants of the prehensile picture remained. A causal theory fails to give a philosophically satisfactory analysis of feeling just as it fails to give a satisfactory analysis of seeing or remembering. An electro-chemical change takes place at the brain end of a nerve—and then comes "I feel an egg." I suspect that knowledge of the nervous system merely gives us a picture of the channels through which we feel: we feel through the nerves.

> Nature also teaches me by these feelings of pain, hunger, thirst and so on, that I am not only residing in my body, as a pilot in his ship, but furthermore, that I am intimately connected with it and so blended that a single whole is produced . . . When the nerves of the foot are stimulated violently and more than is usual, their movement, passing through the marrow of the backbone up to the brain, produces there an impression upon the mind which makes the mind feel something—namely, pain as though in the foot . . . [6]

[6] Descartes, *Meditations*, 6.

> . . . The sense-data must therefore play a double role in perception. In the mode of presentational immediacy they are projected to exhibit the contemporary world in its spatial relations. In the mode of causal efficacy they exhibit the almost instantaneously precedent bodily organs as imposing their characters on the experience in question. We see the picture, and we see it with our eyes; we touch the wood, and we touch it with our hands . . . In the case of bodily feelings the two locations are identical. The foot is both giving pain and is the seat of the pain . . . [7]

[7] A. N. Whitehead, *Symoblism*, (New York, G. P. Putnam's Sons, 1959), p. 50.

THE FUTURE

AND THE PAST

VII

THE PRECARIOUS REALITY OF THE PAST

I am going to attempt to raise a philosophical problem out of the materials from which I think it naturally grows. I want to talk some about the problem —while developing it and after—talk enough that I talk it to death, if I can. So that it will decay back into the materials from which it sprung. The decay, I am sure, will not be very complete; but I am convinced all the same that the way to decompose a philosophical problem is to understand it.

I have in mind a problem which I believe can be grown out of simple materials, the paradoxical idea that the past is inaccessible. I shall try to develop a distinctively philosophical thesis with the words, "The past is gone." I have chosen this sentence because it seems to be one with which we can quickly and happily hit off a particular philosophical theory, and immediately raise a philosophical question. The theory and the consequent question are well illustrated by these quotations:

> The first and most obvious objection to the view that the immediate object of remembering is the event remembered is the objection . . . of time. How, it is asked, can I possibly have before my mind literally an event, or part of it, which occurred, say, ten years ago? When the event happened, it ceased to exist; and in any case, how could an event in my mind which is occurring now (the act of remembering) bridge the time interval so as to have for its object another event which is not occurring now, but finished occurring ten years ago?[1]

> It is surely clear that the argument that remembering cannot have for its direct object the event remembered is an *a priori* argument, based . . . on a theory about the nature of time. It is supposed that when something happens, it has then happened, and is thereafter as unavailable for subsequent observation as it was for

[1] A. D. Woozley, *Theory of Knowledge,* (London, Hutchinson's University Library, 1949), pp. 57-58.

previous observation before it happened, just as if I do not see the lightning flash when it occurs, I cannot hope to see it afterwards (for it is no longer there to see).[2]

On a similar issue, the question of how it can be possible to verify any statement about the past, Ayer considers some "verbal" solutions. One is the decision to say we perceive the past states of stars; another to say that we see the past in a newsreel movie. He observes that such shuffles involve application of scientific theory, theory which one can accept only on the basis of his past experiences. He adds, "And whatever tricks we may be able to play with the dating of physical events, our past experiences are not recapturable. Once they are gone, they are gone forever."[3]

I shall begin with a survey of the materials, the sentence "The past is gone" in some of its back-yard, street-corner, pool-hall uses:

(1) On a brisk, smoky, fall evening, a man burns leaves, leans on his rake and talks to some of the neighborhood: "I remember when on Halloween, we managed to hoist Felger's best cow onto his kitchen roof. She stood there most of the night, and then, just before dawn, started to bellow like all hell let loose . . . so loud they could hear it in the next county. The kids now have no Halloween-imagination, or maybe no guts. Those days are gone. The past is gone . . . (forever)."

(2) A young man tells of his miserable adolescence: "One little slip of speech . . . and hours, sometimes days of self-castigation. I cared so much . . . much too much . . . of what everyone, anyone, thought of me. I was surrounded always with imagined scorn . . . never quite ventilated with laughter. I tried to hide imagined physical defects. I walked so softly, and the twigs crackled underfoot like thunder. Thank God the past is gone. I never have to live those painful years again. The past is gone . . . (gone)."

(3) I see a pile of papers on Paul's desk, and . . . uninvited . . . I read them. I discover page after sick page of childlike stories of his mother, dead for many years. I think, "Paul lives too much in the past. Someone should tell him the

[2] *Ibid.*, pp. 59-60. One can try to distinguish two kinds of problems which the sentence generates: Those having to do with memory, and those concerning the purported "object" of memory, the past. In so far as these are separable, I shall limit myself to problems about the past.

[3] A. J. Ayer, *The Problem of Knowledge* (Baltimore, Penguin Books, 1956), p. 157.

past is gone. 'Come back to the present, Paul,' I want to say, 'The past is gone. You cannot live in it. It is gone. You cannot get it back.' "

(4) A certain queer Croosian artifact has long been exhibited (bearing its proper number) in the archaeological museum. Over the years a more and more complete picture of the Croos culture has been formed. In fact, the Croos culture is now more completely understood than that of any pre-historical people. Still no explanation for the use of this artifact can be given. When considering this state of affairs, an expert on the Croos culture says, "The past is gone (it is simply gone from us)."

(5) As the result of an auto accident, an injury to the head, a man is unable to recall anything that happened before last week. Friends tell him stories, try to jar his memory: they are amazed, unable to believe how complete the amnesia. After a trying session in which his friends insist that he must remember this thing or that, he sighs, "The past is gone . . . absolutely gone."

Now, out of these to grow a problem: I shall try to think the sentence philosophically. I think over these examples quickly, without trying to recall the details. Too bad the past is gone. It is a good thing it is gone. (Do these cancel out?) Some people spend too much of their lives trying to get it back. Large features of it we can never know. The past is gone. We can never get back to it. A little accident and our feeble contact with the past would be snapped. I become impatient, even resentful of the details of particular cases. I fix attention on the sentence itself, "The past is gone." An aura of emotion surrounds it, deriving vaguely from the forgotten details of its various uses. The past is gone, regretfully, sadly—fearfully, for time takes its toll, and moves swiftly on. Feelings about time come in. The past is gone: far away and long ago. The long ago becomes far away. Pictures of time fill my mind, time is a thing, a place, a stream. The past is gone. How can it be remembered? It is gone, how can it be reached? How very queer that it can be remembered. Inexplicable. How can one understand the workings of memory? The past being gone, it is not here. Not being here, we can have no direct contact with it. It cannot be directly known: and if it cannot ever be directly known, it can never be indirectly known. (If I cannot feel pain, I can never know what it is for another to feel pain.) The past cannot be directly known. So it cannot be indirectly known. Therefore, it cannot be known at all.

This is too much, too soon. This is one of those philosophical conclusions we dare not draw. So, the past must be understood in such a way that memory is not impossible. What, then, is the past if it is to be remembered? It cannot be a thing out of reach, a foreign thing, outside the mind, or outside the grasp of the mind. It must therefore be a mode of apprehension of the mind itself, or it must in reality be within the present experience. The past is really in some way present. It must be. But only the greatest of philosophical work and ingenuity could explain how that is possible. This is one great difficulty: how to understand the past, that it is an object of memory.

But there is another: it is hard to understand how anything called the past can be there to contact. The past is gone. And like the rainbow, when it is gone it ceases to exist. This kind of analogy is sponsored and encouraged by the mood which hangs over certain thoughts about the past. Can there be beauty if no beholder? We wonder can there be a past if no memory. I think of some little happening from long ago, a thing which means nothing except to me, and only I remember. And when I die? What will become of that object of my memory? It will be gone, completely gone. How, without memory, could there even be a past? Having lost sight of the particulars at one place in the genesis of the problems (the circumstances surrounding uses of the sentence, "The past is gone"), they return now at another. A great deal of the poignancy of the difficulty comes from our frustrated longing for the preservation of particular —*just those particular*—little things. That just those special things—perhaps only I remember—should be gone, that their existence should be so precarious seems an outrage; that I should be their sole keeper seems ridiculous ... particularly since I cannot keep them. The need for explanation is almost a religious need. That the past is gone is as frightening and outrageous as that a man should die.

What sort of ease can I find for my troubled feeling that the past does not exist? Will it do to say that God remembers everything? So what is gone, I shall say, is not really lost. The solution of this trouble, then, is also the solution of the problem about the possibility of memory. The divine searchlight, shining through our minds and aimed at the past could explain veridical memory. This seems only to replace one set of problems with others—bigger. I want to get at the ground of the problems themselves. I must try to understand that the past is gone in such a way that I can see just exactly why knowledge of it is mystifying, so mystifying that God has been invoked to explain how it can be managed. The past must be gone in such a way that our judgments that it is so gone are on the whole right; but in some deeper way they are radically wrong. I must understand the source of our philosophical urge to say the past is not really gone, but is in the present.

How can I understand the past being gone? I shall look at how things are gone. Is anything else gone in the same way the past is gone?

(1) The gas balloon I tied to the fence is gone. It has floated away. I cannot see it. I could not see it from here: it is simply not in sight. Clearly the past is not supposed to be gone like this. Whereas I cannot see the balloon, others can. If the past is philosophically out of reach of one, it is out of reach of all (except perhaps the dead, and we are out of reach of them). Also the balloon has floated away. "Gone away," we shall say. In none of the examples where someone said, "The past is gone," should we say the past has "gone away." Well, certainly not as the balloon has gone away. The past is not going, going, going and then gone. Also the phrase "gone away" is no part of the way of talking which generates the philosophical problems.

(2) Consider an example where we should not say "gone away." I return to the lake in late spring. I look and say, "The ice is gone." I cannot see it, the children cannot skate on it. No one can skate on it. I do not say it has gone away; it has melted. Is this the way the past is supposed to be gone? Although it has melted in the spring sun, the ice will return next winter. The past will never return, I say, speaking out of my philosophical mood. I *want* to say the past cannot return. It is just because it cannot return that it is such a mystifying object of knowledge. (The snow will return to the mountains, but not the snows of yesteryear.) The ice is gone: it has melted into water. It has changed its state. The past has not melted. Has it changed its state?

There are circumstances in which we might well say the past has changed its state. Photography, especially movies, has changed entirely our mode of knowing and our feeling about the recent past. We have an understanding of and sympathy with the period just before our birth—the time of our fathers' early manhood—which previous generations did not have. The past has entirely changed its state. We should indeed say, "The past has changed its state."

But my philosophical feelings are all against it; my philosophical inclinations lead me to say the past cannot change its state. What is gone is gone. I want to say there are only two changes of state: future to present, and present to past.

The ice on the lake is not gone until it is all gone. Is this like the past being gone? We should sometimes say, "The past is all gone." Suppose only a handful survived a nuclear cataclysm, and only one short history book remained to inform that little group of a past they knew no other way. "The past is almost entirely gone." Now that one book is destroyed. We might well say, "Now the past is all gone." Again my philosophical inclinations lead me away from our familiar ways of talking. When struggling with the philosophical problems, I want to say, "The past is gone," and sometimes with emphasis, "gone, all gone." But this very definitely is not in contrast with "partly gone." I want to say there is no such thing as the past being partly gone. I ridicule the idea of the past being partly gone: "Is the back part of the past gone yet?" When the ice has gone, in its place there is water. But the past cannot suffer a change of state; hence nothing can be in its place. Again, this is quite unlike the way we talk. With the burning of the one history book, all of the past is gone. "Our little of the past is gone. In its place—only this heap of ashes."

What should we say if over all the earth a gas was released which brought about in everyone a progressive amnesia—first inability to remember a few things, then more—and finally total? Should we say the past is going, partly gone, almost all gone? The past is now all gone? In any case, such an example is irrelevant. From a philosophical point of view, the past is not contained in a book or in our minds, and destroying a book or our minds does not make the past go. It was already gone long before the book was burned or the amnesia produced. The past, having gone, cannot go a second time. When anything is past, it is gone. The philosopher thinks he detects a strain in our ordinary ways of talking and seeks to eliminate it.

(3) Following upon "The past is gone," we do not want to give philosophical sense to the questions, "Where did it go?" or, "Which way?" In this respect, "The past is gone," is unlike "The balloon is gone." With announcement that the ice is gone, can there be questions of where, or which way? Yes, perhaps child's questions. The answer consists in lessons in how liquids change form with changes in temperature. It is hard to see how there could be similar child's

questions about, "The past is gone," or similar lessons in the behavior of time.

"My headache is gone" looks more promising. I have been worried about whether I shall be able to keep a very important appointment because I have had a terrible headache, a headache so bad that I could not have driven without getting sick. Just as I am ready to phone an excuse, the headache disappears. "My headache is gone." "At last it is completely gone." As with "The past is gone," there are no questions—"Where did it go?" "Which way—" Still, "My headache is gone" cannot serve as a model for understanding the philosophical complaint, "The past is gone," because my headache may return. I may be afraid to start out on the busy highway, for fear it will return. I wonder what caused it to go—almost miraculously. Was the effect of the aspirin somehow delayed, and did it go to work all at once? When philosophizing, we say the past can not return. But in fact we may have fears that the past will return; we may wonder what makes it return. Many years ago I almost drowned in cold water on a dark, dark night. Quite unaccountably, now—usually when just falling asleep —I live those terrifying moments over, doubled with cramps and struggling upwards, not knowing where the surface is. The past has come back; it returns again. Why does it keep coming back?

My philosophical desires turn my back on this way of talking. "The past is gone," I say. And then I am willing to say also, "The past is not gone. It keeps coming back." This is the way we talk, but it stirs a theoretical revolt. "This talk is careless: not strict. We need something better," I feel like saying. I want to say, "The past is gone: It cannot come back. It must make no sense to talk of its coming back." I want to rule out any questions about why it comes back, and of why it is gone. I may have to watch what I eat in fear the past, my struggle in the cold water, may come back (upon me). We must not allow this idea. I want the past to be gone. But not like balloons, or ice—or a headache. "My headache went away this morning; it has been gone for hours" I say. Or, "My headache, I think, is going away." We must rule out any analogous questions about the past: there must be no room for, "How long has the past been gone?" or "Is the past going away yet? Slowly? Can we make it go faster?"

After a search through the attic and basement, I say, "The termites seem to be gone." "Why do you think so?" is a perfectly understandable question. The past is not supposed to be gone in such a way that one can give reasons for thinking it gone, cite evidence that it is gone. In reply to "The ice is gone," one could say, "No. It only looks like it's gone. There's a bit of water on the ice from yesterday's thaw." Once in a while, when we say a thing is gone, it is not really gone, and we are mistaken. Usually, however, when we say a thing is gone, it is gone, and we are right. Although we often have doubts about whether something is gone, generally we are quite certain. Can we be uncertain, can we be mistaken about whether the past is gone? This brings up a very difficult business. If we are philosophically mistaken or in doubt, it must not be just sometimes, but always.

If I could find out what it is for the past to be gone as the philosopher wants it to be, then it must always *seem* to be gone in that way; yet from another (more profound) point of view, it must not be gone, but present. Could any example show this? Myrtle has just learned to drive. She is showing off her prowess to Francine, and while bragging loudly, drives at 45 miles per hour into the rear of a truck. She strikes the steering wheel with her mouth, knocking out all front teeth. Feeling with her fingers in her bleeding mouth, she screams, "My front teeth are gone." Francine, laughing insanely, replies, "No. They're not gone. They're here on your lap." Is this the sort of correction the philosopher wants to announce with, "The past is not really gone"? How can I tell since I have been unable to clearly understand the judgment which needs correction? Myrtle's front teeth are not gone in the right way, even though their being gone is consistent with their being on her lap right before her eyes. Her teeth could conceivably be returned to the sockets from which they were gone. They could be grafted and grow back. The philosophical past cannot be reseated or grafted; nor can it grow back, nor in any other way returned to its original position.

I cannot find a use of the phrase " . . . is gone" which provides a suitable prototype for the philosophical pronouncement, "The past is gone." Still the one which keeps coming back to mind is the use of the phrase in "The balloon is gone." This example symbolizes my philosophical longings: I cannot blot out from my mind the picture of the past being gone, gone in that way—gone like the balloon. That is the kind of picture which generates the philosophical questions.

Now I think I can see what the trouble is. Something is theoretically wrong with the idea that the past is gone. The sentence, "The past is gone," will not do for accurate and systematic expression. The reason only the pluperfect tense of the verb "to go" applies to the past is that the past, by definition, can never be present. How then can it be gone if it was never here? What is here is the present, not the past. Hence we have nothing, "now-this, then-that." Nothing *goes*. To this we want to say it is not the past which goes, but the present. The present goes away. However this way of talking will do us no better for theoretical purposes; for talk of the present we are confined to the present tense. The present goes: but *it* never becomes past. An adequate style of talking demands that something be first present, and then past: as the balloon is first here, then there; the ice first solid, then liquid; the headache first bad, now better. What is present *becomes* past. That is what is *really* gone. It goes and is gone.

I can see now: the trouble with "The past is gone" is the mental picture associated with it, a picture of some large thing—like the balloon—which has gone away, out of sight. My mind seems filled with such imagery, as if it were drawn on a blackboard, with arrows showing the balloon going, going—and then an arrow pointing to the edge of the blackboard. I have been trying to find a home, an application for this picture, but it leads me always to misrepresent the way we talk about the past, to misrepresent the nature of the past. What is more important, philosophically, it leads me into untenable theory. The picture suggests absurd things: the balloon gets bigger by additions from the present, but it is not next to the present for it is gone. If it is not next to the present, what is in between? Why doesn't the in-between get bigger? The trouble comes from my picture of the past as a *thing*. Perhaps I should try representing the past as a *place*, the place where present things go, a place where they must dwell forevermore. According to this picture, the idiom, "What is past is gone" is philosophically superior to "The past is gone." The things which are here, present, go there, past.

What are the "things" which are present and then become past? This is a perfectly general (a philosophical) question. The answer is clear: events, occurrences, happenings, incidents, episodes, "things" of that category. Some events are in the distant past, some the recent past, some are present; some episodes are yet to occur—in the future. Present happenings become past. Yet is this so clear? Each of these words "event," "occurrence," "episode," strikes its own fear. Anthony: "What happened this afternoon?" Beata: "The cat had her kittens." Anthony: "And what else happened?" Beata: "Don't you want to know how many, what sexes?" Anthony: "I want to know *everything* that happened." Beata: "Nothing else happened." Anthony: What do you mean, nothing else: the clock hummed, didn't it? Its hands moved; the clouds floated by; the wind blew first big, then little; the limbs of the trees swayed, the red line on the thermometer got longer, then shorter. You know, all the things that have now become past. The cat's labor and delivery have no special claim on, or status in, the past. The past takes all, and all alike. It is a perfect democracy."

"Events," "occurrences," "happenings," "incidents," "episodes," each of these words seems to apply, in its own way, only to events charged with a certain human significance. We must change that. Imagine, then, that they apply where they do not. Let us get over our fear of novelty and get on: "Everything that takes place in time, sweeps on in time, takes up a little time, will count as an event." Do all the present events "become past"? Eventually. Remember, we do not talk this way, talk of events becoming past, but we should: and now we shall try.

We are often inclined to adopt this new, theoretically superior way of speaking. Outside of philosophy, we sometimes say something analogous; we say of some present events that they become *history*. Perhaps "becomes history" is an idiom after which we can model "becomes past." The presidential inauguration, taking place today, will become history. But, the incident of the little boy in the garage with the little girl, symbolic of the human situation as it is, may or may not become history. It will become history only if the boy or the girl becomes a person of importance. We have agreed to ignore the question of importance and simply expand the application of "becomes past" to every present event. So "becomes history" will not help us understand this expansion. We must talk on. Just as we can say of everything (everything philosophically speaking) "This too will pass," we must learn to say, "This will soon become past."

A species of bird can become extinct and be gone. The death of some one bird —the last—makes the species extinct. Is there some single occurrence which makes a present event past? A wind uprooted our tangerine tree. In philosophical jargon that event, the uprooting of our tangerine tree, has become past. What came last and made it past? Events do not consist of elements the way species consist of individuals. So there could not be any happening to an element which brought about the extinction or extermination of the event. The death of the last bird makes the species extinct. Perhaps the occurrence of the the last part of an event makes it past? The last bird dies; it does not become dead. It *becomes* sick perhaps, and dies, *becomes* cold, and so is dead. What does the last part of an event become which makes it past? Not sick or cold or old or crippled.

With a nervous tennis star like Fremont, what his wife says at breakfast can ruin his game. She can upset his timing. "My timing is gone," he will complain. His timing can become upset and be gone. An event must *become* past, and thereby *be* gone. Ice becomes water and is gone. A caterpillar becomes a butterfly. When the butterfly has come, the caterpillar is gone. In each of these, something is gone because it has become something else. We do not want a present event, in becoming past, to become something else. It must not be some*thing* else; it must be the same thing some*place* else. What, then, by becoming, can be gone, and yet not become something else? A wound can become healed and be gone. Becoming healed takes time. Time must lapse before a wound is gone. For philosophy, we do not want to make any sense out of "A present event takes time in becoming past."[4] A wound may be partly healed; partly, almost, or nearly gone. Although we sometimes say a present time is partly gone, we do not, it seems, say a present event is partly, or nearly gone.[5] The spring is nearly gone. We do not say, "The spring festival is nearly gone:" it is "nearly *over*."

Timing at tennis seems a more likely example. Fremont's timing cannot be partly or nearly gone. He either has it or he does not; it may be a little off, or

[4] It is easy to be reminded of the times when we might say this sort of thing. A passenger who lived through an airplane crash may awake every night for years with frightening dreams. And then the dreams no longer come, and he sleeps the night through. Later he is in another crash, and he and only one other passenger survive to climb miraculously from the wreckage. That evening he writes his wife, " . . . this event will take a long, long time in becoming past. I am afraid it will take a long, long time."

[5] I am using this category-word "event" in what we might call its unexamined first metaphysical sense. See next footnote.

way off, but it is either gone or it is right. His timing is not gone because its parts or elements are gone. It is gone because of what his wife said. Events are not gone because of anything else that happens. Something that happens may be the result of something else that happens, but something-that-happens-becoming-past is not the result of something else that happens. None of these examples will do anyway. I am trying to apply the picture of the past as a place, a place where events go. A wound, a species of bird, Fremont's timing do not go to some place. The only kind of becoming that will do is becoming transported, transplanted, or something like that. A trunk or a custom can be transported; a tree or a way of life can be transplanted. They *are* transported or transplanted. We do not say they *become* transported or transplanted.

For some technical purposes we use the verb "becomes" as an auxiliary to certain passive verbs. "Water becomes ice," but in a technical jargon we say, "Water becomes solidified at 0° C." Mention of the specific conditions under which a transformation takes place seems to be an essential part of the idiom "becomes solidified," "—vaporized," "—pulvarized," "—carbonized." There are no specific conditions which must be (or even can be) mentioned in saying a present event becomes past. One is inclined to say that in "becomes solidified" there is no reference to real becoming; the word "becomes" can almost be replaced by "is." Compare "becomes solidified at O°" with "is solidified at O° C." In a real case of becoming, such an interchange is ridiculous: "The larva becomes an adult"—"The larva is an adult."

"Vaporize," "carbonize," refer to changes. A substance becomes subject to a certain kind of change under certain special circumstances. A present event by analogy would be host of some certain kind of change. We need a verb form of "past." There is none. How could there be? The closest thing is "passed." Again this applies to times, not to events. "The day passed," we say; not, "The roof being blown off passed."[6] Interesting as they are, these topics are on a

[6] Of course, we say, "The storm passed," "My grief passed." Do we mean, "The time of the storm passed," "The time when I was so sad passed"? To say yes would be to decide that in such cases "storm" and "grief" do not refer to events, that is, that storms and griefs are (at least not always) events. I certainly do not want to decide anything of this kind. Is a storm an event? (or an occurrence?) What sort of question is that? What could it be except, "De we call storms events?" (or occurrences?) Yes, sometimes. Q. "What were the most important events of the year?" A. "One was the great snowstorm on the East Coast." This example does not show what I want. I want to distinguish between "the storm" and

side track. There is a more basic reason why these examples will not do. None of this talk about what birds, wounds, timings, customs, or water becomes is talk about events. We have decided it must be events which become past, not things. We must concentrate on events.

How are we to understand an event's "becoming past"? Just what do events become? A battle can become fiercer, a game sillier. These becomings are no help at all in understanding "becomes past": although a battle may become fiercer it does not remain fiercer. A game which becomes sillier does not there-after remain always sillier. An event in becoming past, remains forever past. What can events become, remaining what they become? The wreck of old 97, an event, an incident, an episode in the life of a railroad. What has this event be-come? A legend. Subject of folk song. A lesson of importance in the development of safe railway travel. Better understood in some ways; more mysterious in others. A reminder of a colorful period in American history. None of these be-comings is like becoming past. Perhaps that is because the event is too signifi-cant. Our old iron pump was once struck by lightning. What has that event, the striking of our pump by lightning, become? The subject of family reminiscences. Symbolic of a past way of life. First of a series of mystifying natural accidents on our property. It appears there is only one kind of becoming of which events are capable: they can take on a new role in explaining the doings of human be-ings. They can be cited in a new way in an historical account. My first fears about the words "event," "occurrence," and others have come back. What can an event of absolutely no significance become? Nothing, if it remains of absolutely no significance. If it becomes anything at all, it becomes of some significance. May-be "becomes" is a bad choice of verbs. Sometimes we want to say present events "recede into the past." But when do events recede? " . . . recede in importance," " . . . recede into insignificance." "Recede" seems to offer fewer possibilities than "becomes": I can think of no use at all parallel to the use we want to give "recedes into the past," and in terms of which we might understand it.[7]

"the storm striking the East Coast." It is the storm that passed, not the storm striking the East Coast. The important event of the year was the storm striking the East Coast.

The reason I say "passed" is not used of events is that no clear-cut example comes to mind. Thus my statement uses "event" in what I have called the unexamined first meta-physical sense.

[7] (a) Of course, we do say "Events recede into the past." See the story of the storm in the

I have been able to find no model after which I can understand the intended force of the phrase "becomes past." I have been trying to think of the past as a place. But the phrase "becomes past" also brings to mind other pictures which suggest not so much that the past is a place as that "becoming past" is a change of relative place. Time is a line stretching endlessly in two directions, one way future, one way past. Events move along the line from the future, into the present. They are then displaced by others which come into the present, and so they move into the past. An event moves from the present into the past— "becomes past." The occurrence of events is like the burning of a long fuse . . . the present burning into the future, leaving the past as an ash, a record behind. Many pictures come easily to mind . . . (Time, mother of metaphors!) How do we apply these pictures? They serve only to suggest such sentences as, "The past is gone," "Present events become past," but in no way help to understand the function the philosopher wants these sentences to have.

These pictures (and their variants) cannot explain why, as philosophers, we want to say the past is gone, or the way we want to say the past is gone—gone so that it is no longer accessible. There is something else at work which quickly expresses itself in more pictures—but more disturbing pictures: the ash of the fuse is always blown away . . . blown away into nothingness. An event moving into the past falls into an abyss; becoming past is like sailing (as Columbus feared he might) over the edge of the earth. The "place" which is the past is not always far away, but it is a very, very different kind of place. One gets there easily and suddenly, and in spite of that it is inaccessible. Becoming past is like dying. Thus it is that memory is either impossible, or always wrong. That is, even those memories which are in the usual sense right are in some deep way wrong, because they imply the existence of the objects remembered.

The reason the past is such a queer place (How could I have failed to notice?)—is that it is nonbeing. So, I suppose, it is no more a place than not a place. Becoming past is just ceasing to exist. Being past is a way of being non-

town, p. 142. (b) How wildly I have been led to misrepresent things. Not only do we not say in the right way that an event becomes past, we do not even say, it would seem, of an event that took place yesterday or ten years ago that it is (in the right way) past. If there is any question, an event is *"over"* we say. Or "It took place in 1863" (an eclipse, say). Perhaps, "It took place in the distant past—no one knows when."

existent. How do we go on with *this* way of talking? How does a thing (any-thing) cease to exist? We are interested in how the passenger pigeon became extinct or why there are no longer any basketball games with scores which total less than 50. But how does anything—anything at all (not any one thing)—become nonexistent? By becoming all past, of course, all in the past. Nothing can cease to exist in any way other than by becoming all past.

A snowstorm visits a small mountain town, causing great damage. It domi-nates the activity and concern of the town for many months afterward. I observe, "The snowstorm has finally ceased to exist." I mean, of course, the damage has all been repaired, and people have found other things to talk about. "The event has ceased to exist" amounts to something like "The effects are gone." The accident has ceased to exist when the scars are gone. This is of absolutely no help in understanding the philosopher's discourse on the past: in philosophical talk an event is gone when it has become past—without regard to its effects—and, I presume, it is never without effects.

One last suggestion. I may have been "misreading" the pictures. After all, the line, the fuse, represents time. The point or region actively sparking and smoking is the present. What is present becomes past. Perhaps what is present is not an event (the burning of the fuse) but simply the point or region which is burning, some span of time . . . the present. What becomes past then, is the present minute, hour, day, week, month, season, epoch. The all too short spring will soon become past . . . and this suggests the idiom, "This spring will join the past (like all the rest, and twenty will not come again)."

Spans of time "become past," "join the past" when they are over. How to un-derstand this talk? What do spans of time become when they are over? As the party goes on, the hours become longer. But not when they are over. The day becomes dark and gloomy, but not when it is over. When it is over it can become, like an event, of historical interest, of great importance, a symbol of human progress. "The hour joins . . . ," "The year joins . . . "; for these there seems no relevant use at all . . . just the philosophical pronouncement, "The present year joins the past at midnight December 31." And in this light, the philosophical jargon suddenly seems familiar and harmless. "A present span of time joins the past at its end" has become a generalized way of representing a host of language, clock, and calendar lessons. The end of the year is midnight December 31. Summer usually comes to an end sometime on September 21. The end of February is the 28th this year. (This is not a leap year, you know.)

A PARABLE THAT TELLS ABOUT WHERE WE ARE

"The past is gone" disturbed us before like a fox starting an uproar in the chicken yard. We went out to see, and he ran. We gave chase. After a little way, we could see it was not a fox we were chasing but our old grey dog—one who ran away from home many months ago. He had gone wild, we discovered. But now he is tired of the chase and of his lean, wild existence. He lies down; we catch up with him, and he is as friendly as ever. Is he ready to go home again?

VIII

THE THINGS WE REMEMBER

We have the idea that in memory we see with our mind's eye into the past. What is the philosophical problem we have with memory? We have philosophical problems about seeing, but our problem with memory is different. If we lay aside the difficulties over seeing, a problem with memory remains. When with the eye we see, let's grant that we do indeed see. We see what is before the eye: the trees, the housetops, the children skating, what is there and what is happening. Something keeps us from straightforwardly saying that we can remember seeing what was once before the eye and what once happened. The trees, the children skating are there; they exist to be seen. The things that once were are things that are no more. No. Of course they are not here: they are *there*. But where is *there*? The past, of course. We are inclined to say the past is gone, so there is no object for our memories. I do not want to get into this troublesome business more than is necessary right now.

Sometimes we are inclined to think that memories are peculiarly private affairs. No one else can have my memory, because my memory is an experience and only I can have my experiences. I do not want to go into this matter either. I assume that we can see that memories are not experiences. They are, usually and among other things, claims to know something of the past. The matter I want to deal with is the "object" of memory: what we claim to know when we remember.

Suppose I am reminiscing with George Garrett about a family picnic he and I attended many years ago. He remembers, and chuckles over, a funny card that Uncle Milton had pinned to his back. He is surprised that I do not remember. I did not see Uncle Milton's back. No good in my trying to remember. One can remember only what he saw or heard, smelled, touched, or tasted. I cannot remember something which happened in China. I have never been there. I cannot remember an event which took place before my birth. The idea of memory excludes anything which is not part of my experience. Although George and I remember the same picnic, his memory will be very different from mine. I was very young at the time. I did not know most of the people. I did not understand the games, the contests, the jokes. I remember it only as a strange and frightening affair. He fondly remembers a warm and entertaining day. Although we remember the same picnic, he cannot remember what I do, I cannot remember what he does. Memories are private, personal things. To remember, we must turn our attention within ourselves.

These are things I am easily led to say about memory. I am inclined to think of my life as an accumulation of experiences. It is built up in layers like the trunk of a tree. New experiences come and cover over the old. My past lies deep in the center. Remembering requires that I drill or bore in some way down into the layers of the past, which have been grown over. But this picture will not do. My past experiences are not literally preserved; they are gone. Another picture, too, enters my mind to complicate the puzzle. If not preserved, my experiences must be somehow recorded and stored. In memory, we must go through the files. Nothing can be found if it was not filed there. But what is it we go through? The stores, the files. They are records, not the originals. Records of experiences. How otherwise could the experience be preserved?

In memory, we must reach a past event, but we are twice removed from it. We have of the event only what we experienced, and the experience is past. We have a record of the past experience. We do not have the original. But we must remember the original; we must know the record is of the original. The things we see, the trees, the hills, the housetops remain. With the passage of time, we remember them, but what we remember is our sights of them: our experiences. And experiences are not things. They do not endure. Wood and brick may be stored, and the wood and brick may then be taken out of storage. Experiences cannot be stored, they may not be taken out again. They perish, leave only a record.

What has storage or keeping records to do with my philosophical uneasiness about memory? Let's invent a machine which is ideal at keeping and storing records. We shall assign a person to dictate to the machine and he will report everything he sees and hears, everything he reads; he will describe to the machine his feelings and thoughts. Now let's suppose it stores all this on miniature tapes and when the machine is addressed a question about the past, it immediately "locates" the relevant sections of the right tapes and plays them back. Does the machine remember the things it is asked about? No, this is certainly not a case of memory. Play a tape recording of your own voice, one you made many years ago, one on which you simply talk about the occurrences of the day. You may have forgotten making the tape. None of the occurrences come back to you. You do not doubt that you made the tape. The things described by you sound right: you do not question their truth. Yet you do not remember. There is much less reason for saying the recorder remembers or that our fabulous machine remembers.

Suppose we complicate the machine so that it sorts and mixes the tape stories together, and then when asked, it picks the highlights, selects and edits. It speaks the modified story in the past tense, and begins the sections of its recital with such phrases as "I was told ... " and "It was read to me ... " In the course of rearranging the stories and picking the significant things, some details become erased. Sometimes when asked a question the machine will reply, "I no longer have a record of that." Does the machine now remember (and sometimes forget)? I should suppose not. Add more features. In editing, the machine will sometimes get its stories mixed and make mistakes. We speak to the machine, saying that it is wrong. It clicks and "digests" that instruction; then the mistake is not made again. Sometimes we wonder whether it is right or wrong and ask. The machine then goes through the tapes and explains how the story was put together from the originals. Sometimes it pauses for a long time making a meditative clicking; then it announces, "Now I remember." Then it goes on to tell its story and explain how it was arrived at.

Now, does the machine remember? It certainly is getting closer; and we are getting closer to fabricating a human being. Suppose we do arrive at something so like human performance that we would not boggle at calling it memory. Having arrived at this, let's suppose that we tear the machine down and examine its construction. We find the insides have fused into a mass whose workings we cannot understand at all. Its performance now would be very remarkable indeed. But would our ignorance of its workings lead us to modify whatever we had decided about whether it could remember? I should suppose not, and so I suppose that an understanding of the nature or workings of storage and recording has nothing to do with our determination of what is or is not memory. An account of memory in terms of storage and records forces itself upon me because I am puzzled about memory. I do not wonder about the mechanical, electric, chemical changes which take place when we remember. I wonder how we *can* remember, how such a thing is possible.

And I wonder how we can remember, whether or not I pay any attention to the things which physiologists tell us. I was perfectly capable of determining whether or not I remember something before I learned anything about physiology. And if I and others were not capable of doing that, physiologists would have no reason to think that their discoveries had any connection with memory. First we must know what memory is, and then we must know something about the workings of the nervous system in order to determine whether there is any kind of connection between the two. Philosophical problems of memory arise in spite of the fact that, in this way, we know what memory is; and they arise whether we know anything about physiology or not.

Although the details of the storage machinery may have nothing to do with my puzzle, still I am impelled to think of remembering in some quasi-mechanical way. The idea of remembering seems to require some mysterious workings which operate between my past and my present. I could not remember the card on Uncle Milton's back at the picnic because I did not see it. Any information I have about the past which could not have been part of my experience could not, therefore, be remembered. If someone claims to remember seeing something which happened before his birth, or something many miles from where he was at the time, we should say he could not remember those things. Not because he could not know such things, but because he could not remember them. Perhaps it seems to him that he remembers them, but they would never be counted as memories. And that, I am inclined to think, is because such things cannot possibly register any effect upon the machinery involved in memory. I have the picture that memory operates like a time camera.[1] Regardless of what

---

[1] The special appropriateness of this analogy was suggested to me by a paper of Mr. P. T. Geach, read to the University of Oregon Philosophy Club, April 10, 1963. However, I am sure he would not approve of the way I here use it.

appears upon the film, it cannot be a picture of cousin Manfred, unless Manfred was before the lens. I cannot have a memory of something unless that something is part of my own past experience. I think that memory records the past as a camera records what is before the lens. What a photograph is, is understood in terms of the camera's workings. If the latent image on the film is not created by light focused by the lens, then what is developed-out on the film is not a photograph of what was before the lens. If the lens had been stopped, and the film had been chemically altered by someone, the outcome would not be a photograph of cousin Manfred, regardless of how much the resultant picture resembled Manfred just as he had posed before the camera.

And so it seems with memory. If I am told over and over of something that happened in my childhood, I may come to think that I remember it. When I learn finally that I was not there when it happened, I know I could not have remembered. I just thought I did. It may have seemed to me that I remembered; but I simply could not have. So I am inclined to think the machinery did not work right: that memory requires a certain sort of machinery like the production of a photograph. Light spans the distance between the object photographed, and the film at the back of the camera where the photograph is produced. Something must span the "distance" between my past and the present where memory is produced. But I do not know how that something works. Worse, I do not see how any such something could work.

Several things go wrong here. The camera is a human invention. Its workings were pretty well understood at the time of its invention. The camera was designed to produce photographs; hence what a photograph is has come to be understood in terms of the camera's workings. If I alter the mechanism of picture production sufficiently, the result—although it is an accurate and detailed representation—will no longer be called a photograph. Or if we call the result a "photograph" we shall put the word in quotes, or we shall feel that some qualification or explanation is needed. Suppose we use a television camera, and make a video-tape of a scene. Later we "play" the tape and expose a sensitized paper upon a television screen. The result is a black and white picture of the original scene. Is it a photograph? Did we make a photograph of the scene? If we called it a photograph, we should feel we needed to add an explanation.

Suppose a man suffers a massive destruction of his nervous system. Large portions of the brain are injured and must be removed surgically. The parts removed are those known normally to be connected with memory; and the man, as anticipated, loses his memory. Now suppose that some years later, without regeneration of any of the lost tissues, the man begins again to give spontaneous accounts of his childhood, his past experiences, and to talk of the past just as he did before the injury. His accounts are the same as those he gave before and they square with the memories of others who figure in his past. Shouldn't we simply say that he had regained, recovered his memory? The video camera-tape-electronic screen picture we might say, will serve all the purposes of a photograph. Surely we should not say the man's stories will serve all the purposes of memories. They are memories.

"Remembering is like taking a photograph of the past." A camera is needed with a long bellows reaching back in time; a lens focused upon the past. Something else is wrong. The lens is part of the instrument: it is focused and stopped by the photographer. It can be pointed wherever he chooses. There is nothing like this in memory. I cannot aim a memory-producing lens at random throughout the past. I cannot remember anything unless once I saw it, or heard it, or tasted it—unless once I perceived it (to use the philosopher's generic word). I cannot remember the card on Uncle Milton's back because I did not see it. Seeing a card is not like aiming and focusing a lens. If my head had been turned right, and my eyes held open, if I had been jarred to assure I was awake, and asked riddles to make sure I was alert, still I might not have seen the card. Seeing is not a matter of arranging all of the equipment just right. To produce a photograph it is enough for the camera to be on the scene, with the lens pointed in the right direction and all the controls properly set. The same is not true for seeing, or hearing, or smelling, or feeling, or tasting.

Another misleading feature of the analogy. A photograph is produced by the action of light and developing chemicals on silver salts or other light-sensitive substances. When they have done their work a photograph results. Remembering is not similarly produced. A memory is not something which is produced, inevitably, as the outcome of a series of processes. A rash on the skin may be produced; hives may develop from contact with peach fuzz. Memories are not like that. I can try to remember something important; I may succeed. When I do, I am told, "We were sure you could do it. You have a good memory." I remember where the key to the safe box was put. I am congratulated; no one else could remember. I am not congratulated for my work in getting an allergic reaction. "You have good hives" is not at all similar in point to "You have a good memory." Someone may say that my memory is improving, or getting better. Also he may say my allergy is improving or getting better. My memory is improving because it is getting more accurate, more complete. My allergy is improving because it is going away.

One may be praised for the accuracy or completeness of his memory: he is praised for having a good memory. The camera or the film is not praised for having a good photograph. Yes, but the photographer is praised for producing a good photograph. He is not praised for what happens in the camera or on the film. He is praised for his skillful use of camera and film; he is praised, if you like, for what he makes happen in the camera and on the film. He has mastered the camera as his instrument; he studied the camera, practiced with it, failed sometimes, experimented and succeeded. I have not mastered my nervous system in remembering; I have not practiced with it, experimented with its use. When I succeed in remembering something, I am not praised for my skillful use of my nervous system, or for what I make happen in it. I do not know what happens in it. What takes place in my brain and along my nerves is irrelevant in determining whether I have a good memory, or whether I remember anything at all. Remembering is something human beings (and by extension, animals) do, sometimes well, sometimes poorly. The words "remember," "recall," "forget," "memory" have grown up as part of it. All this development took place long before the discovery of the facts or the construction of theories in physiology. "Remember" could not *mean* "the physiological machinery has turned." Of course, we should sometimes say of an amnesia victim that his recovery of memory meant the machinery was turning—or something like that. A neuro-physiologist might say this in commenting on just such a case as I have imagined. A patient with much of his brain destroyed amazingly recovers his memory. The physiologist might say to a colleague, "This means some machinery has started. Some other part of the brain must have taken it all over. Let's try to find out." The physiologist does not use the word mean in the sense I had in mind, that is, in that peculiarly philosophical sense (or no-sense) as in " 'Remember does not *mean* 'the machinery turns.' "

Since the nervous mechanism is irrelevant, I feel inclined to say that when one says he remembers he is "giving an assurance that the event occurred, at the same time implying that one is in a position to know that it occurred."[2] When I give such assurance I should generally (not always) be expected to be able to justify what I had said. What could such justification be? Only, I suppose, corroboration by others, checking against journals, records. But that would at most show that what I said was true, not that I remembered it. I can be genuinely confused, thinking I remember something which I do not. I was told it, perhaps glowingly in great detail, so that I came to think I remembered that event I know so much about. Well, others would corroborate it; it would check against newspaper accounts. Still I do not remember. Something is missing. It is not enough to say memory consists in giving assurance about a past event, even when taken with the ability to support or justify the details. It must be the ability to justify what I claim to know directly, from my own past experience. In short, ability to support my claim to remember. I cannot get away from the idea that memory must take me directly to my own past experience.

Sometimes the problem is thought to arise out of the theory that images are essential to remembering. We picture memory as interposing images, its direct objects, between us and the past events remembered. And then we puzzle ourselves about how we could know these images to represent the past. How, if we are directly aware only of images, can we ever directly get to a past experience? This could not be a very deep source of our philosophical anxiety about memory: it is too easy to show that images are not essential to memory. After all, we do often recall something instantly: there is not enough time for the examination of images. If images come they come after the recollection, not before it: they come while we are thinking about little details, while we are trying to remember something that does not come easily. It is hard to see how images could be significant in the memory of sounds or tactual feels, and even more difficult to see how they could function in the memory of odors or tastes. "Image" is a visual word. I have an image or a picture of someone when I visualize him in my mind's eye. We speak of images as we speak of drawings. They are accurate, detailed, blurred. They are vivid or dim. They represent

2 A. J. Ayer, *Problems of Knowledge* (Baltimore, Penguin Books, 1956), p. 147.

faithfully or not faithfully. What would an image of an odor or taste be? How, for example, can you represent an odor? Would the representation be a weak odor? Then we could not represent a strong odor. If images are necessary to memory, then we could not remember a strong odor. But strong odors are often the most memorable: "I remember that smell, that sickening smell—the day the skunk wandered into the cabin." Even a weak odor will not do as an image of a weak odor. It is not a representation of a weak odor; it *is* a weak odor. A visual image may be *of* Uncle Charlie; the image is not Uncle Charlie himself, only in a weakened state (a shadow of his former self).

Most important: even if memory did have images as its immediate object, considering or inspecting an image is not memory. The most important part is left out, namely, "interpreting" the image, knowing it represents something from the past, and from my past. Even more than that is required. Suppose you are shown a picture and are told it is a photograph of a little boy you played with every day when you were four years old. You may *know* it is; it is clearly marked on the back, and you are in the picture too. You can easily recognize yourself. Still you do not remember. Now, you may carry an image of that little boy around in your mind for days, knowing that he was a childhood friend of yours—and still not remember. Then suddenly you remember, and that is something quite different from having an image and knowing it represents a past experience.

What was left out when I had the clear image of the boy, knowing it was an image representing things in my own childhood? The important thing, I want to say, is that we remember *our experiences,* visual, olfactory, or what. The problem arises because I do not see how I can have a past experience as a direct object. I cannot reach out and contact a past experience because a past experience is no more here. The best we have are whatever records the past experiences have left. But I know nothing of such records: I need to know nothing of such records. And even if I had them they would not do. I should need to know directly that the records were records of just this or that past experience. There is no getting around it. I must go directly to my past experiences. Only I had those experiences, and those experiences have occurred in sequence, the present always displacing what was once present into the past. To remember I must get hold of a displaced experience, one now past.

It is as if we saw in a mirror—a mirror which is standing in the past. We look back into a long black corridor of time and into a mirror which reflects what once was. We cannot look out into the past world except by looking back through that mirror, a kind of biographical periscope. As if I could not remember my grandfather's barn, unless I remembered how it looked on some certain day, or unless I could remember myself seeing it. "Do you remember your grandfather's old barn?" (1) "Of course I do. I played there every day for years." If need be, I could tell you the details: where the rickety stairway was, the unused stalls, where the old broken piano was stored. (2) I also remember how the barn looked from the little hill to the south. (3) And I remember one day seeing the barn from my window, when in a storm it appeared chalky white from a flash of lightning. These are not the same kinds of memory. Does the first have to be understood in terms of the second, and that in terms of the third? How else could it be? How else could I remember where the stairway was unless I had looked at it from here and there, and walked on it up and down. But I do not remember any special sight of it, or any one time when I walked up or down the stairs.

I could dissipate the puzzling picture of memory if I did not have to think of it as an inward attention directed on past particulars, if I could always think of remembering as something I could do like walking, as "having learned and not forgotten." Remembering how to do something, for example, to calculate square roots, would then be the basic form of remembering. When I say then that I remember my father giving me a dog on my sixth birthday, it would merely be a case of having learned this fact and of having not forgotten it. I should simply be in a position to correctly answer questions about that time and that gift because I had learned. I remember *how* to answer. If this explanation would do, I should not have to worry about getting to a past experience. In order to remember, I should need only to demonstrate that I had some acquired ability.[3]

[3] Ayer tells us that philosophers have not realized how many memories are "habit-memories." "It covers not only the instances of knowing how to do things ... but also a great many instances in which the knowledge displayed is classified as knowledge of fact. Suppose that I am set to answer a literary questionnaire, and that I have to rely on my memory. I shall, perhaps, succeed in remembering that such and such a poem continues in such and such a way, that So-and-so was the author of such and such a book, that a given incident appears

Can I interpret my memory of the barn along these lines? Maybe from the many sights and climbs that I have now forgotten I learned how to get around in the barn: my memory consists in an acquired knowledge of *how* to get around. Let us try to construct a clear case of remembering how, where remembering consists in demonstrating an ability, where we can see that recalling in any other sense plays no part. When I start out for dinner at Salem's I may remember how to get there, even though I have been there only once before. I need no map. "I remember you go down Maple to the second stoplight, turn left ... " No. Here I may recall the former trip, the lines I drew on a map, the instructions I was given. Each of these will require separate treatment: I want a clear-cut case. But I need not remember any of those things. I could just start out, and as I approached each turning place, I should recall: "You turn here ... " Still I might be remembering parts of the former trip. After I had made the trip to Salem's many, many times I could drive there without thinking. And if by someone who did not know I went there regularly I was asked, "Do you remember?" I should say, "Of course." With a little thought I could tell him the route. Perhaps I could no longer recall any of the details of any one trip, or any of the instructions I was first given or who gave them to me. Better yet: eliminate the complication of being able to tell someone how to get there. I could not tell him but I could take him. "I remember how to get there but I can't tell you" seems quite all right, if the only question is one of getting there. ("I know how to get there ... ," "I can take you there ... ")

Reconsider the question, "Do you remember your grandfather's barn?" Is it just because the barn is not big enough or complicated enough that this

in this novel rather than in that. But none of this need involve my having any recollection of a past event." A. J. Ayer, *Problems of Knowledge,* pp. 136-137.

Ayer cites as paradigm examples of "habit-memory," "remembering how to write, remembering how to set a compass, or add up a column of figures ... " *Ibid.,* p. 135.

Note also Ryle's account: " ... Telling and drawing things are, at best, ways of conveying lessons already learned. So is recalling a conning of something already learned. It is going over something, not getting to something ... " G. Ryle, *The Concept of Mind,* (New York, Barnes and Noble, 1949), pp. 274-275.

" ... Reminiscing, then, can take the form of faithful verbal narration ... It belongs not to the stage of manufacture and assembly, but to the stage of export. It is akin not to learning lessons, but to reciting them." *Ibid.,* p. 276.

cannot be a similar question? But that question was asked by someone who merely wanted to talk of old times. He did not want a guided tour. (There are no guided tours of the past.) When in reminiscing, I reply that I remember my grandfather's barn, there is no question of my getting around in it. If I do remember it, presumably I could get around, and if I were taken there and could not find the stall or the stairway or the tool closet (I have been assured nothing has changed), then I would realize that I remembered little, that my memories were quite vague. If I tried hard to remember such matters, I might pose myself problems: standing here by the door, now where was the stair? Or I might try to picture a floor plan. At any rate, in order to satisfy my questioner (and myself) that I remembered the barn I have to be able to tell about the barn and to answer questions. The trouble is that I could answer all sorts of questions because someone had told me the answers. Someone might have shown me photographs and told me all about what I used to do, what games I used to play and where. In answering questions I might be faithfully repeating what I was told, but this would not be remembering the old barn of my childhood. "I remember the barn," I say, and not just because I could get around, or because I can answer questions. I could get around and I can answer questions because I remember it.

If now I am to think of this as a case of having learned and not forgotten, it is important that my learning came from the original sights and sounds, the lay of things the way they once were—at the right time. What time? The time I remember. Before I get a memory of this kind out of having learned and not forgotten, I must remember when I learned. What would that be? Having learned when I learned and not forgotten? There is still the question of whether I can remember having learned when I learned. Surely that cannot be having learned having learned having learned? I have to break out of this to some time, sight, incident, episode. Also, as soon as I think of other kinds of examples, I cannot apply the formula "having learned and not forgotten." "I remember the great pain on the way to the hospital from my accident." Did I learn of the pain? "I remember the vivid dream I had the night before the voyage." When did I learn of the dream? During sleep? Even, "I remember seeing the barn in a storm." When did I learn of seeing?

I now suspect that I was hasty in dealing with the example of knowing the way to Salem's (but not being able to tell). I let it pass as a case of memory where nothing was involved except being able to do something I had learned. I wonder now whether there wasn't something more hidden in that example. I wonder whether any case of memory can involve no more than that. Another case.[4] Many years ago, with effort and practice, I learned how to swim. When could anyone sensibly ask me if I remember how to swim? Only, I suppose, if I had never really mastered it, not really learned—there being a question about whether I remembered how to move my arms, kick at the hips. What if I had, after my lessons, gone on to become an expert swimmer. For many years I have not swum, but I have no question about my ability to do so. Do I remember how to swim? I can swim if I am called upon. What would it be to forget? I try and can no longer swim. What has happened? Perhaps a nervous disease has affected my coordination in ways I could not have guessed. I can no longer swim; but this is not a case of having forgotten how.

I jump in the water—and what? I cannot move my legs right? I think I am doing everything the same as before, but I sink? When *should* I have forgotten how to swim? There is no possibility here to forget how to swim. Why is this? Isn't it connected with the fact that there is nothing I could do to remember? What could I do that would be remembering how to swim? My difficulty would not be overcome if only I could recall the chart in the textbook, the one that shows the head-position for correct breathing. Losing almost entirely the set of abilities or powers (or what) involved in swimming is not a case of forgetting how to swim. Nor is having them and being sure you have them a case of remembering or of claiming to remember. Of course, we do say that someone has forgotten how to swim but not in the sort of case I have been thinking of. An expert takes a couple of lengths one morning and his style is off. I may say to him, "Austin, you have forgotten how to swim," and he may agree, "Yes, I seem to have forgotten. I need some work."

Now return to the example of knowing the way to Salem's. Against the background of the swimming case, it looks different. I tried to imagine one who,

---

[4] "In a great many cases where one is said to remember something there is no question of one's even seeming to recall any past occurrence. The remembering consists simply in one's having the power to reproduce a certain performance. Thus remembering how to swim, or how to write . . . is in every case a matter of being able to do these things, more or less efficiently, when the need arises." A. J. Ayer, *Problems of Knowledge*, p. 135.

because he had gone so often, could get there unthinkingly. In order to eliminate any features of remembering other than having learned and not forgotten, I tried to imagine that he could no longer sketch a map or give anyone instructions. I eliminated these because I was afraid they would introduce memories of who had shown him, how he had drawn the map, or recollections of former trips, mistakes he had once made. This is a very unlikely, unnatural thing I am trying to think. Try to imagine that this person starts out and does not arrive at Salem's. He tries again and again and fails. What will he say? It is such an untoward thing, I do not know. It might appear nightmarish to him—suddenly to be cut off from his destination, no longer to be able to get to where he had so often gone. He might think he was suffering some mental disorder. He might even think some massive change had been made in the neighborhood: bulldozers had demolished houses, streets had been changed. I am inclined to think he would not say, never say, he had forgotten the way. And part of my inclination to think this is because I am now viewing this case against that of not being able to swim.

Before I was thinking of it against the case of remembering the old barn. It is such an unnatural thing, that I can now see why I made a mistake. One would never be in the position of remembering how to get somewhere, and not able to think of maps, landmarks, former misturns. In a normal case, one might say he had forgotten precisely because he would be trying to recall which filling station or telegraph pole marked a certain turn, and be convinced that if he could recall that, he could set himself right. I think I was unable to keep these factors out. I think they sneaked in and led me to say confidently that my man remembered the way. Now I am inclined to think that he could not forget, and also he could not remember. He could not remember because no one could have a question about his forgetting, except ones I tried to exclude from the example. Such as, did he recall the stop light had been moved, or did he remember there was a new filling station at the corner where you turn right? I eliminated one by one the things he might recall in remembering the way, the order of the turns, a former trip, the lines on a map. And I moved step by step into a familiar mistake. The drift of it can be summarized: if he can remember without recalling any one, he can remember without recalling anything at all.

The formula "having learned and not forgotten" can cause great confusion.

Many things that are learned cannot be forgotten—and so cannot be remembered. When such things are remembered, it is because one can think of lessons, charts, advice, other tries, mistakes, which are helpful in overcoming the performance failure. The main thing is this: my memory of the barn cannot be thought of as just the ability to do or say something I learned. So I am right back on the idea that memory must be of my past experiences. How could it be otherwise? What I now know of that old barn had to be learned from my past experiences of it. But I do not need to remember them, not any of them. I could forget the barn, forget how to get around in it, as I could forget how to get to the library. And I could recall it again and remember how to get around in it. My philosophical picture seems to have a basis in this point: my memory of the barn is related to the events (which I may or may not be able to recall) in a way entirely different from that in which my swimming powers are related to my lessons.

When I swim I need not think of the past at all. When I say "I can swim," I am not professing to remember anything. Being able to swim is not remembering how to swim; it is not remembering at all. In many cases where I do have a memory of something, I make no claim to lay hold on the past. ("Do you remember Abel's telephone number?" "Yes. It's 345-5306.") But that is precisely what I do claim in remembering grandfather's barn: I think of how it once was. Yet I may not recall—may not even be able to recall—one special incident, one time when something happened. I am in a position to tell things, truly, about the past, but what is more important, tell them from my own memory. I am confident that these things are true because I saw them: that and that alone is the source of my present knowledge.

The philosophical picture I have of memory leads me to say that these things I think or tell *must* be an amalgam or a concretion of all the many times and incidents. How otherwise could I know the way it was—and perhaps is no longer? If I go visit that old barn today chances are it will be much smaller than I remember it as being. When I played in it I was a child, and by my standards then, the barn was very large. So my memory was of the way I saw it then, even though I do not recall any certain view of it. Surely I would be more confident, my memory would be more perfect or more complete, if I could recall the times when I saw, and walked, and learned all the things I can remember about the way it was. Why do I think my memory "must" be a compression, an amalgam of many past incidents? What do I mean by this? Certainly I do not remember more than I do. Do I think that if I could see into my memory, break off the top layer, then all these past details would be there? Of what use is this metaphor? I remember the barn, how it was: here there was only dirt, there an old board floor with many cracks. What is the memory? Why do I ask such a question? Well, certainly it is not like a piñata with a papier-mâché shell—and inside hidden all sorts of little toys and candies.

Still, it must be something like that. Why? Because I could not know something by memory that I did not experience. And I must be able to pin what I know to the time of that experience. If we visit the old farm we can see the barn again. Yes, but not as it used to be. That I must remember. I have no access through my eyes into the past. In memory I have access only to the inside world—past experiences. If "I see the mountain" does not report my experience, then surely neither does "I saw the mountain." The past tense is associated with memory, but its use does not immediately drag in memory. "I remember that I saw the mountain" is another step. What introduces it? Some reason for doubt, some room for forgetting, surprise at a feeling of familiarity. Perhaps I am thinking of cases involving a considerable time, cases where a pause and some effort is involved in remembering. These are the cases which abet my picture of memory. When I am trying to remember something, my eyes and ears are closed: it may even be helpful not to be distracted by the sights and sounds of the things around. I am digging into the past, and in that business attention is turned within. I am looking into myself, not out upon the world.

I think that memory must give me knowledge of the past: what I know *now* of the past I must get by memory. Originally I got it from experience, of course. And that is why my remembering now must go through a past experience. I have no way of getting at the past except within myself. Within myself I must go back and fasten my memory to its source, some time, some experience. Sometimes when I stare out the window I think of how it was in spring, in April especially. After the first warm days and the wet rains, the evenings would be cool, but still warm enough to feel soft—soft and humid. How the robins sang then from the budding maple trees! Suppose I am reminiscing with an old friend I have not seen for years and he is incredulous. "Of course I remember how it was." "No," he says, "it was clammy and cold . . . " "That's not the way I remember it." "The way I remember it"? What is that doing here? Are there different ways to remember it? What is the "it" remembered? I am remembering how it felt to me, and he is remembering how it felt to him. So our memories *are* directed to experiences. And we are both remembering the springs of old. And what knowledge do we have? We can take a saving turn. "Are you sure that is the way you felt about it? I don't see how anyone could have disliked the April evenings." "Oh yes, I remember clearly just how I felt." "I know how I felt" sounds in place here, all right. So in remembering, one can know how he once felt about something. This is the kind of example I have been looking for. Here memory gives knowledge about my own feelings (past, of course). This case represents the way it *has* to be.

What about cases, though, where I do not remember how something felt or how it looked to me? "Dale Price died shortly after the February meeting of the committee. It is very important that we know what he said at that meeting. Do you remember?" "I remember exactly what he said." Wouldn't it be surprising if I, as the reporter of what was said, could not add, "I was listening carefully because his voice was weak. I felt there was something wrong"? An investigator is questioning me, "Did you ever see Irwin Kelsey coming home from work?" "Yes. Almost every day. I used to sit by the window around that time." "Do you remember his carrying anything?" Yes, I remember clearly. He always carried a green cloth bag over his shoulder. "Now I might not remember any one time when he came home, or any one thing I thought about the bag over his shoulder. But what I remember must have been taken from many incidents, "abstracted" from them. It is what they had in common. I may never before have thought about what he carried or whether he carried anything. If pressed with questions, I may remember other things. "He always had the bag over his right shoulder, and he had a tight—never a relaxed—hold on the draw string. I never thought particularly about it before. But now that you bring it up, I can remember that grip of his very clearly." Again I may recall no particular day, no particular feelings of mine about the matter. But I had to have seen him. I had to have seen him this time, and this, and that. At no one time did I see what he "generally" or "always" did. I want to say that the separate incidents are somehow "there": they must be available. I *could* remember them. (The details must be stored. But I have dispatched the storage question. If not stored, if that has nothing to do with the question, then at least I must be capable of remembering some one incident by which I can pin my memory to the past, locate it in my life story. Otherwise how could I remember what he did? I was not told. I didn't get it from seeing films. Some details must somehow be available.) Why do I say they *must* be? If there are such details, I do not know "where" they are or how to find them. Still, I want to insist that knowledge of the past has to reduce to memory of particular experiences. Without that, memory has no roots in the past.

I am stuck to the idea that in remembering I must look through the corridor of my past, that I must see there the places I went, the people I met, as in a mirror. Remembered things I see reflected in the mirror of my own experience. My experience is the direct object of memory. If I must see things in the mirror, then by refocusing my eyes, I ought to be able to see the mirror itself; I ought to be able to see its frame. If it is experiences that I remember, and through experiences only that I remember what I do of the world around, then I ought to be able to remember an experience even though I was mistaken about what it revealed of the world. "Do you remember any experiences you had when twelve?" "There is one I could not forget. I had the experience of standing out one night and seeing lightning come from nowhere and strike our apple tree with a blinding flash." "Did you ever wonder afterward why it didn't damage the tree?" "Yes, I always thought that was strange." "Well, we have never told you, but we arranged that for a joke. No lightning struck the tree. We wired and popped off a dozen flash bulbs up there on the tree trunk." Now what experience did I rememember? What do I say? "I remember the experience of thinking lightning struck the tree?" No. At any rate I do not want to say anything which would imply that I remembered seeing a flash and thought it might be lightning striking the tree. "I remember the experience I thought was seeing lightning strike the tree." I am pushing myself to answer an unnatural question. If some time lapsed after I had learned the truth, and another occasion arose to recall, then I should surely say, "I remember the experience I thought was seeing lightning strike the tree."

But also shouldn't I say, "I remember seeing the tree struck by lightning—but I was wrong," or "... my memory is wrong." I look in the desk drawer for my ball pen: it isn't there. "I remember putting it there." I find I did not put it there. I left it at the office. "I remember putting it there—but I guess I didn't." "Remember" here has acquired something of an accent. I could say, "I seem to remember putting it there in the drawer." Here "remember" has come to be much the same as "seem to remember"; it is not used to lay hold of any truth about the past. But I do not want to say, "I seem to remember seeing the tree struck by lightning." Isn't that because I have frequently had the experience of seeming to remember putting my pen, my glasses, my book someplace, then finding them elsewhere. I understand this kind of mistake; I am adjusted to it. I am prepared to give up my claim to remember this sort of thing, because I have come to understand how I could be mistaken. I have come to understand by having lived through such mistakes, and I am prepared for their occurrence.

I am asked to comment on someone I knew *very* well, but I have not seen him for a long, long time. "I remember he has a high voice." Then I am shown he has not, never did have. "I remember him having a high voice," "I remember him as having a high voice." I withdraw as little as possible from the original claim. "In my picture—in my thoughts he has a high voice."[5] I am trying to explain to myself how I could be so wrong. I don't want to say "I seem to remember him having a high voice," that is, I don't want to say that right away. "I remember" now seems to express incredulity. I acknowledge the error, but I do not understand how I could be wrong about this. Suppose instead that I did not know the man well, suppose I had seen him briefly and only once, and later I say, "I remember he has a high voice." What now if I were shown wrong? In this case, I suppose I should say, "I seem to remember his having a high voice." I quickly admit that I do not have the best of rights to my claim. On the other hand, "I remember him having a high voice" is the acknowledgement of the mistake, but not renunciation of the claim-right.

If these observations are correct then when I learn that my bolt of nearby

---

[5] One of the things which makes it difficult to acknowledge error is the vivid imagery which often comes in. "How *could* I be wrong. I remember it so clearly, so distinctly," and we have in our mind's eye a detailed picture of how it was. This may have something to do with our first philosophical thoughts: that imagery is essential to memory.

lightning was a clever imitation, I will not say "I seem to remember." I had a right to be wrong. "I remember so clearly seeing the tree struck by lightning —my memory must be wrong; but how could it be?" Flash bulbs! So unlike lightning. It is difficult to understand the state I must have been in to take that for lightning. I swear I heard a crack; what was that? I cannot really understand the mistake, but I must accept it. I am not interested in this use of "remember," where it carries an accent, expresses incredulity, and acknowledges error. It is not used here to claim any hold on the past. After the error is acknowledged, my philosophical picture makes me say: still I remember something, something of what happened, an experience, "the experience I took for seeing lightning strike the tree."

What has happened to the *experience* I remember? What experience is it? I couldn't have had the experience of seeing lightning, because there was none. I did not have the experience of thinking I saw lightning. I had the experience I thought was that of seeing lightning: now I know it was not. I took the experience as telling me something which it did not. The experience itself must be one which is neither of seeing nor of thinking I was seeing, because at that time I could not have known which, and I only just now learned. I thought I remembered the experience of seeing, but I could not remember that because I did not have that experience. The experience was one of not seeing, but I do not remember that: I just learned that. What to say? "I had an experience and, in addition, I took it I was seeing lightning." What experience? "I was scared half to death. My heart pounded and I ran." That was part of the same experience, but not the part I first reported, not the part that got me out of my experience to the tree and the light. What part was that? "That was the visual part of the experience." What? "A visual experience—one I took to be that of seeing lightning." "Do you remember that visual experience?" I think the answer is "No." I don't even know what a visual experience is here, which is not either that of seeing lightning or thinking I see lightning, but is neutral and could be either. So how could I remember it?

Change the example. I say, "I remember seeing a blinding light." Suppose now the jokers tell me they had put an hallucinogenic drug in my birthday cake, and afterward, had watched me walk into the yard, then cringe and run. They had been afraid to ask me what I "saw." After I learn the truth, what do

I remember? Not the experience of seeing a blinding light. The experience I thought was that of seeing a blinding light? What experience was that? Can I try hard to remember *it*? The experience I thought I remembered I did not have. Hence the experience I remember can be changed by what I learn years later. Yes, but I did not really remember the experience of seeing. What has been effected years later is that I am led to redescribe the relation of an experience to its object. I ought to be free to concentrate on and remember the experience without regard to my "interpretation" of it. But I cannot concentrate on or remember any such experience! I can only remember, sometime after I learn the truth, that it was the experience I thought was seeing a blinding light.

How did the word "experience" get in here? Isn't it only because it was such a memorable thing? And perhaps because it brought fear and sweat and a pounding heart. "I remember that on my twelfth birthday I stood at the top of the stair and saw my aunt eating breakfast just as she always did. What a strangely insignificant thing to remember." Surely, here it would be out of place and wrong to say, "I remember the experience of seeing my aunt eat breakfast." That is, it is wrong to say that, unless I had been aware at the time that it was odd that I should be intently watching that ordinary thing. Then that would have been extraordinary—perhaps an "experience"—of strangely standing and watching, enchanted by an everyday thing. Not all the things I remember seeing are experiences.

Perhaps I had better say I remember my past perceptions.[6] Of course I did not "perceive that the tree was struck by lightning." That is something Sherlock Holmes might do. He might examine the bark carefully, and note the unsymmetrical shape ("It could not have been caused by wind or snow") and then say he perceives this tree has been struck by lightning. No. I mean by

---

[6] "I think we have always to admit that, unless the error affecting a memory statement is the result of the memory process itself, that is, has appeared during the process of retention of the original perception, every memory statement is correct in so far as it concerns what has once been perceived. If we learn or discover that a previous perception of ours which we now recollect was mistaken, there is no change in what we remember of the original scene after the discovery as compared with our recollection of it before the discovery. The only change affecting our recollection is that, as a result of the discovery, we have now become aware of the fact that our memory has all along been concerned with our past perception of the scene in question, rather than with the scene itself." W. Von Leyden, *Remembering, A Philosophical Problem,* (London, Gerald Duckworth & Co., Ltd., 1961), p. 62.

"perception" such things as seeing or hearing or smelling or a combination of these. I thought I saw the flash of light, heard the electric crack, smelled the smoke. All this was involved in the experience. Is it the perception I remember? Take "seeing." "I remember seeing the tree hit by lightning." I learn it was not. What then do I remember: what "perception"? "I remember what I took for seeing the tree struck." And what was that? Was that a perception? I remember seeing something, a great flash. Now suppose that had been caused by a drug, and I just now learn of it. "It was just as if I had seen a blinding flash, like lightning; in fact I took it to be a blinding flash." Was that a perception? It is tempting to say "illusory perception" as if illusory were a type of perception in the way elm is a type of tree. The "type" of perception involved was seeing, and it was a case of as-if seeing, or, if you like, not-seeing. That is a type of perception more similar to the way decoy is a type of duck— if you like, not a type of duck at all.

What do I remember? Well, that would be an "experience," the experience brought on by the drug, an hallucination—as if I were seeing a flash of light. Do you remember *seeing* something? What am I to say? I have all the details before me and nothing I say will change things. If I am telling someone who knows the details I will say, "I remember seeing a flash of light—but my memory is wrong," or "I thought I remembered seeing a light." "I now know that what I remember was an hallucinatory experience—as if there were a burst of light before my eyes." Once the details are known, these sentences no longer support any theoretical load. There is no longer any point in hesitating over fine differences in suggestion—differences we do not quite know how to make. We want the details known. What, in the details, has happened to the perception I thought I remembered? It is gone; it did not exist.

Consider a case of "veridical seeing." Suppose I do remember seeing Irwin Kelsey coming home on one particular day. I remember it was the day of the big storm and I was surprised that he was walking so slowly, nonchalantly. I remember quite clearly his carrying the watersoaked bag over his shoulder. "You remember *seeing* that?" "Of course." I remember that I saw it. "I remember that I saw it," that is, I remember that I noticed it. And I am supposing now that I *did* see it: surely then I must be remembering a perception. What am I supposed to find when I look within and recall that "seeing"? How is the seeing something within? I picture it as if I had been looking out of my eyes, as if I were looking through them upon the scene I remember. And in addition to what I saw, I am inclined to think I ought to remember my eyes framing the scene, and also some effort I put forth—focusing my eyes, perhaps as I might have focused a telescope. What a strange picture to intrude itself here. If I remember anything of this kind I ought to be able to say what I remember. I remember that I noticed Irwin Kelsey's bag. "Do you remember what you did within, or what happened within—in noticing the bag?" Ridiculous. But memory requires my awareness upon the scene remembered. What does this amount to except that I remember *noticing* the bag: I was "aware" that he had the bag over his shoulder. I remember that I was aware . . . ; then I must remember my awareness.

That is a tempting jump. "I remember I noticed . . . I remember I was aware . . . I remember my awareness . . ." I am thinking that my noticing, or my awareness, is a separate thing which I might recall. How easy it is to lose sight of the determining details. I cannot get from "notice" to "awareness" without changing the example. If my questioner knew that Irwin Kelsey was carrying stolen goods in the bag he might well ask whether I was aware of that. I might say, "I was aware all the time that Kelsey was a thief," or "Yes, I was aware of what he had in the bag." But I did not "notice" these things: I noticed he was carrying his old bag in the rain. Well, I might remember that I was aware he was carrying stolen goods. Then I do remember my awareness. "I remember my awareness that he was carrying stolen goods." Is this the way it goes? Are these parallels? I bumped my knee on my way to the office. "I remember my having to limp up the stairway." So, I remember my limping. "I remember my dreaming of a tiny kangaroo, no larger than a mouse." Then I remember my dreaming. (I couldn't remember my dreaming: I was not conscious while I was dreaming of dreaming.) "I remember finding the gallinule in the swamp." Then you remember your finding. What am I to think of as finding—except finding the gallinule. What am I to think of as my awareness—other than my awareness that he had stolen goods? Anyway, such awareness was not something that happened as he was walking along the street, so it could not be something that I remember happening at that time. I could have "become aware . . ." at that time, at the time I saw him walking along the street.

That needs other details: still another example. "I suddenly became aware of the fact that he was taller than before. He must have been wearing very high heels." "I remember my suddenly becoming aware of this." This is like suddenly noticing. Then I must remember noticing; but this is like remembering finding. What of remembering how the April evenings felt, remembering how I felt about the springs? Even this has misled me. I almost thought the spring evenings were remembered *in* the feeling—as if the feeling came first and I somehow pressed the old springtimes out of it. In fact the memory works the other way around. I think of a long-ago scene, I think of walking out into the evening. Then a feeling comes, a feeling of nostalgia, but that, of course, is not the feeling I had then. I remember that feeling, that very particular feeling I used to have in the spring evenings. And in remembering it I have something of that feeling—but not the same, of course. I could not have that feeling without thinking of the trees, the warm evening, the robins' song. And in all of this I am a little hard put for words. If I am talking to someone, I have greater difficulty in fastening upon the feeling than, say, if I am writing or just thinking. My attention cannot be drawn too much without, but I seem to have a wrong philosophical interpretation of this "turning within" in memory. I cannot find a case where I can turn within and discover a past "experience"— or perception or awareness as I had pictured it.

These seeings, experiencings, awarenesses, which I have tried to pack into the things remembered do not seem to be there. I thought of them as the materials, the direct objects, of my memory—and in them, or through them I should come upon the rest, the people, the streets, the doings. Part of the difficulty was that I pictured remembering as twice removed from its final object: my memory, a past experience, what that experience was about. The middle term, the experience, does not seem to be there.

Even if I can be rid of the idea that memory is of past experiences, perceptions, noticings, awarenesses, and with it the idea that in remembering I must shuffle through some inner medium, the picture which disturbs is far from dispelled. What have I done but shorten the route from the remembering to the remembered. That which is remembered is still past and gone. What route, however short, could lead to the past? I have the idea that I send out a tentacle to grasp the thing remembered; the trouble is I cannot send a grasping organ backwards in time. "I'm trying to remember—I think I remember—Yes, now I remember." This may be what has puzzled me all along. I put forth effort to get hold of something—I do not know what now, not an experience, not a perception—but something that has to be reached. "I'm reaching—I think I have it—Yes, I've got hold of it." If these are the analogies which steer my thinking, then remembering is not reaching, but having the thing in hand. Part of the difficulty is that I think of memory reaching the past; and at the same time I think it is impossible to reach or hold the past. And why do I think it is impossible to reach the past? Not that it is too slippery, not that it wiggles out between the fingers. Neither is it completely out of proportion to my size and length of reach. The remembered is not like a fish or a small snake. As I picture it, trying to remember is not even hopeless as reaching for the moon is hopeless. I am not going to allow anything to be a case of reaching the past. I think of trying to remember as something in the present and it is never going to succeed in reaching the past. One cannot break out of the present. In the way I have in mind, holding the past would be like holding something it makes no sense to speak of holding, like holding in my clenched hand a symphony, not the score, not the orchestra, nothing of that kind—but the whole of the music, all the sounds. If it is impossible in that way (if only it were a joke or a dream) what can we say for "*trying* to get a symphony closed in the fist." What should we expect of someone who was trying? Does he think the sounds are made by small flying insects: if only he could get a handful—what a sound that would make in his hand! If he is not mad, he must not understand what a symphony is: also he may not understand what "grasping in the hand" means.

I have seen apparently that I did not know what the "objects" of memory are: I thought of them as "experiences" or perceptions or noticings. But, of course, I *do* know what they are: they are the things I remember. Everyone knows what he remembers. And these are very different sorts of "things." I remember telephone numbers, names, people's faces, dreams, the smell of honeysuckle in Southern summer nights, the sound of an old Army bugle I had when I was about fourteen, my pain on the way to the hospital. I can remember lying in order to hurt someone; I can remember my motives. These things are not all experiences, or perceptions. But when I think of all such things as "objects" of memory, I immediately think of them as somehow of the same kind. The type of memory which is the most worrisome is so-called event memory. Within this type the "things" remembered are various: the taste of roasted corn at a family picnic, what my teacher said to me once in the first grade, what my son did on Christmas when he was four. The idea that there must be some sort of thing, the "object" of memory, is plain silly.

I have been thinking that I remember "the past," and of course I do not. I remember my grandfather's barn, what Irwin Kelsey carried over his shoulder. I remember suddenly becoming aware that he was taller. I remember an hallucinatory experience. I remember seeing my aunt having breakfast. Are all of these memories of the past? Mostly, "No," I suppose. When is it correct to talk about remembering the past? "I read a book in which a man remembered everything that was going to happen in the next century." "You must have misread. He couldn't remember that. One can only *remember* the past." We would demand some kind of explanation. Perhaps it was a long poem or an existentialist novel. "One can only remember the past" is said to establish a basis in plain literal common sense, to indicate how radical the confusion is, how much an interpretation is needed. It points out a linguistic landmark. Or suppose a biologist were to discover a tropical island which had remained much as it was two million years ago. The flora and fauna are those in the geology textbook. He might say, "I see and hear and smell the past all around me. I remember the future, what will not come for millions of years. People who have never had this experience can only remember the past." But these examples are of no philosophical help.

"I know it is 4:05." "Then you know the time." Each case of knowing what time it is is a case of knowing the time, but each case of remembering something is not a case of remembering the past. Or, if it is to be called a case of remembering the past it must be like knowing the time, that is, it is a way of saying that you remember what you remember without saying what it is that you remember. But we do not take it that way. There would be no philosophical sting to that. The difficulty with saying I remember the past is that I thought of it in terms of another analogy. "I know what the living room furniture is like." "Then you know what something in the house is like." As if what I remembered were something in the past, as if the past were a container and what

I remember is in it. If I wanted another look at the furniture, or if I wanted to know more about the living room or about the rest of the house, I should have to take a trip there, or send someone there to find out for me.

Remembering is like sending out a mental emissary. There is no one to go but myself. The subject-object picture tortures me. I must get the object; it is I who remember. It is I who have the memory. As if there were someone who had to do the remembering. An old man is hired to chop wood on a cold winter day, and he sits for a long time near the fireplace telling stories about his childhood. I say to him, "I want some wood split before dark. You split the wood, and I'll do the remembering." But this "remembering" means sitting around thinking about old times. It is as if there were some special question possible about who remembers. The teacher asks her fourth grade class, "Who remembers the name of the shortest tributary of the Missouri?" No answer. She says to Johnny, "You remember. Don't be so bashful." No answer. I put up my hand, "I do. I remember." I had no question about who remembered. That was the teacher's question, and she had the question because her remembering didn't count.

I go into the forest and find a mossy rock. The rock will remain; I can return and look at it again. There is no returning to the past. Everything in it gets farther away. I am thinking of the object going back, escaping, in the past. "The things I want to get are in the past." That is, "My acquisitive instincts are satisfied," or "I've achieved every goal: there is no more excitement of pursuit." That expression is not used to bemoan the impossibility of memory. "The things I am trying to remember are lost in the past." Someone old, perhaps, whose memory has failed sadly admits to the loss of his powers. It is not a philosophical complaint that nothing, nothing at all, can be remembered. I think of objects of my memory as fleeing out of my grasp.

How completely fantastic. This is a parody of the problem, but it cannot be laughed away. Nothing could be running back into the past. Whatever it is, it is fixed. It happened at some time: it cannot change times. If I go to that time I will find it there. What am I trying to represent (or misrepresent) as going to a time past? Sometimes I can recall the time when something happened, but not the exact detail wanted. "I think I can help the investigation. I know where Perry Roe was on November 21. I remember it because that is my birthday. I went out to dinner at the Harrison Hotel, and I saw him there in the dining room. But I can't remember what he was wearing. I can't even remember whether he was there for dinner." But also I remember many things and not the time they happened. "Oh yes, I remember seeing the Talgo train come unexpectedly through town. I was taking a walk along the tracks. But I can't remember exactly when it was: early in June, last year, I think."

Something about memory suggests this picture of a search in the past. Do I "search"? Sometimes I do. "Try to remember. Try to remember whether you were ever taken to Bryton when you were a child. Search your past. Work at it." This is a directive to try hard to remember. Often I succeed. And more often I remember without trying. Nothing could be easier. When I am directed to search my past, I am told to try hard to remember something. I am not expected to turn time around. I am not required to wave an arm around in a time machine. "Search your past" is a dramatic way of saying "Try to remember." "I remember" is not a way of saying "I have searched the past and found." "The thing I am trying to remember has disappeared in the past." Here is a complaint that it is hard to remember details of things that happened so long ago, not a complaint that it is impossible to remember anything.

"It is so clear. I can see it all before me." Yes *sometimes* that is the way it is. I remember it all very clearly. "I can see it now." These idioms fit the picture I have. But such idioms are used *sometimes* for certain memories. They suggest something, they hit off the way it sometimes seems. The picture I support with them dictates what I think memory must be, what it must always be; or if not always, then what it *must* be in its basic or fundamental form. Apparently in thinking with this picture I have lost track of what remembering is. I thought it had a peculiar object, an experience, a perception, and I could not find it. I imagine the object in a place—one which cannot be reached—and I worry myself with the impossibility of memory. The moral should be clear or I can make it clear to myself by saying these philosophical things: memory is *not* of experiences, *not* of perceptions, *not* of the past. It does *not* involve *trying* to get these things. It does *not* involve looking within. It does *not* involve *getting* these things. *Seldom*, in strange circumstances only, do we remember the past. Only *sometimes* does it involve searching one's past. *Rarely* have things I try to remember disappeared into the past. That is, I can make it clear to myself by such sayings, provided I do not then immediately ask, "Well then, if it does not involve these things, what is it?"

I think that memory is impossible, but I *must* remember some things or I could have no knowledge of the past at all. I think that memory must give me too much: I think that I must be able to pin what I remember to some time. So I am inclined to think I cannot remember because I cannot remember that time. Maybe this is part of the difficulty: I have revolted from the "having learned and not forgotten" story. That will not do as a general account of memory, because I must remember when I learned. (It need not be "learned"; it can be "saw" or "heard".) I feel that I must be able to pin my memory to some definite time. But I remember seeing the old barn in a storm, and I do not remember exactly when I saw it. Maybe it need not be the time I remember; at least it must be some particular experience. Well, I remember how it looked, and I do not remember taking any special look at it. And now that seems impossible.

I am in revolt from a philosopical view, and that is often a dangerous thing. So often the revolt is too moderate: it is from one end of the teeter-totter to the other. The "having learned and not forgotten" account will not do because I could have learned in the wrong way. I must have learned by having seen or heard. I should not say "I remember" unless I was sure I had seen or heard. Since "having learned and not forgotten" will not do as a *general* account, I am led to think that being able to recall some exact time or a certain sight or experience or perception must be part of a proper *general* account. This is strong support for the picture that I must turn within and run back through my experiences until I come to the right one. I must pin my memory down there. Of course this is ridiculous. How should I ever know which was the right one unless I remembered that it was?

When do I need to pin my memory to some time or some seeing? When do I need to support my claim to remember by recalling some certain time or sight? Not usually. Not often. Only in those rare cases where there is some reason to suspect I have confused what was told me or what I saw in a home movie with a memory. Only in those cases where I might think I remember, but I do not. What I think I remember I learned in some other way. Then I might say, "I'm sure I remember. I recall the exact time. I recall seeing it clearly from my front step—it was one spring morning." But I do not in *general* have to do that. I would not be expected to. It would be silly to expect anyone to be able *always* to do that. In order to correctly say "I remember" I do not have to be able to do that. Usually there is no question of my confusing hearsay with memory. When there is a question, I will be expected to recall some details or give up my confident claim to remember. Sometimes, even when I am confident, I shall have to give up my claim because I am shown my confusion runs deep. The details I think I recall, the time, is not right. Maybe I was not even there in the proper place: it is shown I could not have been. Sometimes, rarely, I make big mistakes. But there is no reason to suspect every claim. Since there is not, since there could not be, there is nothing I could recall, no added details that would make my memory better or more secure than it is. There is nothing that in *general* I have to do along these lines to pin my memory to some past time or event.

When I say, for example, "I remember the old barn," I may not recall any one day, any certain seeing, any particular incident. But I do imply that I know about it from having seen it, having played in it. I imply that I know about it in that way, but I am not expected to recall details because there is no question of my being confused about the source of my knowledge. If (as generally there is not) there is reason to suspect confusion, I do have to recall details and corroborate my claim. If I cannot, I admit, "I must be wrong. I must not remember."

There is no one sort of object memories must have, and there is no reason why there should be. It is misleading to think theoretically of something remembered as an object. In the failure of the "having learned and not forgotten" theory I find support for my picture of memory. The picture is general; it must fit all cases. There is no reason why some picture must fit all cases. Yet the picture leads a life of its own. It is the old subject-object picture: here am I, looking back upon my past, grasping for my past deeds, experiences, feelings, glimpses and views. It is not that I cannot remember these things. I remember them, but not as I picture it. They are not the "objects" I take them to be.

IX

OF ALL MY FALLACIOUS MEMORY REPRESENTS

. . . de tout ce que ma memoire remplie de mensonges me represente . . .

Here is one of the difficulties we have in thinking about memory. It is not just that the objects of memory, being experiences or perceptions, are particularly elusive. There *may* be no objects at all. The things we remember are past: there may be no past. We can be inclined to think sometimes that there is no past behind us. Then all our memories are delusive. That "nothing existed of all my fallacious memory represents," is one of the conclusions brought on by Cartesian doubt.

The past disappears behind us, each moment ceasing to be as the new, present one arrives. The past then would be gone; it would no longer exist. That is not the worst of it. For once upon a time it did exist, once when it was present, and then it could have registered itself upon our minds, so that we could sometimes remember it. No. Not only may there be no past, there may never have been a past. The world, for all we can tell, may have been created last week or yesterday, or just a moment ago; and we were created with the world and our memories were created with us. We might have come into the world supplied with coherent, but totally delusive memories. Totally delusive just because there was no past, none of the things and events which we remember (or think we remember).

Of course we do not believe there is no past. The difficulty is that we are able to imagine it. It might be so. And the frightening thing is that if it were so we could not find out. Yet it is not really frightening: we think it for a little while and then everything is all right again. It is strangely frightening while we think it, but the emotion evaporates as soon as we turn from philosophy. The important and lasting thing is this: in the process of thinking that there might be no past, we learn something of philosophical importance. We learn that our memories are taking place in the present. They could be created in a moment—complete and self-contained. In order to be correct—true, or what—there must be some past things and doings to which they refer. But we can imagine there being no past at all and, if there were no past, it would not change our memories. Because our memories are in the present, they *could* all be wrong.

One little thing stands in the way of our thinking that all our memories could be wrong. If the world came to be yesterday, and we were created full of memories, then our memories of times before yesterday would be wrong. We could have correct memories of times since then. Since all future times are times since then, our memories from now on could be correct. If we set the time of imagined creation just a fraction of a moment ago, then we need only to wait a little while for something to come which we could remember. Then if we do not remember these things, it is only because we do not think. We cannot take the sting out of the Cartesian doubt this way. Because at any time, any time at all, we can imagine that the world came to be just a moment before. At any time, therefore, we can imagine that all our memories are wrong.

All my memories may be wrong. When are memories wrong? "Where did you put the key?" "Right here under the mat." "It's not there." "I remember putting it there." Suppose now that it is found in the flower-pot by the step, and that several people clearly remember seeing me put it in the pot. I may say still, "I remember clearly putting it under the mat. My memory must be wrong." What is it that was wrong? My memory, of course. But I don't mean that. What I thought I had done I had not. I am looking for that experience of remembering, that something which must be here in the present. There is no other place for it to be. It must all—every bit of it—be in the present, since I have imagined the past away. What goes on here? What is the memory? It may, whenever it goes on, be a wrong memory. What can I say? I may picture myself with the key. I may look at the mat, and thing of myself making a motion as if sliding a key under it. I may shake my head wondering why I have these pictures in my mind, since quite evidently I did not put the key under the mat. I try to recall what I did, and still I have the idea that I put the key under the mat. I remember doing it. That's all I can say. It's just as if I had remembered correctly. Something went wrong, but I don't understand what or how.

I want to find something that could be going on now, remembering, and it could be going on now—even though there were no past. Sometimes we do not say, "My memory is wrong." We say instead, "I do not remember." "Do you remember meeting Filmore? I introduced him to you at the party last year." "Oh, yes. I remember him. He had bushy eyebrows and a high voice." Now I am told that Filmore does not have bushy eyebrows and a high voice. I go over in my mind the people I met. You told me about Filmore before the party. You talked of him many times. You wanted me to meet him. I seem to recall your bringing Filmore over to meet me. But that man did have bushy eyebrows, a high voice. I'm mixed up. I say, "I guess I do not remember meeting Filmore." Now here the same thing seems to be going on. I may picture a man. I may imagine incidents or people at the party. In imagination, I may make a motion as if shaking hands with a man. Filmore does not have the features I had in mind. I do not remember meeting him. What goes on here seems to be the same as in the former case. There my memory was wrong. Here I do not remember. What am I to say? One is a case of wrong memory, the other is not a case of memory at all? The difference between the two is not in anything I can think of that is going on in me.

What have I done here? I have been looking for something which goes on in me, some experience, which is memory. If there were no past at all, it could still go on. I could have that experience. I have assumed that I have that experience before me when I say, "I remember." Then sometimes I change my mind and say, "I don't remember after all." I have taken this as indication that the experience was not there after all. I have been thinking that "memory" is the name of that experience. As far as I can tell, I have the same experience at two different times: once I call it "memory," once I do not. So, I concluded, that experience is not memory.

When I said, "All my memories could be wrong," I did not intend to say, "All the things called memory are wrong." And I did not clearly intend to have what is not to be called a memory determined by my saying, "I don't remember." What was I trying to think? The things I think of as memories are wrong. I say, "I remember." Sometimes I later qualify by saying my memory is wrong. Sometimes I later disqualify by saying, "I did not remember." Sometimes I say, "I remember," and I do not later qualify or disqualify. Then so far as I know, I have a memory or a correct memory. Now I am trying to imagine that these memories which survive without getting any of the well-known kinds of qualification or disqualification are to get qualified or disqualified after all. They are to be wrong or they are to be rejected—because there is no past.

Sometimes I say my memory is wrong. Sometimes I reject my declaration that I remember. I should expect to have the same experience in each case. An experience—or something—which these have in common is what I am looking for. It must be present wherever I have a wrong memory, and also wherever I think I remember but do not. It must be present as well when I remember and my memory is correct. This experience is what memory consists in. I dispatch the distant referent, the past, and in doing so I can concentrate on the experience.

What is there to say about the present? In each case, I presently claim to know something about the past, that is, I say I remember something. The claim is about the past. But there need be no past. I ought to be able to look and see the operation of a claim which has no object. I can awake on the train and think I am in Chicago. The train spent the night on a siding in Milwaukee. I do not have to be in Chicago to think I am in Chicago. There does not have to be a past for me to think I remember something. Of course I can make a claim about a nonexistent thing. But making a claim is not the sort of thing I am looking for. Making a claim is taking a risk, staking the whole thing that I am right. I am looking for an experience which will be the same whether I am right or wrong. It will not be the claim; it will be what I base the claim on. It will lead me to make the claim.

Does one have to make a claim in order to remember? Suppose a ship has struck an iceberg and the radio operator is killed. The captain asks the passenger if anyone can send a message. I say, "Joe, you used to be a ham operator when you were a kid." He says, "I'm afraid I've forgotten." He thinks and thinks, goes to the key, reaches, withdraws, then makes a few tentative dots and dashes—and in a little while is sending and receiving messages at a great pace. "You know," he says, "I really couldn't remember a thing, but it came back to me bit by bit as I worked with the key."

Joe made no claim, but he did remember. He showed that he remembered. There are two reasons why Joe made no claim. There was no point in his saying, "I remember." At first he thought he did not remember. And by the time there was some point in his saying anything, the fact that he had remembered had already been demonstrated. Throughout some considerable time there was no one moment at which he could have said, "I remember the code." It came to him bit by bit. He would not have interrupted his job by saying at intervals, "Now I remember M," "Now I remember X," and so on. In a different situation he could have thought it all over. He could have sat with key in hand, thinking and experimenting. Then, finally, he could have said, "I remember the code. I'm sure I remember it all, even the numbers, and punctuations." This example does not show entirely wrong the idea of remembering as making a claim. If there had been time or some reason for it, Joe could have said, "I remember." And that would have been making a claim.

Take another example: suppose that when I leave home mornings I hide the door key in different places. Very often I forget where I put the key, and when I return I have to stop and think. Sometimes I look in the wrong place. Tonight I return in a hurry: my mind is on other things. I reach into the eve-spout, remove the key, and let myself in. Later I think: "I remembered where the key was and I had never put it there before. Perhaps when I'm in a hurry I remember better." I did remember, didn't I? There is the same feature in this example. There was neither time nor point in my saying, "I remember where I put the key." But if someone had stopped me just as I was reaching, and had asked, "Do you remember where you put the key?" surely I could then have said, "Of course. I remember putting it here in the eve-spout." Later I said, "I remembered." In such past-tense comments, I am not saying that I made a claim. I can remember without making a claim, but it is not clear that I can say (present tense), "I remember" without making a claim. I am trying to imagine that all my memories are to be rejected or found wrong—now. I am trying to imagine that the cosmos was created a moment ago. Therefore I must be thinking of my memories—now. And what could they be except the various things of which, if called upon, I can say, "I remember"? Although it is a bit strong, it does not seem misleading to say these are claims about the past, which if called upon, I could make. Of course, not everything I claim to know about the past is a memory. I know that Cromwell executed Charles I. I would bet anything I am right. But I do not remember the event.

Someone asks, "What do you remember now?" "About what? What is the question?" He tells me. He says, "After all these years, we're trying to collect the facts in the brown-derby murder. You found the body. Tell me everything you remember." And so I shall begin. "Well, I remember . . ." Throughout my story, I should be convinced that I was getting it right.

In any event, what do my examples of remembering without claim-making show? I have been looking for a feeling or experience which might give rise to a claim. Joe could have said, "I remember the code." I could have said, "I remember putting the key here." Whether Joe or I said such things or were only prepared to say such things, there must have been some distinctive feeling. What did he feel while he successfully worked with the telegraph key? Didn't I feel something as I reached toward the eve-spout? Could it be a "feeling of familiarity" which Russell said we had in remembering? That is an odd candidate. It seems to be the kind of feeling I have when I do not remember. As I drive through a small town I say, "The buildings and streets of this town seem familiar. I wonder whether I was ever here before. I don't remember." Suppose I am assured that I have never been here before. Well, it still seemed familiar. Maybe I am told that I was there as a child. "That explains why it feels familiar, but I certainly don't remember being here."

Now suppose that suddenly I remember. "Oh yes. I remember now. You brought me here one day in winter. Just around that corner there was a toy store, and we had an ice cream soda at the fountain over there. Of course." Now I remember. What has happened to the feeling of familiarity? "At first it just seemed strangely familiar. Now I remember." I had the feeling when I did not remember. *Now* I remember. I don't have a feeling of familiarity *now,* do I?

Remembering is something I do within the present. The reference to the past is a venture, a risk. I think that way partly because my memories are sometimes wrong. And so I think they could always be wrong. I think of remembering as something present, partly because my memories could always be wrong—or so I think.

On the other hand, I sometimes think my memories could always be wrong or disclaimed because remembering is something confined to the present. I have been looking for that "something" and I have not found the right words.

Perhaps it is not an "experience," or a "going on." Perhaps there are different experiences or goings-on held together by a certain kind of "object": experiences of something, different activities aimed at one object. There is some peculiar kind of memory-object I am presently aware of, the immediate object. (The subject-object picture.) The immediate object of remembering must be something present. Otherwise how could I have it before me? (1) But there is no one kind or sort of object I remember—the kind of thing I can imagine having before me. I remember how I used to lie with my arms crossed, watching the clouds. I remember how the flies felt as they walked on my forehead. I remember the odd taste of that jam Grandma made of quinces and currants. I remember that I once knew how to recognize the songs of the small flycatchers. I remember seeing John Percy often, but I don't remember how he looked. I remember the telephone number we had when I was ten. What sort of object could be before my mind in all these memories? (2) But is there any *immediate* object? I remember what happened. How can that be? It is not now happening. I must have before my mind something else. But there is nothing else I am remembering. It is what happened; I remember it clearly. If there is something else before my mind, it is not *that* I remember. And if that reminds me of something else, leads me to recall something, then it reminds me of something I remember, it leads me to remember something. The immediate object is not what I remember.

What is "it"? What sorts of things can I have before my mind? Sometimes I have before my mind the very things I remember. "Remember the day we gave the teacher a dead rat in a box?" "Remember it! I have that whole thing —every detail—before my mind!" I am not thinking of that sort of thing. How can that be before the mind? It is past and gone. What else can there be? "Strange thing. When I think of Sally, the little girl next door who died when I was ten, I always have a picture before my mind of a purple iris, a purple iris with a child's head for a pistil." That is not the "immediate object" of my memory. Others can remember Sally without it, and I often wish I could too.

(3) Though the object be past, the remembering is present. If remembering can reach out into the past, it can also fail to do so. There might be no past and I could go on remembering still. What would I remember? There would be nothing to remember. Couldn't I go right on remembering the same things,

but now my memories would have no real object. They might all be wrong, or have to be disclaimed. "No real object?" If not a real object, what object would they have? That is the immediate object: it is in the present. That is what I have before me when my memory is wrong: that is what I have before me when I claim to remember but later disallow it. That is the object of my wrong memory. It is what I think I remember when I do not succeed. And when I do remember and I am right? Then that is the immediate object of those memories.

The real reason for considering wrong or disallowed memories is that they best reveal the features which are present in the workings of all memories. When memories go wrong, their object is not a past thing or deed or happening. In them we see what the immediate object of memory is like. Likewise when a memory is correct, its immediate object is not something that happened in the past. That would, at best, be its mediate or indirect object. What would the immediate object be? When I remember, I am not aware of two different things before my mind. It would have to be just like, almost indistinguishable from, the mediate object. It would not be past: it is present, and before the mind. Then I couldn't *remember* that. One can't remember something which did not happen, but is now happening. While watching a football game one cannot say, "I remember this game, the 1963 Oregon-Stanford game." No. One does not remember the immediate object, but in *having* the immediate object one remembers the mediate. How would that work? Do I direct my attention to that immediate object, and then say I remember the other, the mediate?

(a) The immediate object could *remind* me of the other. Ordinarily, for one thing to remind me of another, the two things must be different. In being reminded, I can remember. I see a cup something like Aunt Mabel's. I say, "That cup reminds me of one Aunt Mabel had when I was little." "I'm surprised you remember that cup of Aunt Mabel's. I never thought of it before, but I can see what you mean. This cup is a little like it." Could the immediate object be like that? Could it be quite different from the mediate, so different sometimes that one had to look carefully to see the similarity? If there were an immediate object like that, I ought to be clearly aware of it; but I am not. I have been thinking that it would be very, very like the mediate object. If they were so very alike, could one remind me of the other?

Would one cup in a set remind me of another in the same set, another which was in the cabinet? "That cup reminds me of one Aunt Mabel had." Should I say that if they were identical: that cup and Aunt Mabel's? Perhaps I do not realize they are almost exactly alike. "That reminds me of Aunt Mabel's cup." "It ought to; it's one of the same set." Could the immediate object serve to remind me in that way? I had not remembered what Aunt Mabel's cups were like. The immediate object must remind me and by reminding me, I must remember the other. Can it remind me precisely because I do not remember the other? When the cups are from the same set I say, "That reminds me of a cup of Aunt Mabel's." Would anyone say now that I remembered Aunt Mabel's cup? "You must not remember Aunt Mabel's cup very well. This one is exactly like it. They are from the same set." I could be reminded in this way only when I do not remember very well or very clearly. The immediate object must function in all memories, clear and unclear alike.

(b) Could it be a faithful reproduction, something like a photograph of the mediate object? Could I see a photograph of a scene and fail to notice that the photograph was one thing, the scene another? That's the way it must be in remembering. But I am not aware of two different objects, the thing remembered, and something like a photograph of it. When I imagine that it might always be as in wrong memory, I am supposed to become aware of the immediate object, distinguishable from that which I remember. Suppose someone devises an optional illusion with a large photograph. A color-photograph of a scene, a backyard garden, is displayed on a rear wall. A window frame is put before it, and it is lighted in such a way that when I look at it I think I am looking out a window upon a backyard garden. Also, I can easily be shown my mistake. Through a real window of the same kind on the same wall, I can see the real garden outside. It is the garden of which the other window frame contained a photograph.

I look at the photograph, thinking, "That is the garden outside the window." Remembering is like looking into the past. However, the past thing is not before me. My immediate object is a representation in the present. While looking at the photograph in the window frame, I am told the truth. I will now see the garden through the other window. "Amazing illusion. I thought I was looking at the garden." I will no longer think that I was looking at the garden when I discover that I was looking at a photograph in a window frame. When I learn the philosophical truth about the objects of memory, am I to think that I have been suffering an amazing life-long illusion? I am not supposed to say ever after that I remember nothing. The illusion at the window was possible because I thought I was looking through an ordinary glass window upon a real garden. If I am incredulous when told of the illusion, I can look out the next window. I can check the panes: I can even open the window and reach out in order to make sure that no opaque surface stands between me and the garden. I can send a friend out into the garden. Then I can talk to him from the window. In memory, there is never to be clear glass through which to view the past-in-itself. There is no such thing as an open window upon the past. There is no sending a friend out into the past as a check on its reality. Yet, if the past were taken away, its disappearance is to make no difference to the memory-experience. There is no way I can have before me any object other than the immediate object, the one given in the present.

When I remember, I often say, "I remember . . ." I often tell what I remember, and when called upon, I tell in considerable detail. As I am looking at the photograph in the trick window frame, suppose I am asked to write a description of what I see. I begin, "It is a lovely garden. Near the center stands a gnarled cherry tree, and just to the left (north that is) there is an arbor of yellow roses . . ." As I go along I think I am writing a rather beautiful description. After I finish I am shown that I was all the while facing a cleverly lighted photograph. Did I write a description of the garden? Now I look upon the garden. I reread my description. I still think I did a good job. "Now write a description of the garden." I do not want to change a word of what I have already written.

An historian can write a description of a scene he never saw. He can describe the inauguration of President Coolidge guided by a very detailed photograph of the event. But he knows as he writes that he never witnessed the event. He would say that he was reconstructing the scene, describing it from a photograph. I could not similarly say that I had described the garden from a photograph. I did not know that I was looking at a photograph. I did not think I was trying to capture the spirit of the original from a photographic record.

Someone reads my description and says, "That is a most perceptive description of the garden." I should think that I had to explain. The praise doesn't quite apply. I wasn't perceptive in that way. "I was looking at an excellent colored photograph, and I had been tricked into thinking I was looking at the garden." I remember my tenth birthday party, and describe it to someone. Now when I learn the philosophical truth about memory I am not expected to think that I must give an explanation of my description of the birthday party. I am not expected to feel uneasy, as if somehow a misunderstanding were likely, and had to be avoided.

Someone who knows all about the origin of my description may read it and say, "All the same, that is a perfect description of the garden." And in this way it could be a perfect description of the garden regardless of its origin. I could just have made it up, a purely imaginative invention. The coincidence of my imaginative invention and the details of a real garden would be most amazing. I could have written it as a description of a garden I dreamt last night. All the same, it might be a perfect description of the garden outside the window. None of this will do for the description of my tenth birthday which I remember in such detail. Suppose I just made up a likely story about my tenth birthday and the story happened to be exactly right. Or suppose I had a dream that I was having a birthday party. It was my tenth birthday, and all of the details happen to coincide with the actual details of my tenth birthday party. I am not going to say that these are memories of my tenth birthday.

My memories are wrong sometimes. This is supposed to teach me that what I remember may not have happened. Yet I have a memory, a wrong memory; or I make a memory claim which I have to withdraw. The immediate object of memory is always to be as it is in wrong memory or in a disqualified claim. Yet sometimes my memories will not go wrong. I do not want to say my memories are always wrong or that I never have genuine memories. I want to say only that I can imagine my memories always wrong, or that I can imagine having no genuine memories. Then I can see that every memory claim has an immediate object. Sometimes the object will be a representation of a real past event. In that case, when I describe the immediate object, I am giving a description of the past. But it would be a description of the past only in the way that a pure invention or a dream account might be a description. And that has nothing to do with memory.

Remembering involves a direct object, a representation—something like a photograph. This idea has a hold on me, mainly, I suppose, because I am thinking of remembering something or some person. I can remember my grandfather's grocery store. It burned down years ago. I can remember the face of my kindergarten teacher, though she died many years ago. I am thinking of things I can remember, things of which I might have photographs. They would be photographs of things that once were, things that are no more. Hence the photographs are records of the past. I think that in memory I am given something which is a stand-in for the past. I am unable to see how being reminded by, or glimpsing, or describing a stand-in for the past could be a memory.

With memories of other things (things of which I could not have a photograph) the idea of a substitute, an immediate object has no strong hold. Not only can I remember Grandma's face, I can remember the taste of the cherry pies she used to bake. What kind of immediate object could I have in remembering the taste of her cherry pies? Someone has found her recipe and has baked a pie. I taste it. "This tastes just like the cherry pies Grandma used to bake." It does not "remind me" of the taste of Grandma's pies. It is the same taste. It does not "stand for," or "copy," or "represent" the taste of her pies. Nothing about the taste makes it the taste of her pies. Eating this pie is the occasion for my remembering the taste of Grandma's pies. Eating a cherry pie with a very different taste could also be the occasion. "This is cherry pie? It doesn't taste at all like those my Grandma used to bake." Of course, when reminiscing, I can just remember the taste of Grandma's pies. I need not be eating. What, in that case, is the immediate object? The idea of a photograph obtrudes even here. I may picture a pie. I may picture Grandma's kitchen, her red-checked, everyday tablecloth. But none of these gives me the taste. I remember that wonderful taste. I do not have a taste on my tongue now.

I'm trying to imagine that all my claims to remember are either false or will have to be rejected as not after all memories. What is involved in rejecting a memory claim? What is involved in having a wrong memory? These are dangerous questions, and ones that in the long run, I think, should not be asked. To discuss disqualified memories and wrong memories, I suppose one must begin with memories. Well, I remember all sorts of things. I say "I remember (this and that)" and tell spontaneously about what I once did and saw, about people and what they said, and all that sort of thing. And usually what I say I remember is taken at full value, assented to, commented on. Others remember similar things. Sometimes many of us remember the same things: we may remember the same school, same teachers, same books, and all.

Then sometimes—not often, but sometimes—what I say I remember turns out to be wrong. Usually I learn how and why I am wrong. For example, when I have met many new people at a party, I learn that I do not always keep them straight. I thought that Filmore was the man with bushy eyebrows. "I probably met someone—I've forgotten now—whose bushy eyebrows impressed me. I thought I remembered Filmore, but I guess I did not." "Evidently not," or "I guess I did not," is what I say. Or, "Apparently I do not remember the person (or the incident or what)." I *conclude* that I must not remember because the incident didn't happen—or something else—and I can see how I should have made the mistake. I think I left my glasses on the table. They are not there. I find them on the desk. Well, I've left them on the table many, many times—and sometimes on the desk, too. But I was reading by the table not long ago. Didn't I put my glasses down there? Even so, I can't recall everything I've done since then. I *must* have carried them to the desk. Jeremy saw me take them to the desk. What now will determine how I describe it? Jeremy sees me looking on the table. "What are you looking for?" "My glasses." "Why are you looking there?" "I seem to remember putting them here about an hour ago." If I'm not very sure I'll say, "I seem to remember." Suppose I'm sure. Then I'll say, "I remember putting them here." Now I learn the truth. Well, I had no good reason for being so sure. When I think back I realize that I have no clear recollection of where I went from the table. "I guess I don't remember where I put them," seems all right.

Sometimes, although I have learned how and why I can be wrong, I do not see or understand how I can be wrong. Suppose I had put the glasses down just a few minutes before. And suppose as I put them down I had said to myself, "I so often mislay my glasses. But not this time: I'll put them right here on the table where I'll need them." Then I get a paper from the desk, walk into the kitchen for a drink. I eat two crackers, close the cracker box, and return to the table to take up reading where I had just left off. And I cannot find my glasses. Now imagine the same conversation: Jeremy asks, "What are you looking for?" I suppose it will come to my saying, "What sort of a joke is this? I remember putting them right here—just a few minutes ago." "It's no joke. You have no idea how absent-minded you're getting." Maybe I'll acknowledge Jeremy's corrections: I'll agree that I have been getting more and more absent-minded. Still, I'll say, "I must have put them on the desk, but I remember clearly putting them here on the table," or "I remember clearly putting them here, but my memory must be wrong." That's what I say in this situation and in others like it.

I say, "I remember, but my memory must be wrong" when I acknowledge, or am ready to acknowledge, that I have made a mistake but I have not adjusted to that kind of mistake. I have not yet understood how I could be wrong in that way. I am more absent-minded than I realize. The point is just that I don't yet fully realize how absent-minded I've become. When later I adjust to it, I shall not be so confident. And when the mistake is disclosed, I shall have a place to accommodate it. I do so by shaking my head and saying, "I guess I don't remember . . . "

I cannot locate any experience or feeling that is present whenever I remember. Nor can I find any kind of object of which I might be aware or of which I might take account in various ways. What of that? Something may go on in the present of which I am unaware, something below the level of awareness of which I cannot take conscious account. But I am looking for something of which remembering consists or something which is the principle element in remembering. Remembering is a claim to have information about the past. The present occurrence must give me the information in some way and it must be given as information about the past. Well suppose that information is handed in an unconscious parcel. Something happens (I don't know what. I am unaware of it.) and then I remember. Something wells up in my mind, and the conscious form it takes is remembering some detail of my tenth birthday, or the afternoon I was lost in the department store.

All right, so it happens: something wells up. And what does it bring about? A memory. I think of something that once took place: I was almost run down by an east-bound freight locomotive. I was standing on the track transfixed by the whir and clatter of a freight train going in the opposite direction on the other track. If there is any point in it, I say, "I remember (that incident)." And

I tell about it. That is like a claim to have some information about what once took place. Something goes on now, and from that I get a memory. From that I make a claim to know all sorts of things about what I once did, what once happened—or almost happened—to me. How could I get a memory, or make a claim from something that goes on now?

My memories are sometimes wrong. I am trying to imagine they are always wrong. Suppose the going on in the present makes me think of my farmer-grandfather, the one who died when I was nine. Suppose it tells me his name was Ralph. I know his name was not Ralph. Shall I remember his name was Ralph when I know it was not? Shall I say, "I remember his name was Ralph," when I know it was not? If I know that the stuff which wells up into my mind is not true, I shall not say, "I remember (that)." When I say, "I remember (that)," I think it is true. I am sticking my neck out on its truth. If someone tells me it is not true my first reaction is to disbelieve him. I remember it.

How can a memory be something which just happens in the present: it just wells up and is there? Whatever happens in the present, full as it may be of details purporting to be about my own past, it must come with the conviction that it is the truth about that bit of the past. The present occurrence, together with its yield of details is not enough. For if I know it is not the truth, or even suspect it, I will not say, "I remember." I will not remember. Even if it came with the conviction that it gave details about my own past it would not be enough. My parents have told me many, many times of how I fell into the rain-barrel when I was four. I know many details of that incident. Still, I am not sure whether I remember it, or whether I know of it because I have been told. Unaccountably, the thought of that incident may well up in my mind, and certainly with the conviction that it is true; still I am not sure I remember it. There is more to remembering something than having it well up in the mind with the conviction that it is true. When I am in doubt about whether I remember something, I want to know how I learned about that something. I may ask, "How did that get in my mind?" The answer might be, "Your parents told you." Then I do not remember. The answer might be, "It just popped into your head." If that was the way it came to me, then it is most remarkable that it is correct; and it is even clearer that I do not remember it. Suppose the answer was: "It welled up from your unconscious." That seems the same kind of answer as, "It just popped into your head." If so, it shows I do not remember. The welling-up-from-the-unconscious story seems to belong with nonmemory. But I was trying to think that it was an essential part of memory.

I can't say that memory is something that happens or results from something that happens. It is something I do. ("I can't remember." "Try and see whether you can do it." "Now I remember.") Sometimes I think I do when I do not. I may say "I think I've done it. I think I have succeeded in remembering the combination." I may be right: also I may be wrong. Sometimes I'm sure that I've done it, and I am wrong. I claim success all the same. Sometimes I do succeed. Is my claim to succeed explained by something that happens in the unconscious or in the nervous system? No: but sometimes my success is. Then it is a question of why I remembered that special thing at that particular time. My memory is unusual or important. Some explanation is wanted. Why did I suddenly remember the details of my sister's death? I have never been able to recall anything about it before. Perhaps something was released from the unconscious, something which was bound there by repression. This might be a significant answer. Why did I suddenly remember my phone number of years ago? I have been suffering amnesia brought on by brain damage. I remembered because something happened in the brain. Perhaps I was jarred. A neuro-physiologist might be interested in what happened in the brain.

I have not been inquiring into that sort of thing. I've been trying to give a philosophical account: a theory of what memory essentially consists in. To answer my question, I do not need to engage neurotic patients in psychotherapy, or to dissect preserved brains. I have the data: I can tell what memory is because I remember all sorts of things. Memory is something like a claim to know in a certain way about certain sorts of things. That cannot be something that happens; nor can it result from something that happens.

I am trying to imagine all my memories wrong. Suppose I do suddenly have all these ideas, and I blurt out, "I remember my grandfather's name was Ralph. He was a tall, thin man and he lived in a brown farmhouse beside a gravel road." This is all wrong. That's the way I want it to be. Someone tells me I am wrong. My grandfather's name was Henry. He was short and fat and he lived in a large white house on a hillside, miles off the gravel road. I thought the things I said were true. I thought I remembered them. What shall I say? "Where did I ever get those strange ideas? Why do I appear to remember my grand-father as tall and thin?" My sanity is at stake. I fully expect answers to these questions. "You were very young when your grandfather died. You heard us talk of him. You have him mixed up with Uncle George. We went to visit Uncle George in the country many times." Some such explanation may work. But it will work only because I listen carefully and think hard and long and succeed in remembering something someone once said, or a trip to Uncle George's. I must get the pieces of my past fit together. "Yes. Now I see. Isn't that strange? I did always think that man was Grandpa. I thought you were talking about him. I never listened very carefully." Of course in this process I shall have succeeded in remembering some things. I shall get them right. In this way I shall never be able to imagine that all my memories are to be discarded.

Then there are the times when my memories are wrong. Those are the times when I seem to have it right, and I can't understand how I could be mistaken. In imagining that I am always mistaken, I must imagine it like that. Some-thing happens. I say, "I remember my grandfather." I go on to tell about him. And I am told I am wrong. I must still ask the question, "How could I have made such a mistake?" It is only after seriously asking that question, searching for explanations, failing to remember the causes of confusion, that I finally say, "I seem to remember, but my memory must be wrong (somehow)." Things went wrong and I cannot understand how. But I can say this only after I have tried to understand how, and that involves trying to remember the crucial times or incidents. I expect to be able to do so. Usually I do. A wrong memory is a puzzlement, waiting to be understood. I know what successful explanation would be. It is a personal thing. It involves memories, reviewing the relevant stretches of my past experience. If I imagine all my memories to go, then I could not understand what explanation of my mistakes would be. So I should never be in a position to conclude that my memories are wrong, that is, that I cannot find the explanation.

Perhaps I do know what an explanation would be, perhaps sometimes I think I find one. But I only *think* I find one, because it in turn is wrong, too. Then I consider it and think I find an explanation, and that explanation is also wrong. Until all my memories are wrong. I can't do it this way. Somewhere along the line I shall come to the point where I shall no longer be able to understand giving an explanation. How easy it is to say this sort of thing, but how difficult to imagine any guts to it. What a fearsome business it would be: doubtless approaching step by step to insanity. If every attempt has gone wrong, I shall no longer have any idea of what I remember and what I do not.

Suppose I never discover that the explanation is wrong. I accept it and the mistaken memories that go with it. But they are all wrong. How would that go? "I remember my Grandfather Ralph." "No. That's all wrong. You have confused Ralph and Uncle George. Don't you remember our visiting Uncle George?" Well, suppose I do, clearly enough to think I understand the mistake. Then I didn't remember my grandfather after all. That purported memory is out. And the memories, on the basis of which I threw it out, are to be wrong; but I do not find out they are wrong. I do not throw them out, or pronounce them wrong. They are what I *call* "memories." I *think* them right. I would not say "I call them memories": I insist they *are* memories. I would not say, "I think them right": nothing has ever led me to suspect them. I do not say, "My memory is right," unless it has been challenged, unless I have some reason to further accredit it.

When I am challenged, I can usually support a memory or at least suggest how I could do so. But any old question is not a challenge. I say, "I remember my grandfather named Ralph," and I go on to tell what I remember. Someone says, "No. You've got it all wrong." The challenger has to show me or help me to understand—or at least be patient with my effort to understand how I could have gone wrong. One cannot doubt or question every claim of mine to remember, not without having some specific reason for doubt or question. That is, no one can do that and be understood. I say, "I remember I got a toy train with a black, electric-type locomotive for Christmas when I was eight." He says "I doubt it." "I remember having a big brown dog named Jack." "I doubt it." Etc. Such professed doubt is incomprehensible. I must ask "Why?" (1) He could tell me that I've got the fact wrong or partly wrong. He has learned the truth from my parents or from a journal. Then I should try to understand how I had gone wrong. (2) He might know that these things were long ago, that my memories of childhood were poor. He knows that I had been told these things over and over by my parents; that they dwelt in great detail with such past trivia. He does not question the truth of what I say; he doubts that I *remember* these things. Again I shall try to understand how I had come to take hearsay for remembering.

When I say, "I remember (something)," nothing will count as a doubt, suspicion, or question unless it fits into some framework within which I can understand the mistake. I am reminiscing, telling all sorts of things about my life and experiences. Suppose someone says that he doubts all of it. He might be implying that I made it all up: I am telling a great long lie. That is not relevant. He says he doubts my memories. How can I understand that? He has no reasons: he does not intimate how or why I may have failed so completely. Maybe I shall think he is joking somehow, but I don't get the joke. "You just *call* those memories," he says. When I sincerely say that I remember, and then say things which there is no reason in the world to doubt, these are not things which I just say that I remember. They are my memories. I cannot imagine that they are all to be questioned for some completely unknown reason or for no reason at all. I cannot then go on to imagine that they are all somehow not memories or are all wrong.

(3) Sometimes a person can doubt my memories because the things I say I remember are so extraordinary, so very unlikely that he cannot believe I've got it right. "Oh, I remember it very clearly," is sometimes enough. But I may be expected to do more. I recall other things. I satisfy myself and the doubter that I never read or heard of such a thing. I find others who were there. They say they remember it also. The details I remember check with the details they remember. Perhaps I can find a written account made by a reliable eye-witness shortly after the event. My doubter was weighing probabilities: the event reported seemed so improbable that my memory must be wrong. But I can establish my memory beyond any doubt. I can corroborate the event and show that I could not have come by my story from some other source. That is, I can show the event happened and show that I remember it correctly. If I am to imagine that all my memories are to be discredited, then this one will have to go too. But how can I count this as a mistake? I have eliminated every possibility of mistake. Am I to say that this is what we think of as a correct memory, that in reality it is not? This is not what we think of as a correct memory: it is a correct memory. I have shown that my memory was correct.

It would not be correct if there were no past. If there were no past, we should not be able to detect that there were no past. It would make no difference in what we do and say. Then I should say, "I remember . . ." I should respond to doubts. I should find corroboration. I could cite eye-witness journal accounts. I could check whether I might have been told and forgotten that I was told. I could do all these things. Then I could remember and I could show that I remembered correctly. The sting is gone from imagining that there is no past, but I am not able to imagine that all my memories are to be disqualified: revoked or shown wrong.

There may be other ways. (a) The correct memories may all have been in the past. The past has now been wiped out: there is no past. And so all my memories are now wrong. But the correct memories were in the past, and now there is no past. So now there were no correct memories. I cannot say there were at one time, and then wipe out the one time.

(b) When I learned to say "I remember," something happened and I said something. Someone told me I was remembering. Suppose I had been told, "You remember," even though I was always wrong. Then wouldn't my memories have been wrong? Now suppose they have continued always to be so. There is a tripper in that "something happened and I said." There is no one thing that happened and by virtue of that's happening I was said to remember. I was told that I remember because I said something rightly about the past, said it on my own and from my own experience. I should not have been told I remembered unless I had been right—and in the right way. But suppose I had been told when I was wrong. Wrong in what way? Just when I spontaneously said anything at all that was not correct? Then I should not be remembering. I should not be having a wrong memory. But couldn't I be having a wrong memory, just not know what to call it? What would that be? Others had observed my recalling, remembering things, but they had never said to me, "You remember . . ." Now I look the same way, do the same things, talk in the same manner, and now I've got it wrong. Then I did have correct memories. So there were those correct memories, and I cannot now imagine that they never were.

(c) There are many, many different ways in which we sometimes go wrong and so say, "I guess I do not remember." I may think something happened which did not. I have considered the possibility that I may have been told. Also I may have dreamt it. A young man says to his mother, "You know, I just remembered your taking me to a wedding when I was very young. I thought the bride was beautiful. Who was she?" "That was Maple Justin. She used to live across the street." "I remember that I jumped up on a chair and kissed her." "Oh, no! You didn't actually do that. But you told me the next morning after the wedding that you had dreamt you kissed the bride. It must have been a very vivid dream. You were very excited by it." What is he to say? "I guess I couldn't have remembered doing that, then."

We can get dreams confused with weddings and birthdays, things we think we remember. Here is a possibility. All my memories are wrong. Or I don't really remember anything. All these things I think I remember came from a dream. I will suppose that I was created just yesterday and all these things were in last night's dream.

I am supposing a philosophical experiment to be performed on myself. I must play two roles and keep them straight. I shall suppose that I was created yesterday, but I who was created yesterday do not know of the creation. I do not know that I have been on the earth for just a little more than a day. On the first night of my creation, I sleep and have a long, long detailed dream—a dream of a past life in all its detail. But, of course, I do not know that all this life of mine, my childhood, all my former friends, are only in a dream.

Upon awaking to the second day of my creation, I start talking volubly about all these things. Why should I say I remembered them? Someone who heard me talking said, "You *remember* all those things." Why would he tell me that I remembered? He should have said, "You dreamt all those things." He is a party to the philosophical experiment. He wants me to think I remembered. Later he's going to tell me that I didn't really remember: I confused it with a dream. What am I trying to think? That I was created as an adult; that I had just dreamt my childhood, my friends, my family; and that I am unable to speak about dreaming and remembering and need an instructor in language. My instructor is going to lead me to think I remember all the things I dreamt. He says, "You remember those things you are talking about." How could I be led to think I remember? I don't know what it is to remember. I shall think that telling a dream is *called* remembering. By these instructions I shall not be confused into having wrong memories or into making memory claims at all. The instructor will have to teach me about reporting memories and about telling dreams before I shall be in a position to mistake a dream for a memory. By the time my instruction is complete I shall have remembered many things: my friendly instructor and his patient lessons, my first taste of food, and much more. By this means I shall not be able to imagine that all my memories are wrong or that all my claims to remember must be withdrawn. Also, when I talked about my dream, I suppose I was remembering it. My instructor could have said, "You remember your dream." However, that would not have been a helpful lesson. How could I learn about remembering and dreaming at the same time?

When I had just been created and needed instruction in the word "remember" and the word "dream," why was I talking at all? When did I learn the other words? I must have been assuming that I had learned the simpler words on the first day of my creation. Could I have learned to talk without remembering? Well, it is easy to get around these difficulties. I, the philosophical experimenter, shall simply assume that I, the subject, was created knowing how to talk. I was created with a mastery of language including a mastery of the phrases "I dreamt" and "I remember" and all the rest. And I know how to say, "My memories must be wrong," and how and when to disqualify after I have said, "I remember." I am so created, but, of course, I know nothing of my unique creation. I have a sound sleep in which I dream all the details of a family, a childhood. Now I say, "I remember my tenth birthday," "I remember the taste of Grandma's cherry pie," and things like that. All this is one big mistake, for I do not remember these things. They were all in a long dream. I do not know it is a mistake. I say with complete confidence that I remember these things.

I make a friend, Boris; and he is surprised at my mastery of language at creation. He questions me to make sure I understand how to talk about memory. I tell him about how a person can sometimes be told a story so often he thinks he remembers; and how sometimes a person knows all about something that happened to him—because he has been told in great detail—and still he does not remember it. I shall tell him about the ways that memories go wrong. Shall

I not have to remember these things? I shall give him examples of all kinds, but I shall never draw them from my past (that is, my dream); I shall make them up. "Where did you learn all this?" he will ask. What shall I say? "I don't know"?

What if he succeeds in raising a question in my mind? Is there something peculiar about my language? What right have I to be so confident? I say, "I talk as all the others do." What others? I have never talked with anyone except Boris. "I talk about such things the way everyone does." Who could I be thinking of? Only the people in my dream. And, of course, if I had been born with a mastery of language and had dreamt myself a childhood, then I suppose my parents and friends would have talked in my dream. But I can't satisfy anyone that I am speaking correctly by appealing to the fact that people talk in dreams. Indeed, does one *know* how to speak correctly when he is cut off completely from ever noting his conformity with others, cut off from ever authenticating his grasp of any idea? I can't satisfy myself that I am speaking correctly by going about and talking to others. There is not time for that. This philosophical experiment does not allow much time. If I talked to others, and checked on my use of words—then I would have to remember that I had done so. I am to have no memories, or no correct memories.

Why would I need to check or confirm my understanding of the language? If I have no reason to doubt, I should only illustrate my lack of mastery of the language by going about to substantiate my understanding of words. Oh, but I am going to have every reason to doubt. Before the experiment is through, I must become convinced that I have no real memories or that all my memories are wrong. Boris has good reason to doubt. He must convince me. He asks, "Why do you think you remember?" I answer, "I don't think I remember. I do." Boris: "No. I mean, how can you understand about remembering and forgetting and all. You have never really remembered anything." Here he lets the cat out of the bag. He will have to tell me that I was created yesterday and that I dreamt all my past. This whole thing is so fantastic that I hardly know how to go on. In order to complete the philosophical exercise, I shall have to imagine that he convinces me. I come to believe that I had no past life—only a dream. What kind of spin shall I be in? I am supposed to say, "Then, I couldn't remember anything," or "All my memories are wrong." Boris has doubted that

I can talk about remembering. Shouldn't I wonder also? I have never had a memory. How could I glibly have talked of remembering all that childhood, all those dear old friends? When Boris asked me to explain memory, I talked about how I think I remember sometimes, but really I do not because I have my times or places mixed up, or because I have heard the story so often I think I remember. What story have I heard so often? I was not talking about myself: I was talking about the idea of memory or the word "remember." But I was talking about my understanding of it. And now I am to acknowledge that I remember nothing. I *seem* to have had a past, I *seem* to have memories. And I seem to be talking to Boris. Everything is thrown into confusion. I do not know how to think of this. Having allowed the experiment in imagination to go this far, possibly I can take one more step. I do not know whether I am talking to Boris or not, that is, I do not know whether he understands me, or whether I understand him. I have every reason to wonder whether I can speak English correctly. (Is that my language?) Specifically, do I know how to use the words "remember" and "dream"? I cannot find out. Perhaps this is as good a way to describe my madness as any. When I say, "I remember nothing. I dreamt it all," I don't know whether I'm talking about remembering and dreaming or not. I don't know what I'm talking about.

It looks as though I am engaged here in a *reductio ad absurdum* argument, the purpose of which is to prove that my premises are not wrong but senseless. Of course one can't do that. One can't make demonstrative inferences from senseless premises. One cannot ask, "If *that* premise were true, what then?" because there is no *that* which can be considered true. No. I suspect I am deeply confused. And if I am confused, I am trying to make inferences from the seeming sense my confusions lead me to think I can make of things—in order to bring out the confusions in those things. And I have gone too quickly. I have crashed through too many barriers.

I tried to imagine myself, an adult, with no history, no biography, no past. I appear full-grown, with all the traits of character, abilities, idiosyncracies, memories, habits, and everything it takes to be an adult human being. I talk as everyone does. I pray; I swear; I write good poetry, make bad jokes.

Suppose I remember murdering my brother. I am burdened with guilt. I wonder about seeking forgiveness from I know not whom. I seek peace of mind;

I am in torment. What will Boris say of me? Will he say I am completely un-justified in feeling this guilt? Surely I can bear no responsibility for nonexistent deeds of a nonexistent past. Suppose I remember writing a poem. I remember every word of it. I write it down, have it published, and I win a literary award. Do I deserve the award? Wasn't the poem produced by a nonexistent person? Should it have been by-lined with "Anon" instead of with my name? Rather, I think the line for the author's name should have been left blank, empty. After all, the poem had its genesis in blank emptiness, the time before creation.

Suppose I remembered years of circus life, years of practice on the high trapeze, many bad falls, and, in particular, one near-fatal fall. I remember re-turning, trembling and fearful, to the platform. Today I put on a breath-taking performance, and it is followed by five minutes of applause. Do I deserve that applause? My talent was not hard-earned; I was given it overnight. Surely I deserve no reward I have not earned.

I murder someone on the second day of my existence. Of course, I remember years of jealousy and many fits of hate for the felled man. I remember plans to kill which I rejected. I certainly remember making the final plan, the one I have just executed. I remember buying the gun in one place, the ammunition in an-other, and so on. Am I guilty, or was it day of insanity out of my life? After all, I am only a day old. How can one tell whether this is a day of insane behavior when there was no behavior before? I did not, in reality, hate the murdered man; and, in reality, I made no careful plan. Where did the gun and the ammunition come from? Presumably they were created in my closet at the time of my cre-ation, because I was created with the memory of owning them.

I have tried to imagine myself created with speech, reasonably good, edu-cated speech. A day after my origination, I can talk very theoretically with Boris about memory and language, and types of mistakes and styles of correction. Suppose I swear at Boris and say slanderous things of him. Should he despise me; should he hold me to blame? And if I speak nonsense, should he blame me? And then if I speak sense, am I to be praised? Aren't the abilities required to theorize about memory and language hard-won abilities?

Boris and others would have all these questions about me. They would not know whether they should treat me as a human being. People do not have reasons to be in constant doubt about whether they should treat human beings as human beings. Am I, therefore, a human being? People have their doubts because of my mysterious creation as an adult. Can an adult human being be created in an instant?

When I came to Boris with my story, surely he would have thought me mad or playing some sort of strange joke. I must assume, though, that Boris accepts the idea that "someone," adult in form but less than a day old, comes talking of his past and memories. If I were Boris, if I were convinced that such a thing confronted me, I should look for wires, record-players, hidden microphones, and such. I should certainly think I was confronted with a life-size, very life-like marionette manipulated by hidden wires. I should think, perhaps, that a ventriloquist was supplying the voice from the next room.

If I tried to think of meeting and talking with someone, an adult, who was created yesterday, I should right away be full of doubts and difficulties. I should not know how to think of a one-day-old adult. How, then, could I have imagined *myself* created yesterday and talking today to Boris? I am afraid I just thought of myself as I am, and then said the words, "I was created yesterday." I now think I cannot think of myself being created yesterday. If imagining all my memories wrong requires that I think of myself being created yesterday, then I am afraid I cannot imagine all my memories wrong.

X

WAS THE SEA BATTLE RIGGED?

Some have been deeply troubled about the law of excluded middle, in particular about its application to propositions about the future. Others have told them that their worry is without foundation, that nothing could be more innocent than a law of logic. But those who are troubled have felt that a metaphysic of determinism or fatalism has been sneaked in under the wraps of a tautology. In turn they have been informed that their fears are misdirected—based entirely on misunderstanding. If logic has under its wraps any metaphysics, it is certainly not such a monster as determinism or fatalism.

Those who defend the innocence of the law, who profess to understand it and see no difficulty in its application to propositions about the future have usually said the misgivings result from a rather crude mistake in reasoning. They claim those who are fearful are misled into something like this series of steps. If a proposition is true and to the effect that a future event will take place then it is not possible for the event not to take place. It is necessary that it take place. Therefore it is not within our power to prevent it. The mistaken step is the last and it is usually represented as an illegitimate move from logical necessity to compulsion. When properly exposed it is a howler: from "If it is true that something will happen, it must happen" to "If it is true that something will happen, there is nothing anybody can do to prevent it." A diagnosis is sometimes made of how this blunder can befool one. People are prone to confuse knowledge and truth. Because we can know the truth of a proposition predicting a future occurrence only by knowing that the causes of the occurrence are operative, some people slip into thinking of the truth of a proposition as an operative cause. They slip from logic into hypermeterology or hyperhistory.

I am sure this does not get to any important source of the difficulty. I *do* have the feeling that the truth of a proposition that a future event will take place does directly involve one in the idea that nothing can be done to prevent it. I am sure that any reasoning which produces this feeling is far more direct and less elaborate than it is represented as being. I do not believe it involves any logical notions of "not possible" or "necessary" at all. The law of excluded middle comes into it because without thinking about the law I should not dwell much on future propositions, certainly not try to envision the truth or falsity of future propositions in wholesale storage.

I shall try here to expose what I believe to be the basis of these feelings. I am going to look into what seem to be very simple considerations, ones which can lead to the belief that the law of excluded middle cannot apply to future propositions. And then to imagine, if I can, what one who understands the law might say to show that these are mistaken or misrepresented (or what). In defense of the law's universal application, I shall probably fail, because I have no clear grasp of what the law means. Part, perhaps a large part, of what follows, therefore, is an exercise in trying to understand the law of excluded middle. My grasp of its meaning is so poor that I may not find what is required to overcome my initial sympathy with those who have had misgivings about it. So, unfortunately, what follows may be no more than wry monologue.

Propositions have "objects." They are *about* things. They are about *things,* events, acts. They are about dogs, battles, past decisions, future intentions. Consider the future. Every proposition about the future is either true or false. For every little thing that is going to happen, or every little thing anyone is is going to do, there is a pair of propositions, one true, one false. Surely then the future in every detail is outside our powers to change. The totality of true propositions about the future is the complete story of what is to come. But the law of excluded middle is meant to be "trivially true," absolutely uncontroversial, completely uninformative.

One of the ways the trouble arises is this: either a proposition or its contradictory is true. Look at the little girl on the walk. It is true that her dress is red or it is true that her dress is not red. To say that a proposition is true is to bear down on it in an emphatic way. From "It's true that the dress is red or it's true that it's not red" I quickly get to "It *is* red or it *is not* red." The dress is what it is regardless of whether I or anyone entertain the proposition. There is no indetermination in the dress: the color is not waiting to spring into being when someone thinks about it. I take the same step with propositions about the future. "I shall die tomorrow or I shall not." One or the other is true. It is true that I shall die tomorrow or it is true that I shall not. Therefore either I shall or I shall not. And this likewise seems quite independent of what anyone thinks or does. After all, just think of one's saying "I shall either die tomorrow or I shall not." Without regard to logical theory, doesn't it have a fatalistic flavor?

Anscombe[1] has made it clear that Aristotle got into the problem in a similar way. Aristotle thought that from "Either a thing is or is not" it followed that either it is necessary that a thing is or it is necessary that it is not. Also from "Either a thing was or was not" it follows that "Either it is necessary that a thing was or it is necessary that it was not." But with future propositions, Aristotle felt this step was not legitimate. From "Either a thing will be or not" it does not follow that "it is necessary that the thing will be or it is necessary that it will not." This is apparently all Aristotle has to say about the problem. It points out a source, but hardly constitutes a resolution of the problem. If the step is legitimate at all, why should it be so only for past and present propositions? No answer is given. And Aristotle thought he had saved the universality of "Every proposition or its contradictory is true." How do we understand "It is true there will be a sea battle or it is true there will not be a sea battle," if it does not entail "It is necessary there will be a sea battle or it is necessary that there will not"?

The word "necessary" here creates confusion. I shall return to my own words. Why is it all right to go from "It's true that it is red or it's true that it is not" to "Either it *is* red or it *is not*," but not all right to go from "It's true that I shall die tomorrow or it's true that I shall not" to "Either I *shall* die or I *shall not*"? I need to find out what is involved in this emphasis on the verbs when specifying the law of excluded middle. I need to think about some examples. Where indeed do I find a clear-cut specification or "substitution instance" of the law of excluded middle?

Before undergoing surgery, a man is about to be given an anaesthetic, "put

[1] G. E. M. Anscombe, "Aristotle and the Sea Battle," *Mind.*, LXV, No. 257, (Jan. 1956), pp. 1–15.

to sleep." He asks, "Where shall I wake up?" and the doctor replies, "Either here or somewhere else." Any specification or instance of the law of excluded middle must be noninformative. This example will not do. It is clear reassurance to the anxious man that he will survive the operation.

A nervous candidate for a high office at the end of an exhausting campaign paces and chain-smokes as the election returns come in. "What do you think?" someone asks, and he says, "Either I will be elected or I will not." Will this do? It comes too close to a resigned piece of self-comfort, something like, "Life will go on either way."

Perhaps he said a completely uninformative thing to make the point, "Life will go on." The uninformative thing will be the instance of the law; the point is another matter. The uninformative thing is said to make the point, and what is said is the instance of the law. But what is said? "Either I am to be elected or I am not." Dare I ask what was said? The words? Am I to stare at the words? They still are a fatalistic effort at self-comfort. Am I to take the words away and forget about the speaker and his situation? Then there are other speakers and other points. But forget entirely about the point. Then am I to think of a completely pointless remark? What am I to make of a completely pointless remark?

On the scene, I suppose, I could make nothing of it at all. But it is not meaningless. Because it is pointless, it is not without meaning. If I were on the scene, I probably should call it a meaningless remark. But we are not talking to the candidate who makes the completely pointless remark. We are thinking theory about his remark. He says, "Either I will or I won't..." and we are quite unable to make anything out of it. But still it does have meaning: that's what we must be concerned with. "It has meaning." Well, I suppose. Perhaps the man is in a coma and muttering. His words come out all mixed up. "Will I either I or won't..." and things like that, and then suddenly he improves in a way. He now gets out recognizable English sentences. "Either I will or I won't..." He says something now with meaning. Surely not every sentence of the right form and with meaning in this sense is an instance of the law of excluded middle. Is it merely a question of grammatical form standing against the background of babbling?

Or perhaps the man has gone insane and is wildly chattering. "Either I will or I won't . . . ," he raves. This may have meaning. It may have meaning to a psychiatrist. The ten-minute psychiatrist in all of us may find it meaningful. It may indicate anxiety about having fallen behind in his logic lessons since the campaign began. Whether something is to be an instance of the law of excluded middle cannot turn on the issue of whether it is meaningful or not. It is to be true in a very special way, "trivially true" or "vacuously true." It has to be a proposition, but one without information content.

Sometimes one's point can best be achieved by saying something that imparts no information at all. I may have no interest in the subject. I can make a trivial remark to show my desire to be let off. "I read that more pancakes are eaten in Brazil than in any other country. What do you make of that?" "Well. They either *eat* the most pancakes or they *do not*." This is said to trivialize the subject, to show that one does not want to be concerned with it. It is not worthy of attention. That troublesome business of point has come back. Even if something like this were to count as an instance of the law of excluded middle, it would not help in understanding "Every proposition is either true or false." The law in this form cannot be interpreted as saying, "Every proposition can be used in disjunction with its contradictory to trivialize the subject in question."

Consider a more important subject. "I see by the papers that the police are looking for you on suspicion of murder." "Well. They either *are* or they *aren't*." Is this a way of saying the papers are not to be trusted? That is not what I want. What is it then? The fatalistic flavor has come back. It sounds like a sigh of resignation. I do not know how to get a trivial truth disentangled from it. I do not know how to state any noninformative truth that is hidden within it.

At any rate, the law of excluded middle is at home in deductive argument. Perhaps that is its only home. When one wants to make every step in reasoning clear and plain, he will sometimes include a specification instance of the law of excluded middle. Dilemmas are commonly posed in this way. "If Congress passes this bill, we shall suffer from oxertaxation. If Congress does not pass the bill, the country will suffer from unemployment. Either Congress will pass the bill or it will not. Such are the times: prepare for your suffering." But is there any temptation here to emphasize the verbs?

If the speaker had said, "Either Congress *will* pass the bill or it *will not*," this would serve to emphasize the skeleton of the argument, a dramatic emphasis that we must take it one way or the other—and so we must in turn accept the conclusion. But within a deductive argument it would make no difference whether this disjunction were a specification of the law of excluded middle or not as long as the alternatives were the only live ones or the only ones we had to seriously consider. Perhaps this is a way to take away from the law of excluded middle its puzzling ontological pretentions, confine it to the generation of explicitly-mentioned premises in deductive arguments. But this is not the way it is meant to operate. It is not just to be sometimes *in* arguments, it is *always* to stand behind them. An argument is valid whether an instance of the law of excluded middle is listed among the premises or not. It has, therefore, unlimited applicability and precisely because it is trivially true and noninformative.

So I have not succeeded in finding an example in terms of which I can examine the temptation to go from "Either it is or it is not" to "Either it *is* or it *is not*." I shall have to be content with examples that come close, where the alternatives are not exhaustive—but practically so. I shall see whether I can gain from such examples an understanding of what is involved in emphasizing the verbs.

We have a deck of cards, and we are turning them up one by one. The next card will be either red or black. But it *is* either *red,* or it *is black* (before it is turned up). Is there a difference between "The next card is either red or black" and "The next card *is* either *red* or it *is black*"?

(1) I have been fiddling around with a mixture of ordinary playing cards and plain white cards of the same size with the same backs. I take some cards out of the deck and put them aside, face down. Then I sort and prepare a pile of those that remain and say, "Now let's guess the colors of the cards to be turned up. What do you say for the first? I say it is red." You hesitate. Then perhaps I reply, "It's either red or black." [I've removed all the white cards.]

(2) I have an ordinary deck and explain the game to a child with whom I am playing on the rug. "Let's guess the first. I say red." No reply. "It's *either red* or it's *black*." [That's the way these cards are—only two colors.]

(3) Instead, suppose that several times I have amazed and amused the child by turning up a card he did not know was in the deck, a card with a purple

elephant, one with a green dinosaur. "You guess the next." He smiles, "You have put a green or yellow card—or something—there." "No. It's red or black." He smiles again. "No. It *is* either red or black." [I mean it.] (But not, I think, "It *is* either red or it *is* black.")

(4) I have cards that by some chemical process unpredictably change color, red or black to any color in the spectrum and then back again to their original color. I have them mixed with an ordinary deck; then I take out the ordinary cards and form a pile of them. "Now let's guess . . . It's apt to change five times while I'm thinking." How about saying, "No, it either *is* red or it *is* black"? [Whatever it is, it is. It is not a changing card.] This will not do. As in the last case, I think one would say "It *is* either red or black."

(5) I have cards which change from red to black and back to red again through all the insensible intermediate stages. So that sometimes one does not know what to say of a card's color. It's red-black, or midway in its change. Now I have these mixed with regular cards, and after taking out the regular cards begin the game. "Which is it?" "Perhaps its one of those who-knows-whats?" "No. It either *is* red or it *is* black." [It is definitely one of these two—no indeterminate transforming cards.]

In all these cases, the "Either x or y" was said to assure someone that there were only these possibilities x and y, where formerly there were others, or where it was suspected there were others. "Either it *is* x or it *is* y" seems used specifically to rule out one kind of real possibility, that of intermediate, indeterminable cases. Part of my misgivings about the law of excluded middle when applied to future propositions was marked by my moving from "Either it is true or false" to "Either it *is* true or it *is* false." I do think that the law of excluded middle forces upon me a denial of indeterminate future propositions. Logicians tell me that this feeling is based on a misunderstanding of the law. This feeling is connected with the way I am inclined to accent the verbs in stating the law of excluded middle. If my series of examples shows what is involved in the accented verbs, then, of course, I have been mispronouncing the law. In all my examples, well understood possibilities are eliminated. "Either true or false" is not intended to eliminate any well understood possibility. What clear alternative could there be? Only, I suppose, an indefinite state of propositions about undetermined future occurrences or actions. But if the law of excluded middle is to be quite uninformative, then there can be no real alternatives on the scene.

Why do I want still to say, "It *is* either true or it *is* false"? Surely I do think this eliminates other possibilities. If I am thinking of this under the influence of "The dress *is* either red or it *is* not," what could have exercised me in that pronouncement? I must have been thinking of "is" as opposed to "becomes."

(6) Suppose we have crossed black and white chickens; and of the eggs produced, half hatch into white chickens, half into black. We number the eggs in an incubator and play a guessing game. "What color chicken is growing in number one?" "It doesn't have any color yet: it doesn't even have feathers." "But it *is* either a black chick or it *is* a white one."

(7) Suppose we have some dye for cloth; but when put to the cloth, the dye does not bring about any immediate color change. Later, when exposed to bright light the cloth becomes either red or black, but which color it will become is quite unpredictable. When treated with the dye, pieces of the same material will sometimes turn red, sometimes black. "Is this a red sample or a black?" "At this point it's neither. Do you mean to ask which it will become? It may become either. Do you want me to guess which it will become?" "No, it *is* either red or it is black." [What could this possibly amount to? "It's not just a question of what it will become. It will become out of and on account of what it *is*. It is either red or black the way the chick embryo is either a white or black chick. The only difference between the chick embryo and this cloth is that we know what determines the chick's color, here we do not know." Who would say that sort of thing and when? Possibly a young and not very dedicated chemist has been assigned the task of finding out why the cloth sometimes turns red, sometimes black, and he appears not to have much enthusiasm for the problem or to apply much energy to it. An older, peremptory supervisor might arrange some such conversation, ending with "It *is* either red or it *is* black. (Something in the dye reacts differently under different conditions. Find out what it is!)"]

(8) Lastly, suppose we have a chemical, X, which will react with Y to produce red, and react with Z to produce black. We treat cloth with X, and then an assistant comes and adds either Y or Z: we never know which he will add. Now we propose a guessing game. Before the assistant has come to add his

ingredient, we point to a sample treated with X, and ask, "Is this red or black?" "What am I to guess? You mean, 'Will it be made into red or black' or 'Is it to become red or black?'" [There is no sense here to, "It is either red or black," but plenty of opportunities for "It will become either red or black."]

When I say every proposition is either true or false, am I throwing out the possibilities "becomes true (or false)" and "turns out to be true"? Am I led to think the truth or falsity of propositions about the future are *in* them something like color in the chick embryo, or in a dye which reacts to light? These are most inappropriate models. They are little lessons in embryology and chemistry, reminders of how chick color is determined by genes, cloth color by light-sensitive dyes. They are intended to exclude other, many other, accounts of determination. The law of excluded middle is meant to rule out nothing: "turns out to be true" is not to be another competing possibility on the scene with true and false.

There remains the possibility that the law is a kind of logical, linguistic, "grammatical" reminder. Let us mix the two sets of examples. (a) We have monochrome playing cards, and we use on them the chemical X which we have been using in our experiments with cloth. It has the same effect on cards as on cloth. We play a guessing game with these colorless cards treated with X. We guess whether the card drawn will become red or black, that is, we guess which the assistant will make it. Then we call him in to add whichever determining ingredient, Y or Z, he feels like adding. (b) At other times, we play a guessing game with ordinary cards, turning them over to see who is right—red or black. Now one day I pull out some cards and say, "Let's play. Which do you say for the first?" "It will be made black." "No, it *is* either red or black" [Oh, you thought I was playing the game using the assistant. No. This is the game with ordinary cards.]

Is the law of excluded middle something like this remark? "Don't think we are going to use other possibilities, 'will be decided,' 'comes to be true.' This is the other game." What other game? Do I sometimes say, "... turned out to be true" and then learn that I have been using the wrong set of words or concepts entirely, ones that do not belong here at all? Surely the law of excluded middle does not say that. By what magical powers can a logician say, "Let every proposition now be either true or false. No more of this 'comes to be true'"? How could he say this and make it work? What would it be to make it work? How could we understand him?

I was led to think that the whole future was something out of my power to control because I was led by a trivial truth to think that either I *shall* die or I *shall* not, either I *am* to be shot or I *am* not. These accented verbs are totally foreign to the intended function of the law of the excluded middle. However, its absolutely unrestricted applicability remains a worry. Another source of the problem is the truth of future propositions. All future propositions are true or false. So half the future propositions tell the whole detailed story of what is to come. What they tell is true. It is true that I am to die tomorrow (perhaps). It is true that I am to be shot tomorrow afternoon (perhaps). I have been led to think about and be puzzled about the truth of future propositions because of the unqualified generality of the law, "Every proposition is either true or false."

How are we to understand this stern generality? *Is* every proposition true or false? "It is true that I had an itch on my shoulder blade yesterday just after two o'clock." "It is true that I ate a peanut about four." What is wrong here? Too much assurance. An over-emphasis about nothing? There is no question, no doubts about those things. The oddity doesn't come entirely from the word "true." "I had an itch yesterday . . . I ate a peanut . . . I saw a dead sparrow." Out of a blue sky, these would be just as peculiar and incomprehensible. How do we get some sense going? Perhaps these things were written in a letter—to show how humdrum life had been: "I ate a peanut at 4:02, another at 4:04. I crumpled a supermarket receipt and threw it in the basket. I missed at 4:08, recovered it and scored a hit at 4:09. The recipient of my letter might ask, "Was all that true? Didn't you just make those things up?" "I might have, but it really is true that I ate a peanut at 4:02, and all the other things were true. I simply reported all sorts of things for about an hour." Or it could be: "Yes. I made them up. Everything I said was false."

Does this show that everything one might say is either true or false? Suppose it is taken as showing either true or false everything anyone or everyone might say in an hour, a day—or even a lifetime. Propositions are not exhausted by what one might say in this manner. There is supposed to be some sense of "possible" in which propositions are all things it is possible to say, assert, or believe, although it would not be possible to say all those things even if everyone talked continuously until the extermination of the human race. Some of the difficulty with future propositions comes in here. For every little thing to happen, there is a pair of propositions about it, one true, one false. And propositions about the smallest part of the most insignificant thing, describing in unbelievable detail, say, the entire span of my future life.

If a letter expressing boredom shows how propositions are to be true or false, how could it show the sense of the law, "Every proposition is either true or false"? In the letter, it was a question of whether I made things up or whether I didn't. All propositions could not be either made-up or not, not if everyone were always writing like a Baconian scientist. But this does not help much. Could one say or write out all the details of my future life? No, but in order to express the depth of boredom, I could write out some. "I shall come home at 5:05, have supper at 6 o'clock, watch TV until 10, read until 11, into bed at 11:20, then to sleep." Is what I wrote true? Is it a question now of whether I made it up? One cannot understand "true" by contrast with "made-up," or we shall be asking for evidence, or reasons. There is no question of anyone knowing the great events of the future, the birth dates of my children, the time of my death. If all the events were known, they *would* be out of my control—or would they? That is another question.

Say the proposition "I shall die on November 6" is true. If in addition someone knew (not just said he knew) that I should die on November 6, there would be nothing I, or anyone, could do to prevent it. Yes, but he might also know what I should do and what my doctors would do in an effort to cure me. But the outcome of it all, he would also know; so he would know the efforts would fail. If he were a normal, reasonably sensitive human being, what attitude would he take toward me, and my efforts? And if all deaths, accidents, tragedies, mistakes, wrongs were similarly known, what attitude should we take toward them? But sometimes it would be known that decisions are right, accidents happy, efforts to prevent tragedies successful. Is it a question, as James thought, of what attitude we are to take toward life as a whole? How is one to size it all up? Most of us take the attitudes we do take toward victories and defeats, successes and failures, one at a time and as the events come up.

We need to get a clearer view of the way an event is determined or fixed— if it is—in being the object of a true proposition. We need an example or two.

"You will die on November 6." Is it true? "Well then, you will not die on November 6." "One or the other of the things I have said is true." Something is wrong here. This does not give us an example of a proposition about the future, because I didn't *say* either of the things. I am in no position to say either. I should not say either of them.[2]

Consider some words about the future, say, "San Francisco will win the 1962 pennant." How do I get a proposition about the future out of these words? Can I draw the sentence, written on a slip of paper, from a hat? Who am I? Suppose I know nothing about baseball. Is it true? I couldn't answer. Who asks? Much more is needed. Suppose a friend, an ardent San Francisco fan, says, "San Francisco will win the pennant this year." I, a baseball-innocent, ask, "Is that true?" He says, "Of course it's true. This is the Giants' year." His words are a half-serious outburst of hope, an expression of loyal enthusiasm. Not a very clear example of a proposition about the future. Several of my friends talk this way, and they have begun to arouse in me an interest in baseball. Then one day I am introduced to the man who is acknowledged the greatest of baseball authorities. He has long been a disinterested scholar and observer of baseball, following each season with a scientific eye from an office full of books and blackboards covered with statistics. Usually he makes only cautious and carefully qualified predictions. To make conversation, I tell him I hear everywhere an enthusiastic and hopeful prediction for San Francisco, and I ask him if it is true. Suppose he says, confidently, "It's true. San Francisco will win the pennant this year." What would this amount to? He is not expressing enthusiasm for San Francisco. How could he say this? Because he knew some of the crucial games were rigged, or because San Francisco was so very superior no other team had a chance. When he says, "It is true...," he does imply that the outcome is fixed, already determined, there is no point in considering any other possibility. Suppose to my question, "Is it true that San Francisco will win?" the expert had said. "No. It's not true." If "It's true" is something like "It's in the bag," then "It's not true" is certainly not its contradictory here. "It's not true" does not amount to "it's not in the bag," but rather "San Francisco will not win," or even "It's in the bag that San Francisco

---

[2] Ryle suggests an illuminating comparison. "Correct" and "fulfilled" he calls valedictory or obituary epithets—like "deceased," "lamented." The use of "correct" is "more like a verdict

will not win." "It's false" seems a less likely idiom, but surely would come to much the same as "It's not true."

In a different context, the expert's "It's not true" might have another meaning. Instead of being a baseball-innocent seeker after an expert's disinterested opinion, suppose that I were a bookmaker. A friendly competitor had told me that something was up with San Francisco. He said he had been tipped off by the baseball expert, who seemed to know more than an expert ought. I decide it is worth a few dollars to check the story, and indicating that I can afford to pay for information, I ask the expert, "Is it true that San Francisco will win?" Now he might well say, "No. It certainly *is not* true." This is a flat denial of the statement, "San Francisco will win," but only where this bears the force of "Some games are rigged." The question we are considering in this context is very close to "Have some games been rigged in favor of San Francisco?" and an answer to this would not be a proposition about the future. I assume that the less limiting context, the answer of the expert to the innocent, gives us something closer to what is wanted. It is more theoretical, much closer to the logician's ideal of a "prediction." But the proposition, "It is true . . . ," in that situation, does not seem to be the contradictory of "It is not true . . . " or "It is false . . . "

In standing for future events that we are concerned to prevent, the example contains a misleading bogy. It follows from "It's not true than San Francisco will win" that no matter how hard they tried they would lose. What of events about which most of us have greater anxiety? "It's true F. E. will die on December 6." What *could* we make of this confident pronouncement? I suppose this: I am in prison for a political crime, and rumors have spread that December 6 has been set as the date of my execution. Is there an "expert" in all of this;

than a description." G. Ryle, *Dilemmas,* (Cambridge, Cambridge Univ. Press, 1954), p. 20.

"True," I should imagine, is also a valedictory epithet, and it is for this reason I should suppose, that we are not prepared to say of most propositions about the future that they are true (or false). This is in effect to say certain events are in the bag—almost to pronounce in advance that they are over, run, the results in.

Rather than dispel the difficulty over the application of the law of excluded middle to future propositions (which Ryle seems sometimes to be talking about, e.g., p. 23, and at other times not, e.g., p. 29 ff.), this observation may merely localize one of its sources, the desire to say that one of the pair of obituary epithets "true" "false" applies to every proposition.

someone who can be asked? Someone with a little pity for me asks the "expert," "Is it true that . . . ?" and after looking through the records the expert says, "It's true: F. E. will die on December 6." Can't he hurry and do something? Who set the date? My befriender has asked a version of the question, "Is it true that December 6 has been set for F. E.'s death?" The reply to that is not the statement I wanted to examine. Instead, suppose a great deal of effort has been expended to get me off, and then a spokesman for my befrienders goes to the "expert," and asks, "Is it true . . . ?" and the answer is, "Yes. It's true that F. E. will die on December 6." The more nearly we get to the pure proposition about my death date, the more clearly it seems to imply that there is nothing one can do to prevent or change the outcome. The truth of a proposition about the time of my death does seem to imply it is inevitable, beyond the possibility of change. But the element of verdict, firm intention, cannot be eliminated from the example.

The fact that "It's not true that . . . " *is* close to the logician's ideal of the contradictory of "It's true that . . . " shows that the original proposition is not a prediction. "It's not true that he will die," in this situation comes close to, "No, we have no intention of putting him to death." The question of whether I may die on that date is another matter entirely. Why such a farfetched example? What other kinds of examples are there? Can't we just suppose that someone, a nextdoor neighbor, says F. E. will die on December 6? Well, try to suppose it. Someone will ask him, "Is that true?" And he will say, "Yes, it's true F. E. will die on December 6." What are we to make of that? Is my neighbor voicing his intention to kill me? That is not what we want. Suppose he predicts the exact dates and times of all kinds of things, deaths, pregnancies, accidents, winners of races, and suppose his record is perfect. He now says, "F. E. will die on December 6." He is asked, "Is it true?" and he replies, "It is true that . . . " Does that imply that my death on December 6 is not preventable? I don't think we should know what to say about this performance. It is extraordinary, even shocking. How do we accommodate this to what we say? We simply should not know what to say. Is it luck? Shall we suggest a psychiatrist to his wife? Such a thing cannot serve as an example.

Could we make the baseball expert understand the question, "I keep hearing that San Francisco will win. Is that either true or false?" Supposing we could make him understand, his answer, I guess, should be, "No." That is, the games are not rigged. Baseball is an uncertain thing: a lot depends on luck. San Francisco is certainly not so clearly superior or inferior that it is true they will win nor not true they will win. It appears we have produced a future proposition which is neither true nor false.

One might say a determined future is not implied by the proposition, "It is true San Francisco will win." It is implied by the fact that the expert asserted the proposition, that is, that the expert was presumably in a position to assert it. No one could be sure that San Francisco would win unless he knew some games were rigged or unless he knew that San Francisco was overwhelmingly superior. The fact that the speaker is an expert and speaks with confidence allows us to infer that the future is fixed. Also, one must not forget that it is a future proposition being asserted. How could one assert a future proposition without the implication that the outcome is fixed? Yet whether it is asserted or not it is either true or false. One could never say it is true or say it is false without implying the outcome is wrapped and waiting to be delivered. Still, the meaning of "It is true" is one thing, what is implied by saying it another.

I must try to isolate the question of the truth of a proposition from: (a) that which justifies one in claiming a proposition is true, that is, the knowledge that a proposition is true, and also from (b) the conditions in which one could say a proposition is true and be understood.

First (a). A proposition (any proposition) is true or false and this has nothing to do with whether anyone knows it is or learns that it is true or false. Something can be so, say there is a marble in the deposit box, although no one has found it out. The police investigators have X-rayed a murdered man's deposit box. The pictures show there is a marble in it. "I am quite sure it is a marble with an American flag in the middle, but no one has as yet found this out." I know the murdered man was an ardent collector of this one type of marble. He had a real "thing" on marbles with American flags: he scorned any other kind. He was very secretive about his collection, and I may well be the only person he ever told. I am sure he would not keep—certainly not in his deposit box—any other kind of marble.

Could I in some parallel way know that a proposition was true or false although no one knows that it is true or knows that it is false? I knew the marble was one with an American flag because I knew something general, "This man collects only one type," or in logicians' idiom, "All the marbles in this man's collection have American flags." I could know that a proposition was true or false only by knowing the right generality : in this case it must be "Every proposition is either true or false." But the status of this law is precisely what I am trying to understand, hence I cannot invoke it.

Perhaps I once got a look in the box, a look at the valued marble. This is really what I must have been thinking of. How do I know a proposition is true or false although no one has found out which? I was thinking of taking a quick secret look or maybe not quite that much, but thinking something was there and I *could* take a quick look. Just a few hours before his death, the man showed me his prize marble locked in the deposit box. The police are puzzled by the X-ray picture, and are speculating. I think, "It is a marble with an American flag but no one has yet found this out." And the proposition about the future? "It is true that San Francisco will win the pennant although no one has found this out." But this implies that the race is rigged or in the bag.

Yes, this is the sort of circumstance in which we should say, "It is true that San Francisco will win, but no one has found this out." That is, the circumstance is this : I have inadvertently stumbled on information, or have been accidentally let in on a plot to rig some games. "No one has found out yet." But that isn't what I meant about propositions being true or false. A proposition is true (or false) although nobody knows—not even me. So I cannot say it is true although nobody knows or false although nobody knows, but only it is true or false although nobody knows. "It is true or false that San Francisco will win the pennant although nobody knows this." This is a hard one, but I have allowed it to pass before as, "It is in the bag one way or another." So it implies it is rigged or settled. Perhaps it should be, "It is true or false that San Francisco will win the pennant although nobody knows *which*." But this is no different. Presumably I know it has been rigged one way or the other : I don't know which way. Maybe I want to say, "It is true or false although no one may discover it." Again this seems to be, "It is rigged, but the plot will never be uncovered." And suppose it is discovered. I keep slipping back into the habit of excluding myself when I say "No one knows." But that is slipping back into the way we use the expression, which is merely observing the conditions for talking sense. But we want it to mean *"no* one, absolutely *no* one." Then we shall have it discovered later that San Francisco would win. No one knows now, but later we learn. When do we say, "It was true that San Francisco would win the pennant, but no one knew it"? What does this mean except that no one learned the games were rigged or that San Francisco had such a very great team? Of course the games could not have been rigged without *someone* knowing. This leaves it that we learn San Francisco had a team so overpoweringly superior that no one else had a chance. The outcome was in the bag from the beginning of the season.

(b) There remains the business of isolating the idea of the truth or falsity of a proposition from the conditions in which it is sensible to say a proposition is true, or say it is false. It is hard to keep this topic separated from (a) because one of the conditions which gives point to someone's saying that something is true (or false) is that he has found out or discovered that it is true (or false). And I am somehow to learn that propositions are (all of them) true or false— independently of the conditions which would lead anyone to say so. A man, Hobart, can learn there are geraniums in the park without realizing the conditions for saying or asserting that there are. He can simply go for a walk, full of childlike curiosity and notice the flowers there. He may have a general interest in flowers. The presence of geraniums in the park is an unremarkable thing. It makes no occasion for saying, "There are," or, "I noticed there are." Of course slightly different circumstances would give him occasion for saying or writing this. He might be looking for material to express the tedium of his life. It remains that he *can* find out or discover there are geraniums without being in a situation where it would make sense to say so.

Can one learn it is *true* there are geraniums in the park without realizing the conditions for saying so? What does Hobart do to learn it is true there are geraniums there? Say geraniums cannot be grown in this part of the country. Perhaps someone, Mervin, says "I hear the park board has been wasting our money planting geraniums in the park. Hobart goes for a walk, and learns it is true (or false). Except that Mervin may not be present, Hobart is in the proper situation to say, "It's true, there are geraniums there in the park." Anyway, he thinks this. The problem is to establish that propositions are true or false—without regard to whether it makes sense to say they are true (or false).

It appears I could not learn that a proposition is true (or false) without being in a position to say so.

However there are other conditions for saying "It is true (or false)." The conditions may come up long after the discovery. Hobart may have taken his uninteresting walk, noticed the geraniums, and not have found anything to remark about. Later, however, it develops that a gardener was paid to remove the geraniums by a certain date, a date earlier than Hobart's walk. And he is called to testify against the gardener. "Is it true," he will be asked, "that there were geraniums in the park?" And he will say, "It is true. I noticed it on a walk." Now suppose such subsequent conditions arise for a proposition about the future. Hobart finds out that San Francisco will win the pennant and thinks it an unremarkable thing. Later an investigation is made and he is called to testify. What did he find out when he learned the truth of the proposition except that the games had been rigged, the outcome fixed? What investigation could it be except one into corruption in baseball? Hobart, I presume, was such a calloused fellow that he thought all athletic organizations corrupt.

But when he testified that it was true San Francisco would win, that he had found this out, did he *say* the games were rigged? Isn't the truth one thing and the rigged games quite another? Well, suppose they are. How else could it be true? Why am I having so much difficulty getting these two things separated? Because it is a question of what it *means* to say, "A proposition is true or false, without anyone being in a position to say it is true (or false)." I do not know how to find out what this means except to imagine circumstances in which it, or something like it, would be said. Hobart will say, "It was true, although at the time I didn't think it worth mentioning," and he will be taken as implying that it was rigged. He cannot say the one without dragging in the other.

The meaning of "It is true" is one thing; what justifies the assertion or makes the assertion sensible are other things. One may say, "I am very hot" implying "Please turn on the fan," but "I am hot" does not mean "Turn on the fan." We know it does not mean this because one may also say, "I am hot" where it does not imply that one would like the fan started. So we can see that expressing the desire to have the fan started is not always associated with "I am hot." "The outcome is in the bag" is always associated with assertions of the truth of future propositions. But not all propositions are future. Propositions about past events may be asserted without implying that they are in the bag, not subject to change regardless of what anybody does.

Looking back upon the events, what sense would it make to say that the Allied defeat of Japan is in the bag, or that the Giant victory in the World Series of 1958 is in the bag? We do say of past things that you cannot change them: "You cannot change the past." The manager of a team holds himself responsible for the loss of an important game. He broods on it. We might say to him, "You can't change the outcome." "There is nothing you can do to alter the result." In the case of events yet to come, there are things one can think of doing, there are things one might try in order to change the outcome. For past occurrences, there is nothing similar to think of. What would it mean to try, to put forth all your effort? It would mean something different. "I can change the outcome a little if I try hard enough" means I can repair some of the damage, make amends, alter the future consequences so they will be easier to live with. "It's true,[3] your team lost the important game, but there is nothing you can do to change the result." If what is said to be true is true, I need not accept the implication that there is nothing I can do.

The meaning of "It is true" will be what is common to all uses. And what is that? What is common to statements about the truth of past occurrences, lives, epochs, present events and happenings, and future outcomes, efforts and changes? What can one answer? "These are the settled things, the things you can bet on, the things you will not have to change your mind about." What can one say? There is an attitude appropriate to all. This is another way of putting the fear about the law of excluded middle. It incorporates the same attitude toward the future as toward the past. These are the things, the truths, we must accept and live with, though we might wish them otherwise. As soon as one loses sight of the details, any formula is misleading.

We say other sorts of things are true: political slogans, theological creeds, moral dicta. It may be that what is common to all assertions of truth is that they are declarations of assurance, issues of guarantees. It is more likely that nothing is common to all. What of that? How does one find "the meaning" so that it is quite clear that every proposition is either true or false?

---

[3] Here is the use of "true" which some writers call "concessive." In connection with future propositions, I do not think it needs any special consideration.

One can see that the meaning of "It is true..." is one thing and "Some games are rigged" is another, because we can ask the expert who says, "It is true" for his grounds or reasons. "It is true" is not an answer to this question, but "Some games are rigged" is. "Is it true?" is one thing, "Why are you so sure?" another. So, "It's true" is one thing, "Some games are rigged" quite a different thing. And what are you going to say is the meaning of "It's true"? One says "it's true" as an assurance or guarantee. But one cannot be in a position to assure or guarantee a future outcome like the National League Pennant unless he has grounds or reasons of just the troublesome kind, games are rigged, one team is uncontestably superior. Suppose he cannot answer the second question, "Why are you so sure?" He says, "Oh, I don't know. That's just the way I feel." Can you understand his saying that it is true? "It's true" is supposed to give a guarantee.

Suppose we run across a man who says "It's true..." about all sorts of things we ask him concerning the future. "It's true that Early Wynn will announce his resignation on August 3." "It's true that Allen Carney will give up smoking on October 22." In answer to, "How can you be so certain?" he always says, "That's the way I feel." Of course he will always or almost always be wrong. But suppose this does not change his behavior one bit. He continues about all sorts of future things saying, "It's true this...," and "It's true that..." Surely after a while we might say, "He's misusing the word 'true,'" or, "He doesn't understand the meaning of the phrase 'it's true.'" Perhaps we might say, "He must be using the phrase 'it's true...' in some peculiar way of his own. Maybe he wants us to figure it out." This is such an untoward example I do not feel very safe with it. Perhaps we might say instead, "He has a funny idea of truth." The first things suggest a difference in meaning. The latter suggests a radical difference in grounds. But the fact that we could say the first things at all— and be understood—seems to indicate that the meaning of "true" is very closely tied to grounds.

Oh yes, but suppose that he was always right. Well, try to suppose it. What could one say? I have already considered this case, that is, eliminated it as no case at all. But isn't this merely a contingent matter? Couldn't it be otherwise? Well, I suppose the language we speak is also a contingent matter then. "It's true" could mean "You can bet it's a silly thing."

In view of all this, there are doubtless many important propositions about the future which we shall want to say (with caution) are neither true nor false. Well, then, all this fuss is merely a question of terminology. There is a quick way out: we shall say that only what is either true or false is to count as a proposition. Such a proposal merely shifts the location of the problem. By this pronouncement, the field where logic can be applied is drastically and arbitrarily reduced. Much we can assert, believe, many things we can employ as premises or conclusions will not, by this fiat, be counted as propositions.

What we assert, the usual doctrine goes, is a proposition. And it is the proposition that is either true or false. All propositions are either true or false. And so future propositions *are* true or false. They are not made to be true or false by things that happen later, nor do they come to be true when something happens that has not yet happened. But the confident assertion of a future proposition does seem to imply that the future is outside our powers. Propositions may also be believed, denied, thought, doubted, considered. Suppose we believe a proposition about the future. "I believe that Clinton Holmes will win the Democratic primary." Then Clinton Holmes does win the primary. Can I now say, "What I believed was true"? If so, it does look like the proposition, that is, what I believed, was true before the election. "What I believed was true" is a rather unlikely idiom and difficult to assess. Some background is needed. No one else thought Clinton Holmes had a chance. But I knew from experience the strange hold he gets on people as they see and hear him often. I knew he would campaign hard, and I believed that before the campaign was over many people would be won over. "What I believed was true." Does this show that true propositions about the future do not wait in time for their truth to be determined by events? I might also have said, "What I believed turned out to be true." This would suggest the opposite, that propositions wait for time to decide their truth. It would not be difficult for someone with a doctrine to defend to choose whichever of these fit his doctrine and then use it as a basis for interpreting the other. "Was true" might be short for "turned out to be true"; "turned out to be true" is a way of mixing knowledge into the pure assertion of truth, "was true."

"What I believed was true" in this case sounds much like "I told you so all the time." In order to make this idiom sound right, one needs to fit it in a case where a belief is held against the majority. The expression is used to call attention to evidence which the speaker noticed or took seriously, evidence which was neglected or misinterpreted by others. "Turned out to be true" would be the natural expression where the belief was more a hunch. It is much less self-congratulatory.

Suppose that instead I doubted that Clinton Holmes would be elected; and then he was elected by a great majority. Should I say, "What I doubted was true," or "What I doubted turned out to be true"? As always, we need some background. Say the experts all believed Holmes's election was a cinch, and I doubted because I knew that Holmes's objectionable traits only came out when he was under pressure, and it looked like there would be a hard and nasty campaign. "What I doubted was true." "What I doubted, namely, that he would be elected, was true." Still, this does not sound right. If anything of the kind is to be said, "What I doubted turned out to be true" would be the thing.

Well, suppose there was overwhelming evidence that Clinton Holmes would win, and because of personal prejudice against him, I simply ignored it or read it off. What then, when he is elected? "What I doubted—that Clinton Holmes would be elected—was true," now sounds in place. And why? Isn't it because I now realize that his election was in the bag, and I refused to see it? Just as "What I believed was true" is self-congratulatory, "What I doubted was true" is self-rebuke. But there is more. "What I doubted was true" fits only where what was doubted was in the bag, where the outcome was definite, past the possibility of anyone bringing about a change. "What I doubted turned out to be true" is less harsh. Is it because this locution is used when one does not willingly acknowledge that the outcome was already determined?

When we take as the mark of a proposition what is believed or what is doubted, we seem again to get the result that we say a future proposition is true only where the events it refers to are determined and in the bag. If that which is believed or doubted is what is always either true or false, it is not surprising that some have felt this implies that the future is in wraps and that it is too late for efforts for or against what is to come.

According to the traditional logical (and metaphysical?) doctrine, another reason I have been going wrong is that I have been considering the truth and falsity of predictions, doubts about future happenings, and other things which are expressed with future tense verbs. A proposition, that which is always either true or false, may be about the future, and it may be believed or asserted or doubted. But the future tense comes in because of the time of the belief or doubt relative to the event described. The proposition itself has no time relative to the event it refers to. Its truth or falsity, so the doctrine goes, is not *at* a time. Neither does it await upon a time. Propositions are true or false, timelessly. Hence, the pure proposition would be expressed tenselessly. Where should we look for anything like a tenseless expression? Suppose that the decisive game between two very equally matched teams is to be played one week from today. A newspaper wishes to have its headline ready in advance. So it prepares both: "Mud-cats win," "Mud-cats lose." No informed person will predict a winner. Isn't one of the headlines of necessity true? One (and only one) will be used. Being used is something that will happen in the future. The truth of a proposition is not to await the future. Suppose someone picks out one of the headlines and says, "That's the one we shall use." Then what he says implies that the outcome of the game is sure. And if the outcome of the game is sure, then what he says is true. But what of the truth of the headline? Would he also say, "That one is true"? I think he would not. Consider carefully looking at the two headlines: (1) "Mud-cats win," (2) "Mud-cats lose." The game is a week away. I am convinced with good reason that the Mud-cats *will* win. I think it is a cinch. Shall I point to (1) and say, "That one is true"? I think not, and I think the reason I should not say that is precisely that the headline reports the outcome of a game which has not been played.

Such a headline is not a tenseless report. It is a past tense report even when prepared well in advance of its use. It is for this reason, I think, that I should not say of a headline prepared in advance of its use that it is true. There cannot be a true report of the outcome of a future game, although there can be a true prediction," The Mud-cats will win." That, if you like, is a report of a result to come. There can be no report of a future result which has come, because the result has not yet come.

So, advance headlines will not do as examples of tenseless expressions of propositions. We can try to force what is allowable in the function of the tense into a date, for example, "The fishing ship, *Maybelle,* sinks with three aboard

December 2, 1966 at 8:15 p.m. PST." How are we to take expressions like this if not in the same way as headlines? Suppose such sentences were produced by a machine and they always turned out to be right. The machine's perform- ance is not in any way limited in time. It produces sentences about the distant past, and distant future as well as the present and the immediate future, and it is always right, or turns out to be right. Are its sentences tenseless? Are they true? Who knows what to say about machines?

The practice of older logicians suggests that timeless propositions are to be expressed by using the verb "to be" only in its copulative function, and putting everything else, including date, into the predicate. Instead of "Sandy Top will win the fifth, August 1, 1965" we should get "Sandy Top is a winner of the fifth, August 1, 1965." This is supposed to be different from "Sandy Top wins . . . " It certainly is not the form of a future headline. It does not have any use at all that I can think of; but the idea is to suggest that "winner of the fifth . . . " is a predicate of Sandy Top. This immediately suggests all the wrong sort of thing. When we say a horse is a winner, we are predicting the outcomes of his future races. If we are to think of this and try to characterize a horse in this way as winner of a certain race, it sounds as if we were saying that the outcome of a certain race were in him now, as if the future were already lying hidden in the present. This is not the way to a timeless proposition. But I have been pursuing a wild suggestion. The fact is the words seem to have no use at all.

I am unable to suggest anything further by way of interpretation of the doc- trine of timeless truth. I am overcome by a sense of strangeness that it should have been ushered in to explain or to defend something which is supposed to be self-evident, uncontroversial, "trivially true," uninformative.

XI

OUR KNOWLEDGE OF THE FUTURE WORLD

When you come to think of it, it is easy to be sympathetic with those old philosophers, like Bergson, who "took time seriously." They are revolted by a certain picture of time: time as represented by a straight line, one direction going to the past, the other to the future. The present is a point on the line. The only difference between past and future is in the relation each bears to the present. There are many ways of elaborating this simple picture. A very tempting one is this: we can imagine the line having a great hidden complexity. If the line were magnified, we could see it is made up of many lines, some very short, some very long, overlapping, like the strands in a thick yarn. Each of these is an event, occurrence, happening—the things which make up time. They take place in time or during greater or lesser lengths of time.[1]

Without worrying about the details, it is easy to get into revolt against this picture: mainly one has to think a little about the way it represents the future. We are led to think that our progress into the future is like the exploration of a cave. We go on and on, deeper and deeper. The cave lies waiting to be explored. We know more or less what to expect around the next corner, but we are often surprised. In any case it has never been explored before and our eyes are the first to see the mammoth rooms and narrow passageways. Here is the trouble. We *are* the first to see: we are the explorers. This dawn is a new day to us. But we need not have been the first. Perhaps many centuries ago some primitive people explored the entire depths of the cavern, and any tracks they left have been erased. We didn't think the future had been entered before; but by the straight line representation of time, there is no reason why it could not have been. We are always told by orthodox theologians something to the effect

[1] I deal with some of these details in Essay VII, "The Precarious Reality of the Past."

that God has explored every nook and cranny: He knows every little detail. Now it is easy to join in Bergson's revolt. We are talking of the future. The future *could* not be like that. I have never seen the corridor which now opens before me. "My seeing this corridor" is not something which could have been waiting in the corridor. If someone else has seen it, he is not I, his reactions are not mine. My present amazement and delight could not have occurred before. This day could not have dawned before.

I am trying to think out the straight-line picture of time. In order to get the idea that the future and the past are alike, that is, that they are segments of a straight line, I imagine the future like a cave waiting to be discovered. Is that so wrong? In one respect at least it is, because my exploration of the cave, my discoveries, my mishaps, and amazements are to be part of the future, and thus they are to be part of the cave waiting for time to turn them up. Did I have that in mind when I thought of the straight line? My exploration of the cave is itself like a cave, waiting, ready to be explored. My discovery of the cave is itself a cave waiting to be discovered. Of course this is ridiculous. Is it just because I have represented the passage of time in terms of discovery and exploration? My surprises are to be represented as waiting for time. How can a thing wait unless it already exists? But we do say, "The future waits . . . "[2] So we do. That is precisely what I have to say: "My future surprises wait . . . " Now I can put my revolt in more general form. *No* future surprise or discovery of mine could be waiting for time to turn it up. Why? Because if my discovery of something waits to be turned up, then I have already made the discovery and it does not wait to be turned up. Suppose that tomorrow I am going to discover a new theorem in number theory. There is the theorem waiting for my discovery, and the event, my discovery of it—both waiting. Then my discovery of the theorem is waiting. All right, so it is. But there is not another event, my discovery of my discovery. The discovery is waiting and it turns up (or will turn up) but it does not (cannot) turn up in the form of a discovery. Still, a discovery that is waiting has already been made. If I know I am going to discover a certain theorem, then I have already discovered it. The point I am trying to make does not turn on *my* knowledge. If *somebody* (anybody else) knows I am going to discover a certain theorem, then *I* am not going to discover it. The person who knows

2 Of course this idiom works the wrong way.

has already made the discovery.[3] A person who knows me, but does not know much about number theory may know I am going to discover some theorem. He knows the way I work and live; he knows all the signs; he knows what I have been working on. But he can't know exactly what theorem I am going to discover, or he would himself have already discovered exactly that theorem. I may know myself that I am going to discover a new theorem tomorrow; I know the signs better than anyone. "Tomorrow I shall come up with an interesting theorem about the squares of primes. I just know it." But I couldn't know what theorem or I should already have made the discovery.

The point must not turn on knowledge. If I am to discover a theorem tomorrow, it does not follow that anyone knows it. But it must be *knowable,* surely. If something is waiting, doesn't it follow that someone *could* know that it is waiting? If there is a silver dollar hidden in my desk drawer doesn't it follow that someone could know there is a silver dollar in my drawer? If my discovery of a theorem is waiting, doesn't it follow that someone could know of the discovery? I am compelled to reason: no one *could* know of the discovery, therefore it cannot be waiting.

If there is a dollar in my drawer, does it follow that someone could know? Suppose I have taken every precaution. I put it there when the blinds were drawn. I shut the door, blocked the keyhole, and made certain there were no cracks, hidden cameras, or any such. "No one could know that I have a silver dollar hidden in my drawer." Now someone I meet on the street (his name is Duncan) says to me, "I know you have a silver dollar hidden in your desk drawer." "You couldn't know that: nobody could." "But I do," Duncan says. And where should we expect the discussion to go from here? He could tell how he watched me hide the coin, he watched through a hole in the ceiling behind the chandelier. So, I was simply wrong in thinking that no one could know. If Duncan has no such account to give, but persists in saying that he knows, I shall deny him. He is making some kind of strange wild guess. Or, he

---

[3] "The finished portrait is explained by the features of the model, by the nature of the artist, by the colors spread out on the palette; but even with the knowledge of what explains it, no one, not even the artist, could have foreseen exactly what the portrait would be, for to predict it would have been to produce it before it was produced—an absurd hypothesis which is its own refutation." H. Bergson, *Creative Evolution,* (New York, The Modern Library, Random House), 1941, p. 9.

is pulling my leg. "He couldn't know. He doesn't." Suppose he becomes solemn, doesn't understand why I do not take him seriously. He insists on going to my desk with me and pointing out that I have a silver dollar in the rear left corner—just where he said that he knew I had one. Yet he cannot say how he learned; he does not show any of my precautions inadequate, or all of them together insufficient. Does Duncan know? Surely this is a case where one doesn't know quite what to say. If his performances of this sort were regular and reliable, we might say, "He knows." At the same time, however, we should say, "He seems to know." I did not originally think of "knowing" and "seeming to know" coming to the same thing. Of course they do not come to the same thing: it's just that in this sort of case we should say either. But we shouldn't say either unless all the details were understood, or we were going to detail them.

I shouldn't think, while philosophizing, that we should want to call this a case of knowledge. If not, then it doesn't follow that because something is there it is possible for someone to know it. If I take all precautions I am correct in saying, "No one could possibly know." The only way anyone could show that I was never correct in saying this would be by maintaining that I couldn't possibly take all precautions. That would be silly.

If I put the coin there it follows that *I* could know. Is that right? I could forget, and then when questioned I could remember—perhaps hesitantly first, and then with complete confidence. I might say, "Yes, I know there is a silver dollar there." That is a situation in which I should know. Of course if I had forgotten and simply could not remember, then even when it was revealed, I should have to say, "I didn't know there was a silver dollar there." I don't need to say it follows that because it was there I should *always* know. I need only say it follows that someone *could* know. At the time I put it there, I know. And if I know then I *could* know. I might know and also it might be true that I could know, but why should I think the second follows from the first? If shortly after I hide the dollar someone needs a silver dollar very badly, I might say, "I have one in my drawer." If he is frantic and says several people have told him the same thing but were not able to produce the dollars, I can imagine saying, "I know I have one . . . ," "I assure you . . . I positively know it."

I am out of the country on a long voyage, and I give my desk and all its contents to Davis before I leave. He loses the key. A discussion arises about whether there is a silver dollar in my drawer. Davis is a fevered collector of silver dollars, you know. If there is a dollar there he will break open the desk. If not, he will not want to harm the desk. Someone says "Before acting let's write Frank, he might know" or, "He's likely to know." "As careless and disorganized as Frank is, he might know whether there is a dollar in his desk drawer." "Let's ask Frank's friend Miles. Possibly he knows."

Here is an example of my knowing, and another of my being likely to know, and of someone possibly knowing. How does anything like the second follow from anything like the first?

In any case, the question of whether I know or could know is not important. It is a peculiarity of the example. What was there was a silver dollar which I had put there. I imagine instead something "there" which I had nothing to do with. Suppose there is a rock in the shape of a man's head in one of the craters on an undiscovered satellite of Jupiter. It is there. Does it follow that someone could know it is there? Surely not. "No one could know whether such a thing is there or not." Return to our man, Duncan, who said he knew there was a dollar in my drawer but had no way of finding out. Suppose he says he knows there is such a rock on such a satellite of Jupiter. What do we say? I don't know. He might be right about this as he has been about so many things. We might say, "He might know"—that is, we might say that to someone who was familiar with all he can do. Is this a case of "possibly knowing"? Even if it is, does it follow that because something is there, someone could possibly know in this way? I should think not, since one cannot say what could and could not possibly be known in this way. When any question comes up, is it fitting to say, "Ask Duncan. Possibly he knows" (that is, he might do what he has so often done)?

I am not voicing my rejection of the straight-line picture of time as clearly as I had hoped. What I really want to say is this: if a thing is there it follows that we can imagine someone knowing it. Not that either. I really want to say: if a thing is there, we can make sense out of a story about someone knowing it. I don't mean that if something is to take place in the future, we can make sense out of a story about someone knowing it in the future: I mean we can make sense out of a story about someone knowing it now. A caterpillar is chewing the leaves on an apple tree. Sometime during the next week or so it will march down the trunk, and go seek an appropriate place to pupate. Can we imagine a sufficiently informed entomologist predicting the exact time it will begin the march and the exact route of its march? Can we understand how entomologists could get such knowledge of the future? Even that would not be enough. The knowledge must be complete: it must cover every minute detail. The entomologist must be able to predict the exact position of every hair on the caterpillar at every moment in the march. Some have assured us that they can understand such an eventuality. Yet even that is not enough. The same sort of predictions for millions of caterpillars, millions of years from now must be within reach of the same techniques. And not only the marches of caterpillars, but every track of every sandpiper on every mud flat for all time to come, every word of every future philosopher, and much, much more.

What sort of story about knowledge could I tell that would clearly apply to *any* future event or occurrence—any at all? It is there to be known. For any piece of it at all, I must be able to understand a story about someone knowing it. The only story I can think of is this. A man has some sort of television set which brings in pictures from a future time. Pictures of the future? Pictures of things that have not yet come to be? "Here is a picture of a building to be built in 1990." "You mean this is an architect's drawing?" "No, it is a picture of the actual building. And here are pictures of the building in various stages of construction." "Oh? Are people actually at work on it now?" "No, work will not start until 1988." Are we going to make sense of this story?

But you see, time is a straight line. Going into the future is like exploring a cave. We need not actually go round the bend to discover what is there. We could send out cameras on motor-driven dollies, we could push forward long telescopes which bend around the corners and had prisms arranged to fall in place at all the proper places. So that these instruments could work in the dark, we could launch lights on balloons and blow them ahead of us with giant fans. If going into the future is like that, then we ought to be able to send out lights and poke telescopes into the future. What I am trying to say is this: If you succeed in finding out about the future, it isn't future, it's now, it's present. If you get a picture on your screen, then it's happening now—or it has happened and you are watching a film or tape. If it's something you see through your telescope, then it's something going on right now.

You invite me to look through your new telescope. It appears to have a large prismatic erecting system: it looks like a periscopic telescope. I look, and I see a cow giving birth to an albino calf. "Where is that?" "It's Jones's cow. You see, it's Jones standing beside her." "That's remarkable. Let's go over and see the calf." "We can't. You were looking at a day next month. The calf isn't born yet. It will be born in exactly 27 days. I have learned that when my telescope is focused in this position it is exactly 27 days ahead of time. In other positions, it sees other dates."

So many strange things are here, one doesn't know where to begin thinking about them. Suppose you see in the telescope your most trusted neighbor jimmy your lock, enter, and steal from your house. Will you change the lock before it happens? Suppose the man with the future-telescope says, "No, I have been watching your door continuously for twenty-seven days, and you will not change it." What shall I do? What shall I think of my neighbor who is going to enter my house and steal from me? I have been working for weeks, off and on, trying to finish a crossword puzzle. I see myself in the future-telescope filling in the long-sought word. Why, then, shouldn't I fill it in now and get the puzzle finished? Don't I know the missing word? I saw myself put it in: I saw what it was. I can't suddenly think of the word in twenty-seven days. Having seen the future, I've though of the word already.

Cameras and telescopes aimed at the future are hard to think about. Does the straigt-line picture of time really require that we make sense of such things? The future is "there." There is no difference in kind between past and future. What do all these things come to? If not telescopes and cameras, then in some other ways we might have knowledge of the future because it is there to be known. After all we do know things about the future. Whatever means we have for gaining such knowledge, can't we imagine them extended or expanded indefinitely so that anything about the future *could* be known? It is not by any means clear that any such possibility as this follows from the straight-line picture of time. We know some things about the future by observing regularities. It certainly doesn't follow from the straight-line picture of time that it is possible to learn everything—absolutely everything—about the future by observing regularities. Neither does it follow that we can make good sense out of a story about learning everything of the future through observing regularities.

I must have felt it did follow, that is, I must have felt that one could infer from the straight-line picture that everything is foreseeable or predictable. The line representation of time has likely become contaminated in my mind. Like Bergson, I was not thinking of *just* the straight-line representation of time. I was always thinking of it as part of a syndrome of metaphysical beliefs of which "complete predictability" is another.[4] The straight-line picture certainly does seem to fit well with the idea that the future is, in principle, capable of complete prediction. If the future is "there" and not intrinsically different from the past, then, at any rate, nothing about the nature of time will rule out the possibility of complete foresight or prediction.

This idea is just as repelling as the cave-representation: the future cannot be like that. It is not possible for anyone to predict *in complete detail* what any part of the future will bring. If anyone knew every single detailed feature of a future event, it would not be future: it would be present.[5] Why do I think that? A storm rages from the south through the valley and then dissipates across the mountain crests. "I predicted the course of the storm through the valley in complete detail." I wasn't thinking of that sort of thing at all.

I was thinking of some "lesser event," say the furious shaking of the leaves on my cottonwood tree just before it went over in the wind. Is that an event? The silver poplar leaves shaking? It is something that happened, that is, the poplar leaves shook in the storm. Had the question come up, I could have predicted that the leaves would shake furiously in the storm. Yes, of course; but I want to say I could not have predicted the complete details, that is, I could not have predicted just exactly the way those poplar leaves would twirl

[4] "The essence of mechanical explanation, in fact, is to regard the future and the past as calculable functions of the present, and thus to claim that *all is given*. On this hypothesis, past, present and future would be open at a glance to a superhuman intellect capable of making the calculation." Bergson, *op. cit.*, p. 43.

[5] "... to foresee consists in projecting into the future what have been perceived in the past, or of imagining for a later time a new grouping, in a new order, of elements already perceived. But that which has never been perceived, and which is at the same time simple, is necessarily unforeseeable." *Ibid.*, pp. 8-9.

in that great wind. What do I have in mind here? I could not have predicted just how those twirling silvery leaves would *look* in the eerie light of that storm. How they looked is not an event, not something that happened. It did happen that the leaves shook. I am thinking that how they looked would be part of a description of what happened. ("They shook fiercely, and looked silvery.")

I seem to be slipping into the idea that one can never know exactly how a thing is unless he sees it. So one can never know all the details of something in the future unless he sees it. And one cannot see something in the future; rather, if one sees something it is not future, but present. If there had been any reason for it, I could have predicted how the leaves would look in the storm. I feel somehow that the prediction could not have been complete. It could not have included everything: not exactly how queer that light was, not exactly the tenacity with which the leaves clung to the tree while whirling madly. What am I to say? "Of course it could not"? And why? Because one cannot know these things without being there, without seeing them for himself? "One who was not there can never know how eerie it was." Of course that sort of thing cannot be predicted, but who thought it could be? Yet having lived through more than a few such storms, I could have predicted exactly how it would look.

In saying of that sort of thing that it cannot be predicted, I am tempted to use the wrong tone of voice. Isn't it like this: it cannot be predicted in the way one cannot know another's pain, or in the way one cannot know how salt tastes on another's tongue? I am trying to lay this on well-covered philosophical ground. In these cases we think in terms of a digram too: a circle represents the mind of another, and in that circle an x and a y, representing his toothache and the taste of salt on his tongue. Now I cannot know what is in the circle, I go on, because I can't get in the circle, or rather, on the circle. My mind, too, is a circle. We cannot attach sense to the idea of this circle and that circle being brought into perfect coincidence. I have an x and a y of my own and they are not the same as his. My pain is mine, his is his. When both of us taste salt, there are two tastes. I try to imagine what would bring about coincidence: it would not result even from the complete fusion of his nervous system and mine. I have tried to read those sentences, namely, "I cannot know another's pain," "I cannot know how salt tastes on another's tongue," or some related sentences in terms of the diagram of circles. Yet in the proper circumstances, I do know another's pain ("Do I know how it feels? I've had that same pain for years"). I do know how salt tastes. ("I see what you mean. That's the saltiest salt I've ever tasted.") In other circumstances, I say that such a tough and well-adjusted person could never understand my pain. A winetaster tells me that I cannot be expected to taste the tinge of salt in the sample of port.

The "smaller event" I really wanted was how someone—perhaps I—felt. The thing whose predictability I wanted to rule out was the way I felt as the storm leveled my barn. I was afraid for awhile, and sad for a longer while, and I had that sinking in my stomach from helpless distress. How is that an event? ("The event of my feeling fear and sadness . . .") It is not even something that happened. "What happened?" "F. E. felt afraid and sad." That could go along with "nothing happened." It is not necessary that what I am talking about here be an event or occurrence; it need not have taken place or have happened. I can dispense with the idea that time is made up of events. My feeling after the storm's destruction need not be an event *in* time; it is enough that it *had* a time. I did feel fear and sadness at a certain time and for a certain time. One who predicted the storm might have predicted that my barn would not survive. Knowing me and knowing my habits he might have predicted that I should be in the house watching at the window, and he might have predicted how I should feel at the sight of my barn toppled by the wind. I feel impelled to say, "He could not have predicted exactly how I felt. Even I could not have done that. How it will feel to lose almost everything in a brief fit of nature's; no one can know how it will feel until it happens." At last I am in a position to say, "If anyone knows how it feels, it is not something that is going to happen, it is something happening (or it did already happen)." "I think I have drawn a line now between present and future, and then thought, or almost thought, "I cannot bring a thing on one side of the line into coincidence with something on the other," or "If two things are in coincidence, they are not on opposite sides of the line." Suppose I had just lost my new building in a fearsome storm. Someone says, "I knew in advance how you would feel as your fine new barn went down." What kind of remark is that? Suppose the speaker was a prying and conceited neighbor, one who took pride in his great knowledge and understanding of people. His theoretical interest in people's problems is mostly pretense, claimed so that he does not have to acknowledge his nosiness. He says, "I knew in advance how you would feel." This is more than I can bear. Is he trying to express sympathy? Suppose I reply, "No one—not even I—could have known how I felt." I am rounding on him for his conceited, feeble effort at sympathy. I am exasperated by his pretense at understanding. Surely I am not impugning his— or my—powers of prediction. Another neighbor, a dear friend, says, "I have been through these storms with big losses myself, and when I saw it coming, I was afraid for you. I knew how you would feel." If a good friend had said that, why should I want to reject it?

It sounds as though I am trying to make the point turn on, "I cannot know how a thing looks without seeing it," or, "I cannot have an experience until I have it." I want these to be profound, and they are profound because I once thought something which I thought denied them; and when they are placed right they cannot be denied. "You cannot know how a thing looks until you see it." That might be biting advice to an aesthetic pretender that the only thing that counts is seeing the paintings. "Put away the books, cut out the prattle, and go look." "You cannot have an experience without having it." A mother says this to her teenage son who is all talk and theory about marriage and child-raising. Such sayings are not to be denied, and of course I did not believe any straight-line theory of time which does deny them. Or did I?

BORDERLANDS

OF METAPHYSICS

XII

WHETHER EXISTENCE IS A PREDICATE

The formula "existence is not a predicate" in one form or another has been chanted over the ontological proof for God since the origination of that argument in the eleventh century. It has had typical success: to many seeming a deadly refutation, to others totally without point. Although the philosophical doctrine was invented as a weapon against the ontological argument, it has been expounded and explained as if it were a singular truth that could easily be understood on its own right. Without regard to its intended target, therefore, I should like to inquire a little into its meaning.

The dictum "existence is not a predicate" is unfortunate, but not in a serious way. No one has wished to deny the obvious linguistic fact that "exists" is often a grammatical predicate. What is intended is that "exists" is not a "logical predicate." The difficulty in understanding the doctrine goes deeper than trouble with terminology. "Logical predicate," one must understand, is a big category. It is explained as including "properties," "attributes," "relations." All of these terms are used in special philosophical senses. For example, in this sense of "property" one may ask what property all red things have, and one acceptable answer is that they all have the property of being red. Supposedly, to say of a subject, any kind of subject, that it exists is not to characterize, describe, determine, define, or give information of any kind about the subject or its connections with any other entities of any kind. "Exists" is held to play a radically different role. The distinction is often expressed in this way: to say *what* a thing is is completely different from saying *that* a thing is. On one version of the doctrine, the word "exists" or any of its synonyms would disappear in a logically perspicuous rewriting of a sentence. Its place would come to be occupied by the phrase "it is true for at least one instance" or some such. I find these things difficult to understand. I shall proceed on the principle that the only way to understand a philosophical doctrine is to look closely at some of the systematic explanations and elaborations with which it is presented and surrounded.

The simplest way the thesis is developed goes something like this. One uses predicates in ascribing properties or giving the characteristics of a thing. Consider the desk I am writing on. What are its characteristics? It is thirty inches high, has four drawers; it is light mahogany, and has a heavily varnished top. What of its existence? I say it has brass knobs on the drawers: that is a characteristic. To say it exists is something quite different. If I say it exists I am not characterizing it; I am saying that something is here to be characterized. If it did not exist, there would be nothing to have brass knobs, nothing to have properties at all.

Does this show that existence is not a predicate? We are to imagine, I suppose, that our attention is fixed on some thing, say an orange, right before our eyes. And we are to characterize it. Perhaps I am to imagine that I am describing it. I come from a country where there are no oranges. I have come to California from a distant northern country; I have seen and eaten my first orange. Now I write home, looking at an orange on the desk right in front of me. I write, "It is a delicious, sweet, and juicy fruit. The one I have here is four inches in diameter . . . " Am I going to write, "The orange exists," or anything like that? "It is delicious and it exists" is supposed to be a ridiculous conjunction. One cannot pair existence with a proper predicate.

Isn't that only because of the situation in which I imagine myself to be characterizing the orange? Suppose that in my home town all we had heard of oranges was what a well-known teller of tall tales had said. Now I might write and say, "The fabulous orange we heard so much about exists." I might well write, "It is delicious and it exists. I try to reproduce the reasoning which shows that "exists" cannot be used to characterize a thing. In order to do that I have to think of characterizing a thing where there could be no question of its existence and, hence, no point in saying it exists. In other situations we use "exists" of a thing right along with and in the same manner as characterizing verbs and adjectives. One could even say of a thing that it exists while looking right at it. Suppose someone from the land of no oranges had joined me in California.

I bring an orange to him and say, "There now, you can see it exists and it is delicious."

What does this consideration show? The only conclusion I can think of is this: To say that something exists and be understood requires a special kind of background. It seems it may be said only to counter an assertion or to settle a doubt or question about whether something is mythical, legendary, extinct. On the other hand, one may say that something is tall, or green, or clumsy, in a much wider variety of circumstances. I may write a description of a Joshua tree standing outside my window just to let another know I am a sensitive and careful observer. I may write a description of the familiar scene in front of my house in order to communicate boredom. But in such circumstances, "The Joshua tree exists," or "The frozen grass on my lawn exists" would not be understandable. ". . . exists" presupposes belief that or doubt about whether the . . . is illusory, a fabrication, a fable thing. If this difference between "tall" or "green" and "exists" is indeed there, it is not the difference between predicate and nonpredicate.

Another method has been used to demonstrate that existence is not a predicate. It is to show that there is a radical difference between the way we think that something has a characteristic and the way we think that something exists. Apparently it is assumed that the way to see what an attribute amounts to is to look at the way we think attributions. Sometimes the explanation has been put in this way: We think things in concepts. Regardless of how completely we think a thing, how many determinations our concept has, the existence of the thing of which it is a concept is an altogether different matter. To think that a thing exists could not be to add a determination to the concept, because then my concept would be different and so have a different object. If existence were a determination, I could never think that something, say A, exists; I would always have to be thinking of something else, B, a thing differing from A by having the determination of existence.[1]

[1] "By whatever and by however many predicates we may think a thing—even if we completely determine it—we do not make the least addition to the thing when we further declare that this thing *is*. Otherwise, it would not be exactly the same thing that exists, but something more than we had thought in the concept; and we could not, therefore, say that the exact object of my concept exists." Immanuel Kant, *The Critique of Pure Reason*, tr. Norman Kemp-Smith, (New York, Macmillan, 1929), p. 505.

In order to interpret this we must try to get the idea that we think things in concepts. We have concepts *of* things. The things presumably may or may not exist. To think that something exists is to think that the concept applies to something. This in no way affects the concept. How are we to understand a concept being *of* a thing, *applying* to a thing? One way to think of animals is to use pictures. They may be more or less detailed, more or less schematic. We have a book of animal pictures with the names of the animals under each picture. Now we want to "apply" the pictures. We may go about through the zoo, book in hand, trying to find out which of the pictured animals are in the zoo. "Do they have one of these? Let's go see." We may find an animal that might be either the one on page 20 or the one on page 21. The animal looks very much like each. It has a black spot on top of the head, but neither picture shows the top of the head. We might say the pictures lack certain characteristics or determinations. A picture cannot have all the identifying characteristics. It has to be a picture of the left side or the right: the animal has to be lying down or standing up.

Suppose we have life-size models. Imagine a building at the zoo which houses hundreds of such models; the names of the animals are on the bases of the models. People look carefully at a model and then go out to see whether the zoo contains one of those animals. Suppose we show Henry the model of a raccoon and ask him to go look. He returns and says, "No. They do not have one of those. They have one just like it, but it is alive." Does this show the model was lacking a certain determination or characteristic? If so, and we gave the model of a raccoon all characteristics, we would end up with a raccoon. Then there could not be any question about the existence of a raccoon, no question whether there was one in the zoo. As soon as we looked in the model building, we should know the zoo contained a raccoon. The concept has become one with its object. Of course Henry made a mistake. The models were of living animals. A model or representation simply cannot have "all determinations" or it would cease to be a model and become a sample. The idea of "all determinations" is a queer one. Certain things simply are not possible determinations of a model, so models are lacking nothing in not having them.

Suppose we have a building full of animal models, some of legendary animals, some of imaginary, some of extinct, and some of existing animals. The problem is to go about the world and determine which of these animals exist. We start out to look for the one labeled "bandicoot" and we find one like that in India. Suppose we wished to save others the trouble and expense of going to and fro on the earth, could we give the model a determination showing the bandicoot exists? We could put an E on the back of each animal found to exist, and in time could mark most of the existing animals. However, this E is not a determination of the model; as a determination it would show the animal represented had a mark like an E on its back. E is a symbol. There was no question, I suppose, about our ability to symbolize existence. When existence is symbolized, the question would be: what kind of symbol is it?

Suppose we simply take the existence of the models as representing the existence of the animals. Then we shall not be able to represent the extinct and imaginary animals. We can simply destroy the models of the nonexistent. But if the nonexistent is not to be represented, how do we have left any representation of the existent? We are now in the position we were with the models representing living animals. As in that case it was understood that the models represented living animals, in this case it is now to be understood that they represent existing animals. (Like Parmenides we have found that what is not cannot be represented.) Existence, like "being a living animal," is not something that can be a determination on this model or that: it is what the models in their capacity as models stand for.

Existence cannot be a determination of a model the way "having a long tail" can. Does this show that existence is not a predicate or characteristic? It clearly does not show what philosophers have meant in saying existence is not a predicate. If existence has been shown not to be a predicate, so has "alive." But "alive," I take it, is to be counted a predicate. What is shown is that there is something wrong with the idea that the existence of a model or the nonanimate status of a model can represent any thing. It is necessary for a model to be capable of contrasting determinations before either of two distinct things can be represented. The existence of a model cannot represent, because a nonexistent model cannot represent. The inanimate nature of a model cannot represent because there cannot be a living model. The same is true of the material nature, the space-occupying character, of the models. The fact that these things cannot be representational features of models does not show they are not properties. Consider a stamp album with pictures of stamps. How many things cannot be represented by the picture?—the date of issue, the type and weight of paper, the country—all the things that are printed under the pictures and at the tops of the pages in the album.

This inquiry with pictures and models is of use only as it applies to the original effort to explain that existence is not a predicate. That had to do with concepts, not pictures or models. Existence, it was said, is not like "having long ears": it is not a possible determination of a concept. Concepts are in the mind, not housed in buildings at the zoo. But if there is not an analogy, how am I to think that "having long ears" is, while "existing" is not, a determination of a concept? How am I to think that the ideas of 100 nonexistent dollars and of 100 existing dollars are the same? I do not know what I was to think except that concepts or ideas or pictures are supposed in some unexplained way to represent things. Then when I make the judgment, assertion, or what, that bandicoots are brown, I must have the concept of a bandicoot and make being brown a part of that concept. When, however, I make the assertion that bandicoots exist, I cannot make the concept represent existence. Do we know whether to say the concept itself exists or not? Whichever way it is, whether the concept exists in the mind or does not exist at all, there is no possibility of an opposite status and, hence, no possibility of either existence or nonexistence being represented by a concept.

The effort was to explain that existence is not a predicate, property, or characteristic. The explanation shows that "exists" cannot, while presumably "red" can be a determination of a concept. The effort fails because the explanatory device does not clearly draw a line between "exists" and the things that I imagine should count as properties, such as being microscopic, being an atom, . . . nonspatial, . . . invisible, . . . the winning move, . . . unlawful, . . . a pleasant sensation, . . . an expert bridge-player. However, it is possible that, with verbal ingenuity, one could interpret "concept" so as to admit of such specifications. There is a more serious difficulty. We are presented with a picture of thinking. The intent is to show by this picture that thinking "x is red" and "x exists" are two radically different affairs. The first involves simply an image or concept; the second goes beyond the concept with a symbol or a mental gesture or something like that. We put an E for existence on the back of the idea. But if we can put an E on an idea for existence, we can put an R on an idea for red. And I suppose on the idea of a dear friend we can put an I for intelligent, D for understands differential equations, and P for being in great pain. Surely this is every bit as good a picture of how we think as that involving concept and determination—both are miserable caricatures. On this modified picture "exist" and "red" are alike, not different; and so existence is not excluded from or contrasted with the predicates. What started out to be an explanation that existence is not a predicate seems to dissolve into an issue over which of two cartoons of thinking one is to adopt. If we must adopt one, the second may be preferable. At least it leaves a place for learning to handle things like "intelligent" and "understands" (though not perhaps "in pain") and suggests that thinking in complex matters is connected with the mastery of symbols.

Along these lines we could easily concoct other pictures, a whole series of them. The models could be very schematic and all alike. Then we could put numbers in various places on them. The numbers are to be looked up in a book in which are listed the characteristics they stand for. We could replace the models with sheets of paper tacked on the walls, and have lines of numbers on the papers. We could replace the numbers with words. The book would then become unnecessary, for we could learn to use the words on the papers, just as we should have had to learn the use of the words in the book. So our pictures would become less cartoonlike and approximate in some ways to our thinking. But they would be just as useless as the simpler ones, except to remind us of how overly simple-minded they were. However all this may be, the effort to picture thinking in concepts hardly makes clear what is meant by denying that existence is a predicate.

The model of thinking as attaching predicates to concepts seems to be the source of the desire to say that hallucinations, illusions, chimeras, dreams, and such, exist. Thus everything *in some sense* exists. The importance of the little qualifier, "in some sense," is lost sight of. The contrast between "exists" and "does not exist" emerges in place of "exists" and "extinct" or "exists" and "illusion." The temptation to say everything exists arises when trying to do wholesale business with very different kinds of commodities. The very different contrasts we mark with the word "exists" are out of sight. The discussion is too general to suggest examples.

This appears to be the way Plato arrived at the idea that existence can be predicated of everything. He speaks of all the "objects of sense." Some are colors, some sounds, some tastes, some odors. The question is whether perception is knowledge. Something besides sense is required to compare, contrast or to articulate the objects of sense. The mind must enter before we have even a likely candidate for knowledge, namely, a judgment. It must survey the objects of sense. The mind is required to take note that all these objects exist.

> SOCRATES: . . . But now, through what organ does that faculty work, which tells you what is common not only to these objects [the private sense-objects] but to all things—what you mean by the words "exists" and "does not exist" and the other terms applied to them . . .
>
> THEAETETUS: . . . there is no special organ . . . It is clear to me that the mind in itself is its own instrument for contemplating the common terms that apply to everything.
>
> SOCRATES: Under which head, then, do you place existence? For that is, above all, a thing that belongs to everything.
>
> THEAETETUS: I should put it among the things that the mind apprehends by itself.[2]

When this arises in connection with the picture of thinking as having "things" before the mind, the next step is inevitable: what can be predicted of everything is not a property. It is not an observable or imaginable mark or characteristic of anything. When you think 100 dollars and 100 existing dollars you think the same thing.

A similar argument has been used more recently, one which deals with words rather than concepts. The newer argument is based on a picture of predication as the juxtaposing of words rather than of ideas or representations. According to this story, a predication in its simplest form is expressed by affixing one kind of word, a predicate or property word, to another kind, a subject word. We thus attribute a property to a subject. In its logically simplest form, an attribution consists in assigning a property to a subject with which we are directly acquainted. We cannot characterize something that does not exist: there is then nothing to characterize. Of course we do talk about and comment on the features of mythical and fictional beings. But such attribution is always deriva-

[2] *Theaetetus* F. M. Cornford translation, pp. 185 B-D, 186 A.

tive, because the subject terms are of an entirely different nature. They do not directly refer: they indirectly describe. A mythical being is "the one I read about in . . .," and this kind of descriptive phrase can be logically unraveled until there remains no subject terms except those which directly refer.

Now we cannot raise any question about the existence of these subjects which are directly referred to. To say one of them existed would be trivial; to deny that one of them existed would be self-refuting. Properties primarily are applied to these subjects. Existence may not be so applied; hence existence is not a property. In the explanation in terms of concepts, existence was held not to be a predicate because a concept and a concept existing were one and the same thing. In this newer version, existence is held not to be a predicate because things referred to and existing things referred to are one and the same thing.

This explanation is very complex and deeply puzzling. It is based, among other things, on a certain picture of the working of language. I think, however, that one does not have to go deeply into it to see that it has shortcomings as an explication of the idea that existence is not a predicate. Unless it can be made clear that predication or attribution must be made up of "property to referred subject," then at most it shows that existence is not the kind of property that can be ascribed to things about which there is no question of existence. A not very remarkable conclusion. Are there any words that we use to refer to things about which there could never be any question of existence? I cannot think of any unless it is Descartes' "I," and that would not be enough for this explanation to work with. My demand may have been too strong. Perhaps the proper question is: Are there any *uses* of words . . .? Do we *sometimes* use words to refer to things about which we have no question of existence? Of course. "The sun is behind heavy clouds today." "Does the sun exist?" Silly. Is there something logically basic about such talk, talk of the sun, and Mt. Shasta, about those things of which we have no question of existence? But that is not the point. The point is this: there is something basic in the ascription of properties to things right before us. Basic in what way? A child quickly learns that his mother is sometimes out of the room, and sometimes fears that she is gone forever.

Even if that picture of the workings of language had some foundation, if some uses of subject words just had to be secured to things, then this consideration would still fail to show existence not to be a predicate. It would show that of those basic things certain predicates could not be used, e.g., "exists," "in the next room," "behind my back," "on a trip," "has evaporated," "deceased." Finally, it is not clear what is meant by saying that attributing existence to a thing which is presently before us is always trivial. A lawyer has built an elaborate case, and is shown a letter that destroys it. He asks for a recess. Holding the letter in his hand, he says, "I had no way of knowing that this letter existed, but it does. And I must ask for time to reconsider."

Another observation has been supposed to exhibit the difference between "exists" and a predicate. If existence were a characteristic or trait, one ought to be able to attribute it to all, few, most, or none of a class. Paradigm predicates can be put with subject and quantifier terms to form categorical propositions (sentences) and their relatives. Consider the tip-cat bat. Suppose all fine tip-cat bats are made by the Ozark Club Company. We may have reason to say, "All Ozark tip-cat bats are made of hickory," "Few Ozark tip-cat bats are made of hickory," "Most are," "None are," "Some are not made of hickory." Against the easy way these sentences slide off the tongue, we are to contrast, "Some Ozark tip-cat bats do not exist," "All Ozark tip-cat bats exist," and the others. The latter sentences, it is said, are nonsense, and the nonsense is produced by attempting to use "exists" as a proper predicate like "made of hickory." This shows existence is not a predicate.

Consider another example. Suppose we are talking about a little book published by a very small company in 1849. Rattle off these possibilities: "All copies are red," "No copies are red," "Some copies are not red." Now consider "All copies exist," "Most copies do not exist." The nonsense effect is not produced and for the reason, I suppose, that we quickly supply a context where existence can be in question. We may have noticed the book listed in an old catalog, and we ask a collector about it. The answer may be "No copies exist. They were all consumed in a warehouse fire before the book left the publishers." "A few copies exist." "Most do not exist." With just a little ingenuity we can supply a background story for the tip-cat bat example.

Suppose the founder and owner of the Ozark Club Company had a secret for making fine tip-cat bats. No others came close to their balance and flexibility. All expert tip-cat players use them, and although they are imitated, any expert can recognize an authentic Ozark. Now suppose the founder dies and with him the secret. The company goes out of business, unable to compete with the imitators. Many, many years later, someone reading the history and development of tip-cat may ask, "Are there any authentic Ozark tip-cat bats?" The answer might be, "None exist," or, "Only a few authentic Ozarks exist." Perhaps they have become so prized that a registry of owners is kept. This may be compared with the company's list of serial numbers. One might be in a position to say, "All authentic Ozark tip-cat bats exist."[3]

What do we learn from this effort? This much: one cannot tell that a sentence is nonsense by sliding it off the tongue. So one cannot tell whether existence is or is not a predicate by saying aloud sentences containing the word "exists" in one position or another. It would seem that, if one wants to show that "exists" is not a predicate, one would try to show that it is not used to describe or to characterize, not used to tell something about a subject. This is so clearly impossible, the philosophical doctrine must come to something entirely different.

The fact that "exists" does not obviously differ in the right way from "alive," "sings," "red," must be acknowledged. "Exists" does sometimes function predicatively. With these uses the doctrine that existence is not a predicate is not concerned. Rather, it must be intended to emphasize that "exists" is sometimes employed in another capacity. It is a common practice of philosophers to speak of "red" and "not-red" as both referring to properties. In general, where "W" is a property-word, then "not-W" is also a property-word. If one adopted this style of talking, then one would presumably have to classify "exists" with the "not-W's." In keeping with this style we might say that "exists" refers to an oppositional property: sometimes to not being extinct, sometimes to not being mythical, and so on. The force of "exists" can be understood on any occasion

---

[3] The original sentences were "All authentic Ozark tip-cat bats are made of hickory," "Some . . . are not . . . ," and the like. One might say my example is a cheat: that by using the long phrase "authentic Ozark tip-cat bat" I had artificially made it a bit clumsy to say about existence what would usually be said, viz., "All *of* the authentic Ozarks exist," "Most *of the* authentic Ozarks exist." The prepositional phrase "of the," which would, perhaps, usually be used in such contexts, is a mark of a closed class. "All exist" will not make sense except with closed classes. How does this affect the question whether existence is a predicate?

only by knowing what it is opposed to. We might say it has a reactionary usage: it gets the content of its position almost entirely from the nature of the opposition. The doctrine is now the insistence that there are other nonreactionary uses of "exists."[4] It is sometimes thought that there is a grammatical mark of nonreactionary use of "exists." When it occurs as a grammatical predicate as in "x's exist," if it is a nonreactionary use, the sentence can be rephrased "there are x's." This must be wrong. The same transformation is possible for most of the reactionary uses we have examined. We can rewrite "oranges exist" as "there are oranges" or "a few Ozark tip-cat bats exist" as "there are a few Ozark tip-cat bats." "There are all ... " and "there is all ... " seem to be senseless forms of expression. However, sentences like "there are twelve," or "there are eight thousand and twelve" are frequently employed, and with the implication that twelve or eight thousand and twelve is all there are. With this idiom, therefore, we are forced to refer to all in the round-about way of using the number. We should ordinarily not say, "There is the fabulous orange." This is too poetic or too whimsical for everyday use. The fact that "exists" can sometimes not be happily replaced by "there are" does not show that, when it can be, the use of "exists" is nonreactionary. Obviously "there are" is often used in a reactionary way. The question remains: when is "exists" or "there are" used in a nonreactionary way?

Talking about the use of "exists" as reactionary or oppositional is, I suspect, a misleading way of noting that, if something is said to exist, this can be understood only if there is a question about or a doubt about whether it is legendary, extinct, or some such. One could not start a conversation as easily with, "Green grass exists, doesn't it?" as with, "There is green grass, isn't there?" "There is" and "there are" do seem to be better starters. "There are roses as big as sunflowers," one might write home on a postcard. But is this the required nonreactionary use of "there are"? "That's nothing," someone might write in reply, "There are roses like that all over Australia." The reader understood, "There are such roses here." Suppose the writer tried to rule out the natural interpre-

[4] Murray Kiteley uses the phrase "exiguous use" for this. I take the following argument from "Is Existence a Predicate?", *Mind,* July 1964. An early version of this paper of mine was presented as part of a symposium, with Mr. Kiteley, at The Elmo Robinson Philosophy Colloquium, San Jose State College, 1961.

tation by underlining "are": "There *are* roses as big as sunflowers." What then could the opposition or rejoinder be?

Consider a flat opposition, "No, there are not." The question is, can it stop there? Children's arguments sometimes go like that: "There *are* flowers that eat people." "No, there *are* not." "Yes, there *are*." Isn't there something distressingly incomplete about such exchanges? The children may be verbally pushing at one another. "There is a Santa Claus." "No, there is not." "Isn't a lot of context required to show what is at stake here? ("Santa Claus is a spirit.") What of an adult who disagrees with, "There *are* giant roses here," by writing merely, "No, there *are* not"? Some background or explanation is needed to make the opposition civil and intelligible. Perhaps he and the writer of the card had discussed descriptions of sunflower-sized roses before and had decided they were gross publicity exaggerations. The man back home feels his tourist friend has become an overenthusiastic instrument of the Chamber of Commerce. Or perhaps he takes the postcard statement as of a kind with, "We are catching twenty-pound brook trout every day." He classes the giant roses as products of conventional and harmless humbug. Then we could spell out the opposition like this: "There *are* roses five feet in diameter." "No. They are all tourist and publicity frauds." So, in spite of the accented "are," this "there are" turns out to be a reactionary use. (Consider how much background is needed to understand, "There are no electrons.")[5]

For the doctrine that existence is not a predicate, one wants to say that it applies to the nonreactionary, *bare* assertion of existence. But it looks as if one

---

[5] J. L. Austin's book *Sense and Sensibilia,* appeared shortly after I had finished this paper. In this book, he labels a class of words (not too appropriately, I think) "trouser words" which behave as I have here suggested "there are" and "exists" do, i.e., in the manner I have called "reactionary": "It is usually thought ... that what one might call the affirmative use of a term is basic. ... But with 'real' ... it is the *negative* use that wears the trousers. That is, a definite sense attaches to the assertion that something is real, a real such and such, only in the light of a specific way in which it might be, or might have been, *not* real. 'A real duck' differs from the simple 'a duck' only in that it is used to exclude various ways of being not a real duck—but a dummy, a toy, a picture, a decoy, etc.; and moreover I don't know *just* how to take the assertion that it's a real duck unless I know *just* what, on that particular occasion, the speaker has it in mind to exclude." J. L. Austin, *Sense and Sensibilia* (London, Oxford U. Press, 1962), p. 70.

To say that one does not know "*just* how to take" an assertion where what is excluded is not known seems a considerable and misleading understatement. And why should a word be a trouser word when its opposite wears the trousers? Why not "no-trouser word"?

had a bare assertion of existence only in childishly blunt, incomplete, and defective communication. It must be some such bare assertion of existence that G. J. Warnock had in mind when he took Berkeley to task for not providing existence with a proper category. Berkeley had pretended to look among the ideas in a collection (thing) for the existence of the thing, and naturally not finding it among the ideas concluded that the thing's existence consisted in its being perceived. Berkeley seems to reason that if existence is not an idea of sense it must be understood as one of the operations of a mind. Warnock quite understandably complains here of a paucity of categories. And what is the proper category for existence? " 'Exist' is a curious word," Warnock says. "It needs to be handled warily." Asserting existence, he says, is like listing or cataloging. His example is that of a librarian compiling a descriptive catalog of books in the library:

> As he comes across each book he writes in his diary (say) "2:30 p.m. Inspecting *Treasure Island*"; he then writes the title, *Treasure Island*, on a card, and writes on the same card a brief description of the book. Suppose we now ask the question —"When he is not describing the book, nor recording his own experiences, what can he possibly be doing?" And here the answer is obvious . . . recording the fact that a certain book is in the library, by writing its title on a card. He may be recording the *existence* of a certain book.[6]

"Exist" is not nearly so curious as this commentary on its use. There are indeed questions about whether books exist and assertions that books exist. A library might possess the only known copy of some insignificant book. A curious historian might inquire whether the book was still in existence. In order to support the statement that the book exists, the librarian would ordinarily need to find the book in the stacks. However, if the right alphabetical segment of the card catalog had *just* been finished, the fact that it was in the catalog would be sufficient proof that it existed. But surely the employee who listed it on the card was not asserting that it existed. A routine inventory is not a set of existence assertions, any more than the hotel guest list for the day is a set of statements about the existence of the visitors. The appearance of an item or name on the list may be taken as proof of the existence of the book or person. But what is used as proof and what is proved are different things. The

[6] C. J. Warnock, *Berkeley* (Baltimore: Penguin Books, 1953), pp. 201-202.

fact that a statement of existence is different in kind from a listing, a check on a roll call, an entry in a guest list, is one of many reasons it is misleading to say existence is not a predicate.

Perhaps the nonpredicative, nonreactionary use of "exists," the *bare* existence assertion would be the listing. I am not inclined to think that that use of "exists" exists.

I started out to examine the meaning of the dictum, "Existence is not a predicate." I reviewed several things said in its explanation and its defense. In each case I seem to have found the explanation simply wrong. One ought not to find something wrong unless one understands it. I proceeded as if I had a good enough idea of what a subject and predicate, referent and characteristic were supposed to be, and I was compelled to find existence turning up with the traits, characteristics, properties. Although I have a very dim idea of what "property" and "attribute" are supposed to mean, they seem to refer to so very many things that it is hard not to find existence among them. A simple consideration of some examples involving uses of 'exists' led me to this result. It is surely no accident that such examples were not considered in the explanations I examined. It is, perhaps, negligence on the part of certain philosophers that they did not look carefully at examples. Perhaps, also, it should be taken as an indication of the nature of the doctrine that its expositors turn away from such details. Maybe an understanding of the meaning of the doctrine consists in taking a certain attitude toward existence, turning away from mundane talk and examples which remind us of it.

I can imagine also that a defender of the doctrine that existence is not a predicate might think that I had cooked my examples, or think that I had put them in a special light, or forced a certain interpretation of them. Suppose I am the curator of birds in a museum and someone comes to me asking, "There is no such bird as a white-throated sparrow, is there?" I say, "Yes indeed there is: we have a speciment in case 9." He bursts into tears and rushes away. I wonder, "What led him to think there was no such bird? Why did it seem so important to him?" Against the background of the examples I have considered one might be inclined to say, "The curator asserted the existence of the white-throated sparrow, but one can't know what it was opposed to." Did the same person tell the questioner about the white-throated sparrow who sent him on a snipe hunt?

Did he think the bird was extinct, mythical, fictional? Perhaps his mother is dead, but he has never escaped her apron strings. Maybe she told him how she remembered, from her girlhood, the song of the white-throated sparrow. He may now have friends who harass him with raillery about his mother: they tell him he should not trust his mother's stories. One tells him the white-throated sparrow is a mythical bird. One tells him the bird has long been extinct. Others tell him other things. His question to the curator may arise out of doubts created in this way. The curator's remark could have several oppositions, working together. The curator knows his remark has some opposition; he does not know what.

One who says existence is not a predicate might give another interpretation of the example. The curator asserted the existence of the white-throated sparrow. He did not know what reason to give, what argument to use, because his questioner did not stay around to converse. Not being extinct and not being fictional are outlines of reasons one might give for existence; mythical and exterminated with DDT are summaries of reasons for nonexistence. Existence assertions consist of two parts: the assertion of bare existence, and the suggestion of reasons. The example of the white-throated sparrow shows that the two elements are distinct because one is absent. What we learn, however, from this and similar examples can be applied to all.

Another consideration might reinforce such an interpretation of existence statements. If existence is a predicate, it is not always the same predicate. Sometimes it is not-mythical, sometimes not-dead, sometimes not-something else. Bare existence is the same ingredient in every existence statement. "Exists" is univocal; it means always and everywhere the same thing. Since only certain examples lend themselves to this analysis, why not say that in those cases existence is opposed to one of the ways of nonexistence, we cannot tell which? But that is not one thing. Existence is one definite thing, the same thing. How is one to know here what counts as "one" or "the same?" Is breakfast in bed and at the table, one and the same thing or two different things? Is there some intrinsic plausibility to the idea that existence is always the same thing, that there is something common and unique present in every use of the word "exists?" Why isn't opposition one thing, the same thing in each case, although that to which there is opposition may be different?

I do not know how to answer these questions. The doctrine that existence *is* not a predicate seems to be a reflection of the urge to analyze existence statements into two ingredients: bare existence, and something like reasons. It suggests a tinkering with categories. The categories involved: property, attribute, characteristic, are so big and indefinite and unbound by any working situation that it is hard to say any tinkering is wrong. Warnock bemoans the paucity of categories in Berkeley. But one of the categories he had available was that crow's nest catch-all: property, attribute. Why can't such a big, indefinite category accommodate existence? It is not clear what is achieved by putting existence in a category by itself, contrasted with this oversized, messy miscellany. Mostly, I must conclude, I have not got clear what philosophers are driving at when they say that existence is not a predicate. And, of course, neither am I clear what one would mean by saying that existence is a predicate.

HERE IS A MYTH TO INSTRUCT US THAT EXISTENCE IS NOT A PREDICATE

Far away there is a barren plain, without horizons. Going to and fro upon this plain are ghostly subjects, the possible things. Their possible characteristics and traits flit like St. Elmo's fires from one subject to another. A proposition is achieved by getting a characteristic firmly attached to a subject. The characteristics have opposites: the attachment of one of necessity detaches others which are incompatible. The plain is full of strife and opposition. But the proposition that something exists is altogether different. It reaches off the plain entirely. Existence is outside the field of opposition and so has no opposite. One of the ghostly things, shrouded with its electric properties and relations, is transported and made magically definite and complete. This is creation, and with this the logical angels sing out an existential quantifier, heralding another addition to the catalog of the universe. An assertion of existence is a whispered mention, a listing in the finest of lines and palest of inks, a token of the magic by which things come to be. The assertion of existence is natural, but absolutely distinct. Think of an announcement that someone gave birth who was not pregnant. (A birth cannot be repeated: that is a logical outrage.) To assert that something exists is so singular it is almost not to assert; a statement that something exists is almost not a statement. It has no proper opposite: death and dissolution end existence but they do not deny it. Opposition is entirely in the conflict of compossible subjects and the antagonisms of their properties. When existence comes, one conflict is over and a new one begins in an entirely different realm. That only God can bring the conflict of existence out of the opposition of properties and possibilities is an idea that may be required to complete the story.

With minor changes, one could make the myth show that existence is a predicate. God completes the story as an agent to bring existence out of possibility. If existence is not a predicate, God will have to operate from outside the realm of possibility, pulling the chosen possibilities out. If existence is a predicate, God can occupy a unique throne, the only existent among the pure possibilities, pushing out those elected for creation. Pure fantasy? The philosophical problem, whether existence is or is not a predicate, did arise out of concern with some such story.

XIII

PERFECTION AND EXISTENCE

In view of these observations on whether existence is or is not a predicate, what of the ontological argument? First, there seems no reason why existence cannot function as a predicate in an "argument." Grant: Does the platypus exist? Nelson: What is a platypus? Grant: An egg-laying mammal with a long flat beak. Nelson: I don't know whether there is any such thing. Why did you ask *me*? Grant: I found it described in Theophrastus. Your uncle is an expert on Theophrastus, isn't he? Nelson: Yes, and he checked the animals in Theophrastus. He found that all of them exist. So, if it's mentioned by Theophrastus, I'm sure it exists.

If I am right, before we can make understandable remarks about a thing's existence there must be some definite question concerning the thing we are talking about: is it mythical, extinct, dead, imaginary? There is another point: it must also be reasonably clear in what way the existence of the thing would be established. Does the platypus exist? We shall consult the natural histories or finance an expedition. Does the gene exist or is it an explanatory fiction? We shall examine photographs made with the electron microscope. I suppose the question about God which the fool raised in his heart and the philosophers sought to answer was whether God was mythical, a product of the imaginations of the folk historians, the bards, the priests. It is no ghost of a lost leader, no sprite in the bushes that the ontological argument is intended to establish. The philosopher will not allow that a rainbow following a long rain, or bolt of lightning striking after a prayer will show the existence of God. The way a thing's existence is shown depends upon what kind of thing it is. The philosopher's God is the thing we are dealing with, a God purified of myth and superstition. He is not to be seen glowing in the swamp at night; He is not to be painted or sculped; He is not to be found here or there, or even everywhere. Then what is it for Him to exist and not to be merely mythical? If the philosopher's interest is religious, then perhaps the main thing is that for him God shoud be a fit object for worship. If anyone says foolishly to the worshipper that God does not exist, and he feels inclined to reply, perhaps the correct answer is "He exists." A being that exists is a fitter object for worship than something that does not. But what exactly is the question, "Does God exist?" The ontological argument attempts to answer this question with a proof which rules out the possibility of God's being mythical.

The ontological argument is based on the presumption that one appropriate way to show God's existence is by proof. "Does there exist a prime number between 10 and 20?" "Yes, I shall give you one." "Does there exist one between any two numbers, x and y, where y is $x + 100$?" "I don't know, perhaps we can prove it." I'm told that mathematicians talk like this, and that they demonstrate or prove "that there exists a prime number such that..." and things of that kind. Here perhaps is something like the ontological argument: a knockdown proof that "there exists..." something. To follow the mathematical proof, one needs to know mathematics. To follow the ontological argument, one needs to know what? How to speak and think, I suppose. The analogy will not take us very far. Numbers are not thought to be mythical. There are no doubts about whether or not prime numbers might have been invented by priests or charlatans. "God's existence is like that of a prime number or the solution to an equation." Who could be satisfied with that outcome? Surely not the worshipper. And the philosopher cannot forget that God is the object of religious adoration and awe.

The mode of establishing that God exists and is not an historical, literary figment is to be proof, demonstration. Anselm addresses his proof to the alternatives: "God exists in the mind only," or "God exists in the mind and in reality." Perhaps this is pale philosophical language for the very real question, "mythical or not?" But there is a danger here. In Leibniz's language the alternatives are "possible" or "actual." With this we are invited to think there is one and only one contrast, and that among the possible things some are marked out as actual. We are tempted to think the realm of the possible can be imagined, conceived. Then there is the matter of determining which among the possibles are actual. Most philosophers will not go along with the rest of Leibniz's story: they tell us we can never determine which possibles exist merely by inspecting the possibles. We must look to another realm entirely, and after observing there, we can turn back and check those among the possibles we have observed to be actual. The checks we make to mark out the actuals are not characteristics of the possibles. Historically, Kant's doctrine that existence is not a characteristic or property may be appropriate, but it distorts existence-questions as much as the doctrine it is intended to refute. How are we to imagine one and the same existence-question arising for the hippogriff, for my best friend, for ghosts, for the sun, for the neutrino, and for God?

"Legendary" of an animal may be contrasted with "inhabits the mountain valleys of India." The fact that an animal inhabits certain valleys can be determined in much the same way as the fact that it produces ten offspring in one litter. The question of whether God exists is to be answered by proof, not by search party. Well, by proof mathematicians show that "there exists a prime number for every n-segment . . . " This contrasts, I suppose, with "is not inconsistent with the systematic principles of cardinal arithmetic." Similarly the ontological argument is an effort to show that the nonexistence of God is inconsistent with some self-evident principle or principles. Can this show that God is nonmythical? The mythical and the inconsistent are not the same. I suppose that if some mythical being is characterized inconsistently, then it cannot be nonmythical. God is a being some suspect is mythical. We are to show that there is an inconsistency in characterizing God as mythical. Could a being that many have seriously thought mythical, now be proved to exist by showing in a simple step or two that it is inconsistent to say that being is mythical? The philosopher's characterization of God must be taken for the proof. It may well not be what others were thinking of as God.

It is not enough for the ontological argument to have existence function as a predicate. We must be able to conclude by proof that existence belongs to something on the basis of a simple delineation of it as conceivable. To deny existence of the thing so characterized results in inconsistency. I meet an old friend, a person I have not seen for years. Since I saw him last he has become an avid collector of paper money. He has a large album which contains every type of paper money in use today. He wants me to see his collection and I am impatient. I should rather talk—after all these years—about old friends and all. Facing me with his album, he asks: "Is there anything you would like to see? I: "I don't know anything about money. Show me a bill with a yellow border." He: "There is no such thing." I: "How about a purple border?" He: "No such thing." I: "I'd like to see just anything. Show me one, then, which either has a purple border or does not have a purple border."

The ontological argument must go something like that. I was imagining possible kinds of money. I finally fell on a formula, "a bill such that it either has a purple border or it does not." To make this parallel the ontological argument, I want to say that such a bill must exist. The first two sorts I thought of were purely imaginary. But the third: there *must* be one of that sort. The point of what I said to my friend was this: I didn't care at all what he showed me; any piece of paper money was all right with me. I wanted to get this money business over with; so I asked for a bill such that any bill at all would do.

There is one important respect in which this cannot parallel the ontological argument. The existence of the thing characterized should not turn on the "mere fact" that human beings use paper money, sheets of paper which have borders and hence are printed in colored inks. We have the feeling that the example could be patched up by my saying, "Show me something—anything—which either is red or is not red." Well, suppose an insecticide I used had turned all the reds in my house blue. I say to my daughter, "Get something red." She gets the joke, "They're all gone." "Can't you get me something red? Then I'll give you some work to do: get something which is either red or not." Now of course this "presupposes" that there are things which can have colors. The ontological argument must not lean on the existence of anything like that. It must not "presuppose" the existence of anything at all.

We think we can patch this up too with a phrase like "something which has weight or does not," and now we shall try to make it clear that among the things which do not have weight we are going to reckon fugues, differential equations, and fairy stories. In the paper-money case, there was a question about whether something was imaginary or real. In the red-object case—and we need to stretch here—the question was whether every red thing had changed color. ("No such type of money exists." "There are no red things any more.")

What is the question with fugues, fairy stories, and stones? Purely imaginary? Change of color? Extinction?

We have tried to stretch imagination over such a range of things of different types that no one kind of existence question could arise about each of them. Of some it is not clear that any existence question could arise at all. What question could there be about the existence of C above high C? A physicist may have reason to suppose that no means of producing sounds will yield exactly a certain number of vibrations per second and remain constant over a period of time. He might doubt whether there is any "true" or "strict" C above high C. This concerns "C above high C" in some very special sense, not C above high C at all—not the note produced by a tuning fork or a violin string. Someone might doubt whether that note could be produced on a trombone with a large mouthpiece or by a baritone in falsetto, but these are different questions. I do not know what the question could be about whether "C above high C" exists.

This does not miss entirely the drift of the ontological argument. We move to the phrase "something which either has weight or it does not." We want a characterization such that something so characterized *must* exist. Suppose we call a thing which either has weight or not a "weightor." Then we want to say a weightor must exist. A weightor might be a dream, a devilish plan to irritate the dean, a chess problem, a cloud of dirt. Whatever it is, *it,* the weightor, must exist. Unfortunately, because of the mixed bag of its "nature," there is no comprehensible question about the existence of a weightor. One cannot make head or tails of the idea that a weightor must exist. "Must exist" is what we require of the argument. We want to say that because of its nature it must exist: its existence follows from its nature. It necessarily exists, or necessary existence is part of its nature. Just as having angles equal to two right angles is part of (or follows from) the nature of a Euclidean triangle, existence is part of (or follows from) the nature of a weightor. A triangle necessarily has angles equal to two right angles. It is part of the nature of a triangle that it necessarily has angles equal to two right angles.

We want a phrase which characterizes God's nature. Existence must be part of this nature. Hence God *must* exist. God's nature must include necessary existence. Malcolm[1] is undoubtedly right in his insistence that Anselm pre-

[1] Norman Malcolm, "Anselm's Ontological Arguments," *The Philosophical Review,* LXIX,

sents two different arguments in the *Proslogium,* one in which he endeavors to show that existence is part of the nature of God, another which turns on the point that necessary existence is part of the nature of God. But if the first argument were successful, that alone would show necessary existence was part of the nature of God. There are many different things one can think about the nature of God. If one understands what God is, he sees that He must exist. If one understands what God is, he sees that He could not exist contingently. The second can be thought independently of the first. But once the two things are thought clearly, one sees that the first implies the second. If it is part of the nature of a thing, weightor or God, that it exists, then it exists necessarily. Necessary existence is part of its nature.

If we could carry the weightor case through we should show that necessary existence was part of the nature of a weightor. We should somehow have to establish some use for "exists," such that everything that has weight "exists." The things with weight are not all the things. There are those without weight: ideas, fugues, C sharp. And our fabricated use of "exists" must apply to these also. All these things exist. This is apparently what Plato was trying to think in the *Theaetetus.*[2] Then "nothing," I assume, would be something which did not have weight. We can talk about nothing—and it does not have weight. And so a weightor would necessarily exist. It would necessarily exist, although it could be nothing. Even if one could get this far, the parallel goes wrong. The nature of a weightor allows it to "exist" in any way, as a stone exists, an idea exists, a dragon exists, or as nothing exists. And what are these? What are the questions? "I do not know what to trust in the histories. Does the Rosetta stone really exist?" "Did anyone really have that idea or are you making it up?" "Are there really dragons in literature?" "When you looked under his pillow was there really nothing, or are you telling me that because you think I can't stand the truth?" The characterizing phrase we use for God must make it clear that God cannot "exist contingently." It is compatible with the nature of a weightor that it be a mere thought, an imaginary being. The point of the ontological argument is to deny that being a figment of imagina-

No. 1, Jan. 1960. Reprinted in *Knowledge and Certainty, Essays and Lectures* (Englewood Cliffs, N.J., Prentice-Hall, 1963), pp. 141-162.
[2] See Essay XII, "Whether Existence is a Predicate," page 244.

tion is compatible with the nature of God. Also, the weightor characterization is not of the right form. Anything—everything—is a weightor. If there must be a weightor, there can be and are billions. The characterization of God must fit *only* one.

More like the characterizing phrase of the ontological argument would be "the winner of yesterday's fifth race." There *must* have been a winner. Yes, if the race was run. The race might not have been run: there was a storm or an epidemic. It might have been run, and resulted in a dead heat. "The fastest gun in the old West." There may have been no gunmen in the old West. The stories are purely fictional, or the last two shot each other dead at Skidoo Bend. Which was the fastest gun? Neither. How about "my childhood?" I *had* to have a childhood, and just one childhood. I cannot doubt the existence of my childhood. No, but others can. Suppose an inveterate teller of tall tales, old Clinton, had described my childhood. Then a listener might think Clinton had invented the story. There might be no such childhood, no person who had such a childhood: you can't ever be sure of what Clinton says. The same story is told by Pearce, a most reliable person. The details of the story might lead to suspicion. ("A strange and unlikely story. Could anyone have had such a childhood?") Both Clinton and Pearce could be good story tellers. The character in their stories might speak in a lively way: he could be a dead-ringer for me, he could have my name. They could make that character use the phrase "my childhood." There remains the question whether the childhood in the story is fictional or real. Of course if *I* use the expression "my childhood"—outside of story-telling contests—I must be referring to a real thing. The characterization of God is not to depend in this way on who makes it. God's existence is not to depend even upon the existence of the person who talks of Him. Again, we are inclined to think that the difficulties can be overcome with a phrase like "the universe." What is the question about the existence of the universe? A cosmologist might say Hoyle's universe is pure fiction. But I didn't mean somebody's model of the universe. "I'm not talking about a model or theory: I mean everything there is, just everything." (And I wave my arms all around). Now that has to exist. The ontological argument requires that nothing like that *has* to exist: the universe might not exist. This is awfully hard to make sense of. There might be no winner because a storm stopped the race. A description of my childhood might lead to doubts about its existence because the describer might like such fictions, or the description might be odd. "The universe" is not odd or suspect in any such way. I am talking about the universe: I am not making up things for fun. There is no question of a storm, an epidemic, a cosmic accident. We have no fears that something—something we know nothing at all about—is threatening the existence of the whole universe. Still, the universe doesn't have to exist because, regardless of what characterization I intend to make, there just might not be anything matching that characterization, even if I just waved my arms around. Even "everything that exists" won't do, because it is possible that nothing of all I am waving at exists. "There was such a great storm, it's possible the race was not run." "He's such a liar, it's possible there was no such person." How can I get to the possibility of no universe?

Fortunately we can get on. "The universe" is not the characterization of God required by the argument. If the universe is God, we cannot learn that from the argument. It has to be found out by other means. It is not because God is the universe that He necessarily exists. He necessarily exists because He is "the supremely perfect being" or "a being than which none greater (or more perfect) can be conceived."

The argument leans on some connection between perfection and existence. An absolutely perfect being must exist. If you deny existence of the absolutely perfect being, then there is a more perfect being than that, namely, that being existing. The absolutely perfect being which does not exist is not after all the absolutely perfect being. One cannot deny existence of an absolutely perfect being without being inconsistent. How are we to see that when we try to imagine a nonexisting absolutely perfect being that we can immediately imagine one more perfect, namely, one existing? We need some principle connecting perfection and existence.

"In a perfect vacuum, a pendulum would swing forever." "How do you know? You have no way of producing and studying a perfect vacuum." "We have found that as the vacuum increases, the time of the pendulum's swing increases. The rates can be determined exactly. So we calculate that in a complete vacuum, the time would be without end." The conclusion is arrived at by using a known connection between vacuum and time of swing.

Similarly, I should think, we have no way of seeing that absolute perfection implies existence—unless there is some definite connection between perfection and existence. Only a complete vacuum will produce an endless swing. That is because of the connection between degree of vacuum and amount of resistance to motion. Only absolute perfection entails existence. The connection between vacuum and resistance to motion is studied by experimentation. The one needed between perfection and existence is not like that. It must be found in the very ideas of perfection and existence. Existence must be connected with perfection the way the sum of the angles is connected with the idea of a triangle. I must not forget that "existence" here has—partly at least—the force of "nonmythical," "nonfictional," or something like that. What is the principle of connection? "The more nearly perfect anything is, anything which is suspected of being mythical or fictional, the better it would be if it were nonmythical?" That isn't right, of course, but something of that sort is the connection we need to find. Perhaps the exact nature of the principle of connection will become clear if we examine cases where we talk of perfection. If we are to discover the principle at all, we shall have to find it there.

(A1) Imagine a game. I make up a story about a murder. Each person invents a clue. We write down the details of my description and each of the clues. Now who can solve it? Each person writes his solution and then reads it aloud. All agree, "Alden has a perfect solution." He has accounted beautifully for every detail of every clue. (A2) A friend takes me to the ball game. He has not bought the most expensive seats. They are midway up, just beyond first base. As we are led to them by the usher he offers apologies. "They give a perfect view of the field. Why these are perfect seats," I reply. (A3) After a party, I say to the hostess, "It was a perfect evening. Thank you so much." (A4) After a pleasant day on the stream with a good friend, I comment, "It was a perfect day." (It was June, too. Then, if ever, come perfect days.) The circumstances which lead to these perfection-comments do not provoke any detailed examination of whether the remarks are right or not quite right. My hostess *might* reply, "Not perfect. I must apologize for the dessert. But I'm glad you had a good time." Even so, the matter stops there. It is hard to see in such examples where there is any foothold for a question about whether something is mythical or not, or the connection of perfection and existence. (A5) After a complete and careful physical examination, my doctor says, "You are in perfect health." "But what about those aches?" I ask. "For your age you are in perfect health." "What about those aches?" "You'll get used to them. Everybody does as they get older."

(B1) A physicist might say in an introductory lecture: "A perfect thermodynamic system would be one in which there was absolutely no gain or loss of energy from the system as a whole. To any other system, application of the laws of thermodynamics is always something of an art." (B2) A mechanical engineer will explain to his students that a "perfect machine" is frictionless. Eliminating friction is one of the guiding ideals of engine design. (B3) When someone worries too much about his little faults and failures, we know what it means to say, "No one can be perfect." (A perfectionist is one who continually suffers excruciating frustration because he has set his standards too high—so high, perhaps, no one could meet them.)

There are many different related ways in which the phrase "the perfect . . ." would play a role in explanation and technology. Physicists explain things in such a way that the explanations involve talk about "ideal systems," "a perfect vacuum." In turn, their explanations are related to the ideals of engineers, designers, and builders in such a way that "the perfect machine is frictionless," "the perfect bridge has stress-members of zero thickness." In explaining all this to a novice, such sayings as "A perfect machine cannot be constructed," "No engine is a perfect machine" can play a useful part. Along analogous lines, I imagine, we understand the force of "There is no perfect woman," "No one can be perfect," "no one can make it perfect. Just get it done well." But in most such cases, there are no standards to be stated, adopted, or reviewed. There are no explanations in terms of which useful engineering ideals are understood. Sometimes it is easy to start in that direction. A job could be explained in terms of "the perfect": "A perfect mail-sorter will dispatch 100 letters a minute for eight hours and never get one in the wrong box." In the A-cases, by contrast, it would be inappropriate to say, "No solution can be perfect," "No seat is perfect," "No evening (or day) is perfect." In those cases things were just fine, just right. (A6) You gave me a shirt for Christmas and you guessed at the size. "It was a perfect fit." There was, then, no need to exchange it. (B4) Shirtmakers might see reason to say, "No shirt can be a perfect fit." They might specify "a perfect shirt." I was not concerned with that when I tried on my Christmas gift.

Where in these B-examples is the connection between perfection and existence? Would the perfect machine be better if it did exist? Who could think it was mythical? How could it be better if it were nonmythical? These questions are based on complete distortions or misunderstandings. "The perfect ... cannot exist" calls attention to the way we use certain ideas in order to make explanations and to guide design. ("Don't think I'm talking about a bridge I saw last summer.") Sometimes we take ideals too seriously or in the wrong way. Then, too, we need reminding that no one can be perfect. There can be no question in this of perfection implying existence.

The ontological argument requires that we draw upon a connection between perfection and existence from which we can say something about the *extreme* case. We need to say that *absolute* perfection implies existence. The way we are to get this suggests analogy with "At absolute zero, chemical action ceases," or "In a complete vacuum, the time of swing is limitless." We can say, "Josh would be a better mail-sorter if only he knew the routings for the northeast better." But "the perfect mail-sorter" is not the end sorter in a long line. It is not a detailed description of the way the last one would look, if only we could find one or hire one. That is not the way "the ideal mail-sorter" enters into training, judging, and hiring. As in the A-cases, there is here no room for a question about existence.

In these B-cases, the question "Does the perfect ... exist?" can arise only out of radical misunderstanding. There seems to be a closely related use of "perfect," in which some type of thing is denominated "perfect" and there can be a straightforward question about whether there is such a thing. (C1) Someone wants to learn handball. I take him to the court and explain the game. "When I hit the ball, what should I try to do?" "Hit it so that your opponent cannot return the ball. The perfect shot is one driven into the angle between the wall and the floor. It hits the wall and floor together, and then rolls back. It does not bounce at all." Now he might ask, "Can anyone do that?" And the answer is, "Yes. An expert can get it off quite regularly." In this case there is no connection between perfection and existence. The novice asks whether anyone can make that shot, and I answer yes because I have many times seen it done. In other similar cases the answer would be "No" or "I don't know." (C2) We criticize a mystery novel because of the contrived solution of the crime. Worse than that the author left many strange things completely unexplained. "He painted himself into a corner." "I wonder whether there is any perfect solution to the crime he contrived? Let's try to think of one."

I have grouped these examples of perfection talk according to the way "the perfect" is (or is not) related to existence. In the A-cases, there is no question of existence at all. The thing judged perfect is here before us or with us or upon us. There is no question of comparing it with other possibilities. In the B-cases, nothing is judged perfect. The perfect bridge or machine may be appealed to in judging, designing, or building bridges or machines. There is no question about its existence, except, it seems, the one which arises through misunderstanding. In the C-examples, there is a head-on question of the existence of the thing called perfect; but there is no connection between the perfection of the thing and its existence. There are many other related ways we talk of the perfect this or that, but I can think of none which illustrate any other connection (or lack of connection) between perfection and existence. The three types can be illustrated by talk of the same subject.

(A7) Our Siamese tom has just shed his kitten fur. Suddenly I notice his grown-up grace and elegance. I whistle and the cat leaps to my lap. Although he now has cat-dignity, he is still full of kitten spirits. Rubbing his head, I say, "There is a perfect pussy-cat." (B5) Now suppose that sometime later I am talking to a friend, a breeder and expert judge of cats. What shall I say of my cat? I shall not say, "I have a perfect Siamese tom." Maybe I'll say, "I think my young Siamese tom is a real beauty. I'd like your advice about putting him in the Fall show." "Bring him over. I'd like to see him." So I take him to the expert, and he says, "He's a good one all right. I'm not sure I've ever seen a better. But he's not quite perfect. Look at the hind legs here, and the shading here." So I ask, "What makes a perfect Siamese?" or, "What is a perfect Siamese?" These questions can lead to elaborate lessons in the standards, how they are determined, what the breeding problems are. "The features we want don't run together. You get a strain with the right kind of shading, and the points are not dark enough. You get a strain with distinct points, and the shading is not smooth and even. You find the long thin tail and along with that you get those crossed eyes in the male. And those damned tabby marks keep coming back. The perfect Siamese would have no tabby marks at all; large, round, well-spaced eyes, no hint of crossing." In breeding and judging cats, standards are adopted and changed. "The perfect" at any given time is so specified that it gives a standard for judging. But also it sets an ideal which exercises even the breeders of the best cats. Of course there is no question about the existence of "the perfect Siamese." The expert is not discussing some type of cat described by an unreliable world traveller. There is no question, "Did he actually see such a cat, or did he fabricate it in order to make his readers take notice?"

(C3) There is another possible outcome. There can be no question of the existence of "the perfect Siamese" of the breeders' guide or judges' handbook. But my cat might amaze the expert. After very careful examination, my friend, the expert, might declare, "That is indeed a perfect specimen. He will be a winner in every show in the country." My friend can't speak for every judge. Suppose, then, I enter my cat in the shows and that all the experts concur, "He is a perfect Siamese tom." They will tell people, "If you want to see a perfect cat, go look at F.E.'s." These judgments are something like those in A. But these result from serious, careful, studied comparisons. They come from the application of stated standards. They are not B-style talk of perfection: they are not lessons in the standards.

After years of watching my friend judge cats and talk about them, "not quite perfect this way and that," I might ask, "Is there anywhere a perfect cat?" He could say, "Yes. Go look at John Dale's," or, "I don't know. There just might be. There are a lot of fine cats bred by people who have no interest in showing them." Here there is a simple question about the existence of "the perfect Siamese," but no connection between the idea of "the perfect" and any answer to the question, "Is there a perfect cat?"

I think there is yet another kind of talk about perfection. Suppose we are on a camping trip with a baseball manager. We are sitting around the campfire listening to his baseball yarns. He has made uncomplimentary remarks about several very good shortstops, implying they were not so very good, not as good as one expects in the majors. I ask what a really good shortstop would be. He thinks I do not know much about baseball. "I don't know what to say. He could go to the right better than Phil Rizzuto, get a better jump on the ball than Lou Boudreau, and be as good at the plate as Hans Wagner."

We have a big bottle, and the fire is crackling. (D1) "You're too much involved in the thing. The perfect shortstop would never make an error. He would go after everything down the left side. He could fire the ball like a bullet, and sometimes beat his own throw to second to start a double play. There once —a long time ago—was a shortstop just like this. His name was George Mulligan. I'll tell you what happened when he turned up on the sand lots at age ten," and so on. Perhaps something like this is the origin of legendary heroes. (D2) Paul Bunyan *may* once have been "the perfect lumberjack." Santa Claus, perhaps, "the perfect, children's wintertime friend." Santa Claus can visit every single child all over the earth—and in one night—and take to each just the gift he wants most. He goes down and up billions of chimneys in less than twelve hours. (He has to do it in the winter, though. The summer nights are not quite long enough.)

Such talk is not always—or has not always been—just for fun. But it is fun. And what of the connection between perfection here and existence? Would Santa Claus be a better Santa Claus if he were real, and not just fictional? Would Paul Bunyan be a better lumberjack if he were to be a nonlegendary lumberjack? (He does live in the north woods). Being a manager of Weyerhaeuser Lumber Company, I might say Bunyan would be better if we could put him on our payroll. In saying that, I'm back again at the campfire; and though the drinks may be gone, they have not worn off. Anyway, the ontological argument is what we are interested in. So it is not a question of whether the manager of Weyerhaeuser Lumber Company would like it, not a question about whether it would be better for him, his company, or for all of us that Paul Bunyan should exist. It is a question about whether Paul Bunyan would be better—a better lumberjack—if he were not just a figment of folk imagination. What is one to think about the idea that Paul Bunyan or Santa Claus might exist? "Not possibly" is the thing that comes to mind. "Not likely" is not right. I feel inclined to say, "Santa Claus couldn't conceivably exist." These are the things which come to mind, but do I know what I'm talking about here? I am not addressing myself to any question about the existence of Santa Claus. Am I trying to be candid with a child who has just about outgrown Santa Claus?

"Think about what Santa is supposed to do. He couldn't possibly be real, could he?"

How are we to think of God's perfection such that it implies His existence? Is God perfect the way an evening is perfect, the seats are perfect, my health is perfect? In these cases, there is just this much to fit the need of the onto-logical argument: there is no question of the possibility of a more perfect, a better. If we were buying seats and talking with the ticket agent, there might be better seats than these, but that is beside the point now that we are in the stands. These seats are perfect. One at my age could not be expected to be in better health. I'm in perfect health. When my hostess says, "Not quite perfect," she is being humble; she may find it hard to accept such strong praise. If she wants to be theoretical about it—most inappropriate—she will shortly be say-ing, "No evening can be quite perfect." "A being than which none more perfect can be conceived" suggests that we are trying to look both ways: less perfect and more. Only there can't be anything more. In these A-cases, we do not look both up and down: we look only down to the worse. The perfect evening, seat, solution, fit of a shirt, is not one of the worse: not boring, not too far back, not too large nor too small. We are *not* looking upwards at all. We are not thinking of whether under this special condition or that the seat or the fit could be better yet. We are not saying this is the best, the very best that anyone could have at any time. We are not saying, "No one could think of an evening, a seat, a state of health, a fit that we should think better—if we were seriously to compare."

In trying to make a footing for the ontological argument here, we are tempted to slide into the kind of thinking appropriate for the C-cases. We are attempt-ing to think of the perfect or the absolutely perfect and then ask seriously whether its perfection would be increased by this or that. We want to ask seriously whether it exists or not. Starting with A-type examples, we cannot get there. There are no questions such as "Is there a perfect day?" "Are there perfect seats?" "Is there a perfect state of my health?" We must take subjects, things, doings which are specified as perfect after considering the possibilities and the characteristics of excellence. "Can anyone make the perfect shot?" "Is there a perfect specimen?" Are we to think of God's per-fection as like a perfect shot or a perfect specimen? Nothing follows as to whether such things do or do not exist. There might be one or there might be many. We are to think of God's perfection such that it is absolute, highest, complete. There can be but one: it is *the* absolutely perfect being. Here we are thinking of the B-cases. Is God's perfection like that of the perfect machine, the perfect mail-sorter? There is no way to consider the existence of such.

However we are to think of God as perfect, we must think of Him in such a way that we can ask whether He would not be better or more perfect if He existed. How can we get an issue about the existence of "the perfect"? Here is a possibility: the A-uses of "perfect" can be fictional as well as drawn from real life. In the case of the A-uses, there could always be the question of whether the perfect so-and-so was fictional or real. Suppose I am telling a story about a party. I just make it up, a pure invention. I end the story with my telling the hostess it was a perfect evening. "That was not a real party you were talking about, was it?" someone might say, someone who just heard the tail-end of my story. "No. I was just telling a story." What comes next? Will he say, "It would have been a better party if it had been real?"

While under the spell of the ontological argument, I shall want to say, "Nothing fictional can be quite perfect—not absolutely or completely perfect." "Only things that exist, only things that are real, can contain one of the ingredients to complete perfection." This suggests ranking, judging—as if we always had an eye out for possible improvement. That sort of thing is out of place as a commentary on my remark to the hostess, "It was a perfect party." How could I understand "It would have been better if it were real," or "It couldn't be absolutely perfect?" Do these comments mean my judgment of the party was not quite right? I made no judgment of a party. I have already straightened that misunderstanding out: there was no party to judge. I was just telling a story.

Am I to imagine looking in on a fictional party from outside, from some point in real life, and there rank it among parties? How? Shall I have to taste the fictitious food, engage in the imaginary conversation? Or, from some standpoint outside fantasy and fiction, am I to rate it only among fictional parties? How, for example, does it compare with the Mad Hatter's tea party? Was the Mad Hatter's party a good one or a bad? No. I have to consider "possible parties," "conceivable parties," each as a candidate for existence. Will the Mad Hatter's party be among the possibles? What question could arise about its existence? On Saturday mornings, a librarian reads classics to a group of children. Could some child who came late to the reading think the librarian was recounting a party she had seen? If some child could, then he would raise the right sort of question: fictional or real? But the Mad Hatter's is not the "perfect party." It is only "the perfect party" that could offer a useful parallel. I cannot imagine what "the perfect party" amounts to unless I slip back into thinking of some situation, say, where plans are being made for a party. A very inexperienced hostess, perhaps, is seeking advice, "How should I do this?" "Which is the better way?" "Would it be a better party if ... ?" But surely, in no such case would there ever be anything like a detailed review of all the possible parties. What about perfection here: the perfect party? "The perfect party." Where could such a phrase occur except at the beginning of a book on entertaining guests, perhaps. And then might follow a rough description of each of the proper things to be done: the correct invitation, the right reception, the appropriate drinks, the best appetizers, a chapter to be devoted to each. Then "perfect party" is employed in a way similar to "perfect mail-sorter" or "perfect lumberman." It is used as heading for a specification of guiding ideals. And for this "perfect party" there seems to be no question of existence except that which arises through the wildest and most unlikely misunderstanding. If such a question should ever arise, then I suppose the author of the book would have to say, "No, that is not a description of any party I or anyone else ever hosted or attended."

From "the perfect so-and-so" we must get to the existence of the so-and-so by concluding that the existent so-and-so is better than the nonexistent. How can we find a connection or situation in which a thing would be better if it existed, and would not be best if it did not exist? I go to an employment agency and tell them I want someone who can lift the rear end of my car which is stuck in such a position that no jack or hoist or other machine can be used. He says, "I've got these men available," and he shows me photographs of each. The pictures are full views. I can see the build and height of each man. I can pretty well determine the age of each. The agent asks, "Which do you think would be best?" I point to one: "That one," I say. He consults his files. Then he looks up and says, "Sorry. He is not the best ... He died last week." "He would be better if only he were not dead." What sort of joke is that?

In thinking of who is best at some little job, I have no model on which to conceive of the perfection of God. Well, suppose I simply want the best worker, the best lifter, mover, or something like that. "A dead man can't be the best lifter." "The one you picked would be a better lifter if only he were not dead." I seem still to have in mind some particular lifting to be done. What am I picking one for? I want to get rid of any taint of "best for this one little thing." The very best, or very greatest, lifter of all may have lived in the early nineteenth century. Who is the best lifter now? Clearly not that man: he died in 1879. "Who will be the best lifter in tomorrow's meet?" "Certainly not Benson; he died this afternoon." The nineteenth-century champion is not an entry in today's ratings. Benson is not a contender in tomorrow's contest. He cannot be a winner because he cannot be entered. "He can't be best," is a grisly way of saying, "No comparison can be made." Also, there is no contest among dead men: no conceivable determination as to which among the dead is the best lifter now. And then on to the conclusion that the worst among us now is better than the best of those who are dead. Of course we do compare the living and the dead: we compare Willie Mays with Babe Ruth. We do not reason that Mays is better than Ruth because Mays is alive and Ruth dead. When we compare a dead man with a living one, we compare the performance of the dead man when he was alive with the performance of the man who is now living. We compare two real performances; we do not compare a real performance with an unreal, mythical one.

There are many mythical beings. Some have been called "God." Some are clearly more perfect than others. "God" is the most perfect conceivable. We can imagine or invent all sorts of beings, some with this perfection or that. Some superior in that way or this. But "God" is absolute perfection. Now the question is, "What if He were merely mythical?" (or dead?) I am not to compare the past performance of a dead God with the present performance of a living God. No. I am to compare the excellence of this real God with the same God, only unreal. This seems like comparing the two performances of the lifter, Benson: the one he might have given in tomorrow's contest with the one he gives (or does not give) because he has died. Consider Benson alive and consider his performance tomorrow. Think of him dead and think of his performance, dead. Then compare the two. Consider God existing and consider

Him mythical; then compare the excellence, the perfection of the two. By analogy with the lifter case, I say, "No such comparison can be made between the mythical and real, the dead and living." This cuts out a necessary move in the argument. I cannot now say "the most perfect or absolutely perfect" would not be "most" or "absolutely perfect" if He were merely mythical. In this series of examples, I can give the appearance of comparisons between the dead and living (nonexistent and existent) by allowing for some bad jokes. The jokes may be jokes precisely because they suggest the incongruous comparisons. Between the dead and living, the bizarre comparison is introduced by the questions "Which is best?" or "Which will win?"

Could something less bizarre be introduced by a question about "the perfect?" I could say, when looking for someone to lift my car, "He looks like the perfect man." Then the agent will say, "Not quite perfect. He is dead." This is the same kind of joke. He looks like a man to whom, after the job was done, I should say, "That was excellent. You did exactly what I wanted—and not a scratch." When I said, "He looks like the perfect man for the job," I was not at that point comparing him with the others. I wasn't looking back and forth, weighing the several requirements. Perhaps I had to do some of that. But now that was done. There is nothing grudging about my selection now: the comparisons are in the background, and I fasten on just one, with a superlative, "He looks like the perfect man." The agent can say, "He might have been just your man. Unfortunately, he is dead." Can we spell this out in such a way as to get rid of any suggestion of the jarring joke? "You sized up the men well. You picked old Rupert Scott who was the strongest man in six counties. Unfortunately, I just for the first time saw the note in his file: he died last week. He would have been able to do the job for you."

Is this the way the step in the ontological argument is to be taken: "With good reason you picked him as the most perfect being. Unfortunately he is merely mythical"? I got myself into this position by looking for a candidate of whom I might make an A-type judgment: "He is the perfect man." Then I backed into the question of existence by learning my candidate was dead (or mythical). I was thinking of the job being done, after which I should make an A-judgment, "You did a perfect job," "My hunch was right. You are the perfect man for this sort of job." Religious language addressed to God is often language of praise: "Almighty," "Ruler of heaven and earth." Is that enough for the ontological argument? Can I hear of God, and say He is perfect, and then for a moment or a day think that He is dead or that He is merely a mythical being? That will only get me to "He would have been perfect," "He would have been ... if only He were not mythical." Then I could find out for sure that He was not mythical, and so He would be perfect after all. No. I must be able to find out that He is not mythical by noting that I should not say "perfect" unless He were real. "Think of the being you would call perfect if he were real." "All right. Then he is real." There is no chance here.

There is no chance of an argument here because I can understand quite well what it is for a man to be dead (or mythical). And I know it is only a joke to rank or compare the dead or mythical with the living or real. I can say of poor old Bentley, "He's the only man who could have done it. He would have done a perfect job, too—if only he had survived the flu." But I cannot think such things and follow the ontological argument. "God would be absolutely perfect if only He were not mythical." No. God is a being of which I cannot imagine that He would be better or more perfect only if ... He cannot possibly be mythical. I should not be able to think clearly or consistently of His being mythical. I must see that being mythical is not compatible with His being perfect, and I must see that it is not compatible by noting that if He were mythical He would not be what I have said He is, namely, "the absolutely perfect." Now I want to read all this as, "I wouldn't call anything absolutely perfect if it were mythical." But how can it follow from that that I do call something absolutely perfect? I cannot get the ontological argument by using the model I have here, that is, the situation in which I rule something out as perfect because it is nonexistent.

I must, it seems, think of a perfect being and then think of His being mythical and of His being real. Finally, I must see that a mythical being is not the absolutely perfect being, and not because a mythical being drops out entirely as a candidate, not because no comparisons can be made except jokes. I must seriously compare and ask myself which is the perfect being. This sounds like a kind of multiple-choice question one might be asked in a physics class. "A perfect thermodynamic system is one in which (a)——— (b)——— (c)———." Checking the right answer shows that one knows what is meant by "perfect thermodynamic system." I am now thinking of God's perfection as a B-type perfection. But one who understands "the perfect" in this sense knows there is no question of existence, especially no question "mythical or real?"

How about a C-type case? I have studied the descriptions, photographs and judges' comments of several cats. "This one, Bung-Po, seems to be a perfect specimen." "No. He is not a perfect specimen. We just invented him for fun. We faked the photographs." Bung-Po would be a perfect specimen, perhaps, if only he were real. I shall not say of any cat that it is a perfect specimen unless I know there is such a cat. There is the same trouble here as in the A-cases. I cannot just imagine a cat which would be a perfect specimen if he were real, and then conclude that there is such a cat because he would not be perfect unless he were real. I can imagine a specimen that I should call "perfect," but I cannot imagine a specimen that I *do* call a perfect specimen. The existence questions that arise about C-examples are not of the right kind. We can ask whether there is such a shot, a perfect one, or whether there is such a specimen, a perfect one; but we cannot ask whether there is this shot we have just applauded as perfect or this cat we have just judged perfect.

We do need, it seems, to compare something with another just like it except that the second exists, is nonmythical. And we cannot do that with A or B or C cases. There remains only the D ones, the mythical beings. Are we to see the connection between perfection and existence, then, in the perfect shortstop or the perfect lumberjack? A child might ask perhaps (who else?) whether or not Paul Bunyan or Santa Claus was real. Would it be a question like whether or not the hoop-snake was real? Something like it, I suppose. And to the extent that it is, I suppose the answer is "not possibly." We have the wrong connection here between perfection and existence. Of course, in the case of hoop-snakes, nonexistence has nothing to do with lack of perfection. But Santa Claus must never die. That is the way we feel now. Santa Claus is what people think he is. Sometime in the future, people may turn the stories about him into past-tense stories and add the appropriate, moving, symbolic details of his death: a sacrifice, perhaps, out of deep love for children all over the world. But "Santa Claus as we understand him now" cannot die.

I am asking the wrong questions. The question is not whether Santa Claus can or cannot die. Even if he were to die it would be a mythical death of a mythical man. And if he could not die, it would be mythical immortality. The question is: would Santa Claus be better if he were nonmythical? If Santa Claus can be thought of as the child's perfect friend, then remember how he came to be that. We took off on a wild flight: he goes down every chimney in one night, guides reindeer through the sky. Could he be a better children's friend? If you can think of some way, we shall tell the story to include it. No caution need be observed. Is there one more way he could be a better child's friend—by being nonmythical? We shall tell the child that he is real. One day the child will come and ask us whether or not it is true. Would it be better for the child if it were true? Maybe, for a little while. But the question is not whether or not it would be better for the child. Would Santa Claus be a better friend to children if he were to exist? Would it increase his perfection? We have made him perfect, as unrestrainedly perfect as we can. Have we fallen short; have our imaginations failed in not making him nonmythical? What shall we tell the child? "Think, child. Santa Claus is a man, a man who lives at the North pole; he does not die, he travels faster than light, carries by flying reindeer a load heavier than a mountain range. There could not be such a man. It's a wonderful story." "Is he real? Does he exist?" A *man* who cannot die? "No child, there could never be any such man. It's a wonderful story."[3]

---

[3] I have been talking about talk of perfection. I have been asking "How does talk of perfection go?" In view of what Norman Malcolm says on this topic, I wonder whether or not I should be asking, "What language game do we play?" In commenting on the view that logical necessity is based on the use of words and so existence cannot be a necessary property of anything, Malcolm writes: "That view requires us to look at the use of words and not manufacture a priori theses about it. In the Ninetieth Psalm it is said: "Before the mountains were brought forth, or ever thou hads't formed the earth and the world, even from everlasting to everlasting, thou art God." Here is expressed the idea of the necessary existence and eternity of God, an idea that is essential to the Jewish and Christian religions. In those complex systems of thought, those "language games," God has the status of a necessary being. Who can doubt that? Here we must say with Wittgenstein, 'This language game is played!' " N. Malcolm, *op. cit.* (above, note 1), p. 156.

Now it has been and is questioned by many Hebrew scholars whether anything like "necessary existence and eternity" was part of the Biblical conception of God. It has been and is doubted whether anything like that is essential to the Jewish and Christian religions. Grant that those ideas are part of the religious beliefs of many people. What has that to do with the ontological argument? Two solutions necessarily exist to every quadratic equation, but the religious attitude of worship is not directed to some solution of an equation, a solution which must exist. Presumably God, a being worthy of worship, must be unlimited, absolutely supreme, the sum of all excellences, supremely perfect. And such a being must,

But why need we be so wild in imagining our hero? We could invent a more realistic Santa Claus or Paul Bunyan. And then when the question arises, "Does he exist or is he just an invention," the answer will not be, "Of course not," "Not possibly." It will be "No," or "No. I don't think such a person exists." It will be like, "No, there are no living dinosaurs," or "No, I don't think there is a thrush with a green back." Now conceive, with reserve, this tamer type of a god or hero. Can't I imagine one more perfect? Wouldn't Bunyan be a more perfect lumberman if he could fell a giant Douglas Fir with one or two strokes of an axe rather than having to gas up and pull the starting rope on a chain saw? Would he? What is the question here of perfection? How should I specify "the perfect lumberman" so that there was a question left about whether he was real or legendary? I could not be making ideal specifications for judging contests at a lumbermen's festival. Nor could I be giving to a group of new men the ideals to work toward in their training as loggers. In these connections, "the perfect lumberman does not exist" are the right words with which to forestall certain misunderstandings. What could the misunderstanding be which would lead to the question "mythical or real?" or "fictional or actual?" Perhaps someone arrives at the end of a lecture by a contest judge or a trainer and hears just some of the talk about the perfect lumberman. He asks, "Does such a man exist or were you talking about a fictional figure?" What is the proper answer? Maybe the best short one is, "Neither." "I was talking about judging the contest," or, "I was telling these new young men the ideal to work for." I have fallen back into a B-type situation.

Novelists can write so realistically about a character that one can wonder whether there was such a person or not. Yes, and in what way is a fictional character the perfect this or that, perfect stocking salesman or perfect king? Such a one might be "the perfect tragic hero" or "the perfect clown." Then he

---

by nature, include existence. He must exist necessarily. Religious language must lead us from one attribute of God to another. That must be part of the "complex system of thought" Malcolm is talking about. We must see that perfection requires existence. Is this the "language game" that is played? How many "language games" do we play? When and how do we play this one with "perfection" and "existence?" I think I have been trying to find the answers to these questions.

Perhaps religion is not that kind of "language game." It does not require that logical connections be unfolded into the "necessary existence of God." Then what has that "game" to do with the ontological argument, or with philosophers' criticisms of it?

is judged with respect to the fictional work of which he is a part. A real person might be "a perfect clown." Yes, that is, his performance was perfect, it was just right. "He made us laugh 'till we split."

In trying to think the ontological argument through, I am required to borrow a little from several uses of "perfect" and to mix them in a mystifying way. I am to think about characterizing something such that the possibility of anything more perfect is ruled out by the nature of my characterization. That sounds something like a perfect evening or a perfect fit. I also have to think seriously about whether this something would be better one way or another (that is, existing or not). That suggests thinking about what the characteristics of "the perfect" are. It suggests a situation which leads to talk of the perfect Siamese or the perfect mail-sorter. It suggests something like serious consideration of what to say in a breeders' guide, or a training handbook. However, there is no head-on question about the existence of these "perfections." But to follow the ontological argument I must be able to ask of the most perfect being whether it is mythical or whether it exists. This suggests the perfect shortstop or lumberjack, something which is mythical, and here we are not involved in serious specification or characterization which will be used in making definite rankings, ratings, and gradings.

But couldn't we discuss seriously and in an orderly way the characteristics of a perfect legendary or mythical being? When we try, we get one result which might seem to support the ontological argument. At least we get one result which seems to fit the requirements of the argument. Start with the characterization of a being which might be mythical. Take a being of any type, say a shortstop, and specify that being as a coach or manager might. Then ask seriously, if you can, whether the perfect shortstop wouldn't be better if he never grew old, never slowed down, never struck out. Now we have gone wild: we have no guide except unfettered imagination. But we must be serious and theoretical. Yes, that is just what you should expect. If you ask these philosophical questions about the perfection of any being other than God, the concept of that being goes to pieces in the mind. One does not know what to say in this philosophical mixed mode about the absolutely perfect shortstop or the absolutely perfect white onion. Hence there is no clear question about whether the absolutely perfect shortstop must exist, no clear question any more than there is a clear question about whether the perfect shortstop should have ten fingers and two thumbs on each hand.

How, after all, are we to characterize the perfect shortstop? We are not now stamping the performance of Hans Wagner with one more unneeded approval. We are not telling a new recruit to the little-leagues what he must do to play the position best. What shall we say? The perfect shortstop is always young, always at the peak of his powers, not subject to ailments or slowing down with age? Will he hit a home run every time at bat? Wouldn't that ruin the game? Shouldn't he have the human virtues? Isn't any man, baseball player or not, more perfect if he is capable of deep love, sympathy, compassion? Is this so clear for a shortstop? Surely, our shortstop would be on the base paths often. Are sympathy, love, good things on the base paths? If I am not allowed to create a purely mythical shortstop here, how am I to know what to say? The idea of a perfect shortstop slips away in unanswerable questions. For defensive play why not, after all, give him fifteen arms or ten prehensile tails with gloves grown onto the ends? Why not have his hand grow into a glove the size of a bushel? Do the rules of baseball govern the size of a glove of living human flesh and bones? This glove *is* the hand: do the rules limit the size of the hand? All this fits with the ontological argument. After all, we do not want our proof to establish the existence of the absolutely perfect shortstop or the absolutely perfect island. It is to work only for God.

God is unique. He is not of any kind or sort. God is not the perfect lumberjack or shortstop. He is not a perfect example of this or that type in a drama or novel. God is a perfect being. Whatever unqualified perfection is, God is it. And for a being to be perfect He has to be. The perfect being is perfect in being. His necessary existence just is His perfection. What conception of perfection can be used to sponsor this line of thought? I have run out of examples. Besides, no example, now, is relevant.

If this finally is the way the argument must go, then what is the connection between perfection and existence upon which it rests? In no being other than God can the connection be understood. None of the ways of talking we understand will show it. It is an absolutely unique kind of argument. How does one distinguish this from no argument at all?

Some think that light is shed on the argument by looking for the connection between perfection and "necessary existence." That connection exists only for God, and it is this: being mythical or imaginary is incompatible with the *nature* of God. An absolutely perfect being is *necessarily* nonmythical for the reason that it is an absolutely perfect being. If that being were mythical or fictional it would not be an absolutely perfect being. Now this seems to lean on the same idea: a perfect mythical or fictional being would be more perfect if it were nonmythical. It is hard to find even the possibility of a connection there. I have looked to several uses of the word "perfect," and they hold no promise. Are there other relevant uses I have overlooked?

Malcolm thinks that one can find the required connection between perfection and necessary existence by taking "necessary existence" as "noncontingency" or "nondependence."

> ... [God] cannot be thought of as being brought into existence by anything or as depending for his continued existence on anything. To conceive of anything as dependent upon something else for its existence is to conceive of it as a lesser being than God.[4]

Note: the language here suggests that the question of whether God is nonmythical and the question of whether God is nondependent are not quite the same thing. Also, one who approached the question in this way could not bear down very hard on the analogies with mathematics. When "there necessarily exists a solution ... " or "necessarily exists at least one prime ... , " these are not cases where something noncontingent or nondependent exists. Malcolm finds the needed connection between perfection and nondependency:

> If a housewife has a set of extremely fragile dishes, then as dishes they are *inferior* to those of another set like them in all respects except that they are *not* fragile. Those of the first set are *dependent* for their continued existence on gentle handling; those of the second set are not. There is a definite connection in common language between the notions of dependency and inferiority, and independence and superiority.[5]

The connection we want is one in which we may learn something about the

---

[4] *Op. cit.,* "Anselm's Ontological Arguments," *Essays,* p. 147.
[5] *Ibid.,* p. 147.

extreme cases. We must see what follows upon absolute or complete nonde-pendence. The universality of the presumed connection ("between the notions of dependency and inferiority . . . ") suggests china-grading or china-manufac-turing. Perhaps (I have no knowledge here) a ceramics engineer would say, "The perfect dish would be virtually indestructible." But this does not mean that it would be a good thing to fill the world with indestructible dishes. What should we ever do with them? All those indestructible dishes would not be thought of as "good dishes," "excellent dishes," or "perfect dishes"—except ironically. The connection we need is that between nonfragility and perfection. What would a trap-shooter say after scoring several direct hits to find that his clay pigeons did not break? He discovers the whole shipment is made of some virtually unbreakable material. The manufacturers of clay pigeons would not say, "The perfect clay pigeon is virtually indestructible." I suppose that the connection between perfection and strength or indestructibility is to be found in "common language," but what connection we find seems to depend entirely upon what we are using "common language" to talk about.

"Indestructible" is presumably the thing you would get if you ran along the series, "fragile" . . . "less fragile" . . . "much less fragile" . . . "strong" . . . , and so on. But this series of words is not used always to apply the same kind of standards. The material used in a fragile jet engine compressor would make a virtually indestructible coffee cup. Even if we can imagine this series leading off in one direction, it would not lead us to "noncontingent" as an attribute of God. God is not to be "much, much less fragile than a rocket nose-cone." A happier rephrasing of noncontingent as applied to God might be "not fragile and not nonfragile, not easily broken and not indestructible." "Independent" like "indestructible" is not always used in reference to a virtue. How inde-pendent can a pet be and still be a good pet? What of a computer that was inde-pendent? "It goes its own sweet way." An increase in independence does not always make just any old thing better. Barlow can be a most independent, self-sufficient fellow. He can also be much too independent. A person who is too independent necessarily lacks certain virtues: proper concern, deep love for people and things, loyalty, the ability to make concessions and to cooperate.

XIV

WHERE THE ACTION IS

Consider these two answers to the question, "What are you doing?" (1) "I'm still trying to think of that word for last night's cross-word puzzle: the one for 24-across." (2) "I'm sharpening the barb on this fish hook." Both answers specify "actions." What does the second involve which the first does not? We are inclined to answer, "It involves certain movements of the hand and arm." An old classification quickly comes to mind: the first is a mental action; the second a bodily action. Consider just bodily actions, and now ask this general question, "What does a bodily action involve?" The answer must be, "Some movement of some part of the body." That question certainly seems an easy one.

The answer cites something simple and easy to understand. We have no deep questions about bodily movements. Now we can turn about and ask the hard question. Take some bodily movement. What must a bodily movement have in order to be an action? Our willingness to ask this question seems to come from the fact that we view the world philosophically as a scene of things and motions: rocks and flowing rivers, fiery stars and revolving planets. The movements of human beings belong to this world, they fit in it. We are ready to believe that some simple explanations (scientific, of course) can be given for all these things and motions. But human actions do not belong; they spoil the simplicity of the world-order; they even threaten its existence. Praise and blame, good and evil—the things which go with human actions—are mystifying. We can understand human bodily movements, but we are led to ask questions about human actions because, by contrast with bodily movements, it is difficult to see how they fit in the world.

We have no deep questions about bodily movements because we can see them all about us; we can point them out to others. Being a part of the "physical world" they are things in motion: they are like rolling balls and falling snow. The simplest kind of vocabulary is sufficient to refer to these movements. A child can be taught the basic words of this vocabulary because these goings-on can be pointed out to him. They occur at certain places and they have fairly definite beginnings and endings in time. Actions are notoriously not simple in this way. Think how long it takes a child to understand that by marking an "X" on a paper his father is voting for the president of his union. There is nothing one can point to, nothing which begins at one time and ends at another, which will give the child the idea of what voting for the president of the union amounts to. In this way, too, bodily movements are simple; and actions are bewilderingly complex.

So we ask this puzzling question: in addition to a bodily movement what is involved in an action? This is not a new question: and we have already tried many answers. Long ago we tried to answer by specifying an action of the mental kind as part of a bodily action: some kind of mental movement which acted as a thrust on some part of the body. We may naively have thought of these thrusts as "acts of will" or "volitions" or even as "motives" or "intentions." Then we saw that no such "causal" answer could account for the characteristics we know actions to have. We tried again with more sophisticated "concepts" of volition, motive, intention, and we found that we could not give a satisfactory answer in that way either. It is easy to think of actions which do not involve any of these: volition, motive, intention.

We were led to see that while these things and many more enter into actions in all sorts of ways, no one of them, nor any combination of them can be the *defining* characteristic of an action. At last, it was pointed out that we were asking the question, "What is a human action?" against the wrong background. We were exercised by a misleading model. We were thinking of the question as like "What is a natural pearl?" "How do you tell a real war-surplus store?" "What is scarlet fever?" The question "What is a human action?" is more like "What is a move in chess?" or "What is a shot in billiards?" The question we *should* take as a parallel is this, "In addition to being a movement of a piece of wood on a checkered board, what is a move in chess?" With this model in mind, we are supposed, now, to see that no answer such as "intention," "motive," "volition," "reason," will do. Of course, in certain answers to certain questions about certain actions, reference to motive, intention, volition will enter just as "queen's gambit" may enter into a description of certain—but not of all—chess moves. We are supposed to see that "human action" cannot be understood without something like the rules and conventions of chess, without something like the training, and practice involved in a mastery of the game. Actions cannot be understood apart from human social life; its laws, regulations, rules; and the training and education involved in the development of sane, sensitive, and responsible human beings.

In taking this new model, it may seem that we have changed the question. This is standard procedure in philosophy. We must struggle to understand a philosophical question. Coming to understand a question is not changing it. Through struggling with the question, we have made it clear. At first it suggested that we look for some occurrence in, or just preceding, an action, something like a mental thrust. We now see that the question, "What does an action involve besides a bodily movement?" cannot be answered in that way. The addition to a bodily movement is not some occurrence in or near an action. The answer to the question, now more clearly understood, is this: A bodily movement in certain circumstances is an action.[1]

Surely there is philosophical progress here. But on second and third thought, much of the mystery first surrounding our question returns. Certain very obvious things are sources of uneasiness. What do I now take the question "What is an action?" to be? Is the question "What is a move in chess?" any clearer? A committee, attempting to codify the rules for a certain type of tournament might ask this question. They might answer thus: "Any movement of any piece within a three-minute limit, once the hand is removed, constitutes a move, and the three-minute limit begins immediately for the move of the opposing player." This is not the question I am supposed to ask about a move in chess. A child has been watching his father play chess with friends. He has listened to the players and has mimicked their voices and mannerisms while moving his

---

[1] It will be obvious that, in part, I am taking my lead here from the writings of A. Melden, particularly from "Action" in D. Gustafson, *Essays in Philosophical Psychology* (Garden City, Doubleday, 1964), pp. 58-76, and from *Free Action* (London, Routledge & Kegan Paul, 1961). I hope it is equally obvious that I am just taking a lead. I want to engage in no polemics, and I am reasonably sure that the philosophical predicament I have fallen into here is not one in which I share Melden's company. Cf. Ryle's use of the billiards analogy. G. Ryle, *The Concept of Mind* (New York, Barnes and Noble, 1949), pp. 79-81.

blocks around on the floor. He asks his father to play, and his father—thinking he will begin the child's instruction in the game—humors him. The child moves two of the white pieces about and then says, imitating his father's voice, "That's my move." His father says, "That's not a move at all. You're just shoving the pieces around." Can we imagine the child now asking, "What is a move?" If so, the father might answer something like this: "A move is when you move a piece in the proper way. Each piece has its own proper way. You get only one move each turn. Now, these are pawns, these knights..." The father's answer is intended to go on and on, with talk and demonstration, until the child has learned the fundamentals of the game. At least, so the father hopes.

Can I imagine any similar child's question, "What is an action?" Part of the difficulty is with the word "action." It is a word of high rank, used in very general or very theoretical connections. It has become a philosopher's "technical" term, and we do not always have a clear idea what it is supposed to mark. Consider instead the distinction between "action" and "happening." As in the chess game the child wanted the distinction between "move" and "shoving a piece" around, so, too, a child might be concerned with the difference between "action" and "happening." Can we imagine the child asking, "What is the difference between something someone does, and something that happens to him?" This, too, is hokey. The child's question will most likely be, "Why did you punish me, and not John?" Then he might get an answer in terms of motive or intention. So I have lost the general question I want. But, after all, isn't any answer to the child's question just a beginning? Won't he have to learn about accidents and guilt and punishment and excellence and failure and politeness and rudeness and love and hate and all the rest before he knows about "actions"? Isn't it like learning to play the game—just much more complex? There are reasons to be suspicious here.

In order to get a question whose answer had the right form, I allowed myself to invoke the wrong question about a move in chess. The chess simile is supposed to help us see that there is something in a chess move analogous to a "bodily movement," and also something analogous to an "action." The child's question was an appeal for a grasp of the distinction between a move and shoving a piece around. These are both actions. A move is supposed to involve something analogous to the bodily movement which is involved in all actions.

What could it be? The chess board is set up on a small table, and the board is shaken in an earthquake so that one white pawn is moved one square forward. Here, surely, is the "movement" of a piece. Can this be involved in a chess move? Two people might have agreed to start a game just before the earthquake began. "White" now looking at the result of the earthquake, says, Amazing, that's my move." And the game might go on from there. The cooperation of an earthquake *might* be involved in a chess move, but it couldn't be so involved in every chess move. If it were, even in the most earthquake-prone region of the world a chess game would take a long, long time—longer, I dare say, than any player would live. When he died, a player's game would have to be taken over by another. One game might last for many, many centuries. Chess is usually played—and better played, I'm sure—without the help of earthquakes.

To make the chess simile work, I need a "movement of a piece" in chess which is involved in every move—of every game—earthquake or not. The question, "What is a move—in addition to the movement of a piece of wood?" is intended to be perfectly general. Can't I just say that I'm talking about the *bare* movement of a piece of wood on a checkered board? That is, I'm talking about something in complete detachment from persons and players and in complete detachment from the fact that the wood or the board are recognizable parts of equipment involved in chess—or even involved in a game, or in any human enterprise whatever. I can say that, all right; but can I say it without being mystified? I cannot imagine a child asking the right question, "What is a move—in addition to being *this*?" Well, hang the child's question. I brought in the child so that I could begin with someone's question against some understandable background. Why do I need that? The question is one which philosophers propose. Isn't that enough? Perhaps that is one of the reasons for my uneasiness. There is another reason, though, for bringing in the child. A bodily movement is supposed to be a simple thing. I brought the child in because I imagine a bodily movement to be the sort of thing a child can easily see.

I must not become lost in preliminary misgivings. The chess move business is meant only as a simile, an analogy. It is intended to shed light on the question, "What, in addition to a bodily movement, is a human action?" It may still fulfill its purpose if it helps me to see that an action involves, besides a bodily movement, something analogous to the rules of chess. There is no good reason why I must find something in a chess move which is the exact counterpart of a bodily movement.

Return, then, to the original question: "What is a human action?" In addition to being a bodily movement, it involves something like the rules of chess. A difficulty arises immediately. An action which involves something like the rules of chess, does not seem to directly involve anything which could qualify as a "bodily movement." A motorist raises his arm before making a left turn. If asked, an observer quite naturally says he is signalling a left turn. This action, signalling a left turn, certainly involves an understanding of the rules of the road, as they are written in the state drivers' manual. But what is it that, in terms of these rules, is signalling a left turn? The answer must be, "raising the left arm when approaching an intersection." Someone can ask, "What do you do to signal a turn?" Of course, the answer is, "You raise your left arm." That's what you *do*. And that is an action. That action in the right circumstances, according to the rules of the road, is signalling. Here is something in a situation governed by rules, which in the context of those rules is an action, namely, signalling. The something, however, is not the "bodily movement" I want; it is itself an action, namely, raising the left arm.

One of the things which went wrong in using "motive," or "intention," or even "reason . . . " in the philosophical formula for an action was this: we can ask, "What was his motive or intention or reason in doing *that*?" only where *that* is already understood to be an action. We can ask about one's motive for, or intention in doing some particular action. Hence we can identify the action and characterize it quite independently of our knowledge of a person's motive or intention. Motives and intentions are not identifying features or "essential" features of actions. They do not make actions actions. Hence they do not make bodily movements into actions. It makes sense to say that one has a motive, intention, or reason only for an action: we can talk of motives, intentions, reasons only in connection with actions. We want something we can talk of in connection with bodily movements.[2] We want to say that a bodily movement

---

[2] I think this argument is important in giving form to the philosophical need for a "bodily movement." The argument I use here is a very general version of a type of argument used by Melden and Anscombe. (A. Melden, *Free Action,* pp. 76-77; G. E. M. Anscombe, *Intention* (Oxford, Basil Blackwell, 1957), pp. 28-29; see also p. 187.)

becomes an action when that something surrounds a bodily movement. A bodily movement is a simple thing. We can easily see it, identify it, describe it. Sometimes a bodily movement is an action, but sometimes it is not. We want to know what is present when a bodily movement is an action, something which is absent when it is not an action. Of course we no longer expect mental events or thrusts to provide the answer. Neither will motives nor intentions. The answer is to be in terms of context, circumstance, rules—the things suggested by the game simile. We want to explain what makes a bodily movement an action. A bodily movement cannot by itself be an action.

Now it appears that the chess simile involves me in a similar difficulty. When I look for a thing whose character as an action is determined by rules, that something turns out to be an action itself. Raising the arm becomes signalling in terms of the road-rules. But raising the arm is, of course, an action. Is there something which in a situation governed by rules, becomes the action of raising the arm? What would it be? Of course, it must be the bodily movement with which I want my account to begin.

The chess simile is supposed to make things clear. But I am having trouble with the very starting point of the question "What is an action besides a bodily movement? I am beginning to wonder whether I understand what a bodily movement is. At least the chess simile suggests how we are to think of bodily movements in connection with actions. One action becomes another when it is performed in circumstances governed by certain rules. Shoving a piece around can become a move in chess. Raising the arm can become an act of signalling a turn. The chess simile indicates the role bodily movements are to have in actions. It invites us to think that a bodily movement becomes an action in the same way one action becomes another. It invites us to think of actions as organized into a complex hierarchy. When an action enters the scene of application of a new set of rules it becomes an action of a higher order. Going down the scale one comes to simpler and simpler actions, until finally one arrives at the simplest actions. Bodily movements are one level lower than these. Bodily movements enter into the simplest actions in the same way simple actions enter into more complex or higher actions.

An example of an action built on simpler actions, and based on a bodily movement, will go something like this. A man may lose the game by swinging at a bad 3-2 pitch. At the same time he strikes out, he swings his bat at the ball, he takes his turn at bat, he moves his arms and twists his body in a fierce swing. Each of these actions is characterized by reference to a different rule or group of rules. The last one is different. That motion can be made in the batter's circle as well as in the batter's box; it can be made with or without a bat in hand. A person who knows nothing about baseball can be shown how to make that movement. The same or a similar movement is made while playing other games or while engaged in other activities: the motion plays a part in stick-ball, and in an energetic beating of the edge of a rug. I am led by the game simile to think of it as a neutral and preliminary sort of action, one whose character is partly determined by its potential. Into that simple action, I must now say, a bodily movement enters; and entering into the simple action, it thus enters into the more complex actions above it. This example is presumably representative of every bodily action and its underlying bodily movement. So, in this way I shall now be able to say that a bodily movement enters into every bodily action. Well, if it does, it is not easy to see how it does. Twisting the body while swinging the arms is an action that would be called a bodily movement. It is not easy to see how the "bodily movement" with which my philosophical question begins enters into that bodily movement.

Again the difficulty may result from my pressing the simile too hard. My examples have been dictated by a too simple-minded use of the simile. Thinking of chess, I have looked for actions which involved rules. The simile is intended to have perfectly general application, and most actions do not involve conformity to rules. Most are not characterized by reference to rules. I must be able to think indifferently of turning on the bathroom light, picking an apple from the tree, aiming a gun at a target. I must be able to think of any bodily "action" at all. The point of the simile is to call attention to the social background in which actions take place and against which they are characterized, and appraised. The chess game is to remind us of all this by giving us a sample of the things which actions in games involve: cooperation, competition, tutoring, learning, tactics, plans, purpose, excuses, plaudits. The purpose of the analogy is to remind us of the social life of actions. Rules are just tokens of the sorts of things involved in actions: admittedly, most actions do not involve rules. Of course, the simile should apply primarily to simple actions. The simile may work to suggest how simpler actions become more complex actions by becoming involved in more complex social settings as swinging the bat is involved in striking out. But primarily it must shed some light on how bodily movements become simple actions. Otherwise it will not give a hint of what kind of answer is to be given the question, "What is involved in an action besides a bodily movement?"

At this point it should be clear that the game simile is not important at all. There are many others which might serve the purpose just as well. The outline answer we are urged to adopt might be illustrated by this story. A tribe on a distant island lives in grass huts. On a shelf in one of these huts, a small boy finds a ball about the size of a hedge apple. It rattles when shaken. He is naturally fascinated, and he takes it down to play with it on the floor. His mother comes screaming that he must not play with that ball: he must not touch it. It must always be picked up first by the juju man. The juju man will then pass it to others: sometimes when they marry, sometimes when they are going on a long trip, sometimes when they are sick. "When you are sick," the mother says, "the juju man may give you the ball to play with." Of course the boy will not understand all this until he has learned the rituals, the religion, the superstitions of his tribe. He saw it only as a ball. He will one day come to see it as a special, sacred ball. Bodily actions, we are to think, are like this special, sacred ball. We come to see many of them as actions as we gain adult membership in our tribe.

There is a danger here. In describing the social development of the tribal boy's life, I suppose it is all right to say that he comes to see the ball as a sacred object. As an adult he will not say he sees it *as* a sacred object or *as* a juju ball. Suppose that when he is grown, he becomes the juju man's assistant. The juju man needs the ball, and it is lost. The grown boy, now the juju man's assistant, finds it. When he finds it, he will say, "I see it there in the corner" or "I see the juju ball over there." He will not say, "I see that as the juju ball." Even if he is wrong and the ball he sees turns out not to be the real thing, he will not say, "I saw it as the juju ball." Likewise as we develop, we shall come to see bodily movements as actions. We shall not say we see them as actions. If we do learn to see a bodily movement as an action, we ought to be able to see the bodily movement which we see as an action. It ought to be easy to see the bodily movement. It is simpler than the action; it is right before our untutored eyes.

I must go on. I shall worry the similes no more. Bodily motions are determined *as* actions by all sorts of things: the many, many things which distinguish the development of the human being from the development of the sow-bug. With such a generous and indefinite supply of things, surely the simplest of actions will involve or be involved in at least one of them. Consider raising the arm, the thing one can do while taking exercises, while pointing out a bird in a bush, relieving a writer's cramp, seeking recognition at a meeting. Raising the arm is something which calls for coordination, it calls for a bit of practice on a child's part to bring it under control, to make it easy, rhythmic, and accurate. One must learn when and how to do it on command; one must learn to do it when one wants to be called on by a teacher, or when one wants to go to the "lavatory." Certainly some social things are relevant to the action of raising the arm. In a context where these or some similar factors are effectual I should be able to see that a bodily movement becomes the action of raising the arm. Similarly I ought to see that a bodily movement enters into every simple bodily action. A horse-shaped piece of wood can be moved in dog-legged hops. Given the right circumstance, that dog-legged hop is a knight's move in a game of chess. A bodily movement, given the right circumstance, becomes an action. I ought to be able to see a bodily movement before it is in action. And then, in a new setting, I ought to be able to see the action of which it is a part. Where shall I find a bodily movement which is not an action, but which could become an action in a different setting? I do not know how to proceed except to look to some of the things we think of as bodily movements.

(1) A girl just from the country has answered the advertisement of a city place for a "girl dancer." She tells the manager that she has had some experience and asks about the job. He says, "We want a belly dancer." She does not know what that is. The manager calls one of the watiresses, who used to be a belly dancer, and the waitress gives a demonstration. The country girl says, "I simply could not make those bodily movements.' 'She is morally offended. Making those bodily movements is something she will not do. So these bodily movements are not the things which enter into bodily actions: they *are* actions. And as actions, they get the country girl's censure.

(2) Bodily movements are, of course, not actions. Sometimes we contrast them with actions: we are inclined to speak of "actions as opposed to mere bodily movements." So we think of a tic in the cheek or a spasm in the muscles of the calf as a bodily movement. There is also that jerk of the body which sometimes occurs just when one is going to sleep. The phrase "jerk of the body" certainly suggests "bodily movement." The trouble with tics and spasms and jerks of the body is that they are things we cannot control. Certainly no such things as these enter into every action, although there may be actions into which they would enter. Imagine a drummer whose violent and rapid beat set his arm muscles into uncontrolled spasmodic action. He may execute a final long rapid roll in this manner, and then quickly leave the stage to take antispasmodic pills and to relax. This would be a rare and unusual type of action. Nothing of this kind enters into all the simple actions involved in walking, pointing, eating, sitting, writing, climbing, in which we engage throughout the day. In most cases, muscular spasms would prevent our carrying out an action. We might have to give up sawing wood because of spasms in the back and arms. At best we should be able to carry on in spite of the spasmodic muscle contractions—not with the help of them.

(3) "Spasms are uncontrolled bodily movements." In saying this I have, after all, called them bodily movements. They are just the wrong kind of bodily movements. Controlled bodily movements, then, must be the kind which enter into actions. We do sometimes say that a person has his bodily movements under perfect control. We might say this of a dancer who can be counted on to give a magnificent performance of a most difficult ballet. In summarizing the ability he shows in his performance we might say, "He has every bodily movemen under perfect control." What we should mean, I suppose, is something like this: he has practiced and practiced before mirrors and with the help of tutors and critics until he can unerringly put his body in the right positions. He can move from one position to another, and one place to another in a manner to create the most appropriate flow of motion, of arms and legs—and body. His bodily movements are part of a piece of art. We are commenting on his mastery of the parts and his ability to work them together. He has practiced the parts, the bodily movements, by themselves, and in various sequences with others. He has become exceedingly skillful at, say, raising and holding his arms

just right. Now raising the arm, or kicking the leg sideward, are actions. Although in commenting on the dance we speak of them as bodily movements, they are not the "bodily movements" we want as an ingredient in our philosophical account of actions.

(4) When one pushes his arm hard against the wall and then moves away from the wall, his arm rises. "His arm rises." That sounds like a bodily movement. However, it will not do. As with tics and spasms, this rising of the arm is an uncontrolled movement; not the sort of thing which enters into every simple bodily action. Then a bodily movement must be just like that rising of the arm, except controlled. What would that be? Raising the arm? But that is an action.

(5) Someone else can hold my arm and lift it upward. If blindfolded and asked to comment I should say that my arm is being raised. This could not be the "bodily movement" we are looking for. Nothing like this enters into bodily actions.

(6) Sometimes we speak of parts of the body as subject to movements in other connections. When telling a scary story around the campfire, I may say, "The hairy arm moved toward me out of the darkness..." As this story unfolds, I shall be horrified but not surprised to learn that the arm was not attached to a body. "The hairy arm moved..." This is a way of giving the arm a frightening agency. Nothing like detached members is to be involved in the bodily movements which enter into human actions.

Yes, but we use the same language in describing the movements of an attached arm—and in circumstances that may not be fictional. "I stood riveted to the wall with my hands up. I could not take my eyes off the gun. I could only look at his hand and arm. His arm moved—up and down, as he pointed the gun first at my head, then at my belly." In describing this I said, "His arm moved—up and down." This is the kind of language I imagine appropriate for "bodily movements." But here it serves as a dramatic way of isolating the gunman's movement of his arm. It is as if the arm were the only thing. I could look at nothing else. As far as I was concerned, the arm was operating almost as though disconnected from the body. When describing the same experience again, I might well say, "He raised his arm—up and down—always pointing the gun directly at me: first at my belly, then at my head." I now describe it in the language of an action. Is it both an action and a bodily movement? Yes of course.

Every such action must involve a bodily movement. However my first description did not serve to isolate the bodily movement. It was a dramatic way of describing the action. In any case, I am looking for a bodily movement which is not an action, and I have not found one in this example.

(7) An old man sits all day on the porch rocking in his rocking chair. All day long the neighbors have their radio on, turned full volume. I know the old man is nearly deaf and he seems neither bothered nor entertained by the blasting of the radio. Perhaps he cannot hear it. One morning program always begins with the *Colonel Bogie March,* and at this time the old man changes the rhythm of his rocking, and he seems to beat time with his hand. I am curious, and I ask him, "Why do you always beat time to that march?" He says, "I didn't realize that I did. I'm almost deaf, you know. I do hear a little of it and I like it—but do I always beat time to it?" When I tell someone what I first noticed about the old man's behavior I shall say, "His hand always moved in time with the music." "His hand moved" is the language I expect to be used for bodily movements. But here the man is beating time to the music, and that surely is to count as an action. "His hand moves in time with the music" is a way of saying that he does not realize what he is doing.

(8) We say of someone who talks too much, "His mouth is continuously moving." This is a way of saying that his mouth is out of control: it seems to go by itself. He cannot control his talking. This is different, of course, from the way tics and spasms cannot be controlled. But bodily movements are not supposed to be out of control or unregulated in this way either.

(9) Let us tie a black cord to a man's wrist, and run the cord over a pully, so that by pulling the cord from some distance away we can raise his arm. That is, we can raise his arm providing he relaxes his arm muscles and does not resist. We make a movie of his arm being raised in this way, and we take the pictures against a black background so the cord is invisible. Now we have him stand in the same place, before the same background and have him raise his arm normally. We make a second movie of that. Look at the movies one after the other. The bodily movement is pictured in both: it is what is common to the two. Compare them: in each the arm is first down here, then up there. How do I say what is common to the two? If I saw the first only, I should say that I saw the man's arm being raised. If I saw only the second, I should say that I saw a man raising

his arm ("I don't know why"). What is common? I see the movies again some-time later, and now I do not know which is which. "Look at that one. Describe what you see." What should I say? "Either he is raising his arm, or his arm is being raised." No, I want something neutral: something common to the two things. "I see his arm moving up." Perhaps, at last, this is a bodily movement.

The important thing here is this: bodily movements are to be simple, easy to see. They are common, and can be pointed out, anytime and anywhere. They are conspicuous items in any inventory of the physical world. "I see his arm moving up" in this example can only be understood against the features of the example: it must be understood that I am talking about something neutral and common to these two incidents. This sort of situation is hardly common. In cases where this special background is not present, "His arm is moving up" will not do. When a calisthenics student raises his arm on command of the instructor, how can I say that I see his arm moving up? How can I say that I see something properly neutral between raising the arm and having the arm lifted?

(10) I tell someone that through a large, glass laboratory window he can watch a robot I have constructed. "The robot, you can see, is more or less hu-manoid in form, with arm-like and leg-like appendages. I control his movements from this panel here." "Now I shall put him into action, and you tell me what he is doing." I turn a dial, and the observer says, "The arm-like appendage is moving up." I carry the experiment on for a while, and then I reveal to the ob-server that it is all a hoax. He was watching a man in a robot costume, and I had no control over him other than through hand signals: one means "raise your right arm," one means "kick your right leg," and so on. So the observer was watching the bodily actions of a man. Am I to say that his first descriptions were of the bodily movements involved in those actions? Everything is wrong here. The observer's first descriptions were of movements he presumed to be controlled by dials, electric currents, radio signals, and the like. They were really not such movements, but the observer would not have described them as he did unless he had thought they were. Simple human actions do not involve movements controlled from some master switchboard.

Now, suppose that I tell the observer that he may be watching a robot: or it may be a man. "I shall not tell you yet." "Describe, now, what you see." I am back to the difficulties of example (9). He must describe what is common to the controlled movements of the robot and the actions of a man. His description can be understood only in these very special circumstances.

(11) Suppose a space-explorer were to meet something on another planet: a moving humanoid thing. It may be a man-like animal, an amoeba-like animal. It may be a robot. How is he to describe its movements? I think he would not know quite what to say. Certainly his description could not be understood unless we knew the details: maybe a man-thing raising his arm-like appendage, maybe an amoeba bubbling up his pseudopod-like appendage. We do not know. Can one describe the actions of his next-door neighbor in that way? Would that be a description of his bodily movements?

What is the difficulty in finding a "bodily movement?" Perhaps I am having trouble because my efforts have been directed to examples on the scene of human actions. The bodily movements which the country girl finds morally objectionable are actions. Tics and spasms are intruders on the scene of actions. Etc. A dance is made up of actions. The talking mouth is an unregulated action. Certainly this is excusable because bodily movements enter into every action.

Tics and spasms *are* bodily movements. They seem, somehow, the best candidates I have found: they are just not the kind of bodily movements found in actions. My philosophical picture leads me to think that something *like* that is involved in actions. The important thing is what I mean by "like that." I have not kept clearly in mind the origin of the question. I mean that a "bodily movement" is "like that" in that it can be explained in nonhuman terms: it can be explained by the principles of mechanics, chemistry, and electro-magnetics. We can ask what causes that muscle jerk, and the answer presumably is something like this: "excitation of a nerve due to an infection of the throat. The muscle is excited by a nerve whose trunk passes through the neck near the infection." The picture I have here is this: a "bodily movement" is an occurrence in the nonhuman, material order of things and hence enters into mechanical, chemical, and electromagnetic relations with other things of the same kind. At the same time some "bodily movements" enter into actions, and hence become explanable in terms of intentions, motives, reasons. They become subject to appraisal as right or wrong, elegant, skillful. The movements of the balls on the billiard table are explainable in terms of shape, mass, velocity, direction of movement, force of impact. At the same time they are billiard shots which are explanable in terms of tactics and intent. They are appraised for the way they exhibit skill, cunning, mastery of the game.

All along this idea has been operating. A "bodily movement" is primarily the sort of thing which is subject to physico-chemical explanation. Perhaps I have not kept clearly enough in mind the philosophical genesis of the distinction between "bodily movement" and action. The distinction grew out of worry over the old free-will problem, and it seemed a likely—but I'm afraid unsuccessful— way to get disentangled from the picture that all our actions are determined. It grew out of that picture of the world which is the Eden of mathematical physics, a picture which all of us sometimes have. Human actions are mystifying intruders in that world, and we are in need of an explanation of how actions are possible. The distinction between "bodily movement" and action was supposed to give us the explanation. "Bodily movements" may be determined, yes. Physics and chemistry may own them. Actions, no. The categories of physics and chemistry do not apply to actions at all. "Bodily movements" may be like the movements of the billiard balls on the table; but actions are like the shots of the players—good ones and bad—that go to make up the game.

Imagine a man with electrodes installed in the brain. When a certain current is sent through the electrodes, his arm rises. Why is this? The explanation is in terms of the structure and arrangement of bones, the nature and location of muscles, the effect on muscles of the nerve-currents excited by the electric shock to a portion of the brain. Now won't this same explanation do when he raises his arm, because I ask him to do so? Why not? I am now regarding his raising his arm as the scene of nerve-current propulsions, muscle contractions, the motions of bones in their sockets. Surely the same nerve-exchanges, muscle contractions take place in both cases. Here, at last, is the bodily movement in the action of raising the arm.

I get to the bodily movement, not by seeing anything as I imagined that I might look and see before. I get to the bodily movement involved in an action by regarding the action from a different point of view, by putting it against the background of tics, and spasms, and by asking for a certain kind of explanation. I regard it as a subject for certain kinds of questions. They are sophisticated questions: my physiologist colleagues warn me that I expect answers which are more appropriate to the workings of an old-fashioned hand water pump than to the workings of the human body.

A bodily movement, we might say, is a human action regarded from a certain point of view, as like a tic or a spasm, in that mechanical, chemical questions may be asked of it. This is not what the game similes led me to expect. My original question, "What is an action, in addition to being a bodily movement?" was based on an altogether different idea of a bodily movement. My original question, and the game similes which came to its rescue, were based on a different picture. I was thinking that a bodily movement was simple, an action complex. I was thinking that bodily movements were simple in the way that moving his blocks is simple for the child who does not know chess, or simple in the way that playing with the ball is simple for the boy who does not understand juju. I was thinking that the language of bodily movements is elementary; the language of actions, sophisticated. I thought that bodily movements were visible to the child's eye: they were seen as the bouncing of a rubber ball or the quivering of leaves in the wind. I thought that the vocabulary of bodily movements would be learned by a child in the way he learns the words "block" and "ball" and "chair," that is, by watching, and having things pointed out to him. And then the movements of such things would be described with the simplest verbs, "roll," "bounce," "slide," "fall."

A chess board would first be a checkered slab of wood, or a piece of cardboard. Then there would be various pieces of black wood and white wood. They would have different shapes. They could be made to slide and hop in various ways across the board. All this is first and easy. Then comes the more difficult business of learning to play chess, and so to talk of castling, check-mate, queen's gambit, *en passant,* and all the rest. It would be a long time before one learned the rules which apply to the repetition of positions in end-play. So I imagined bodily movements to be simple things which one could have pointed out to him as part of the material world of moving, changing objects. And actions: much more complex, requiring socialization and civilization. I thought, too, that bodily movements were easy to explain, and actions were not. Actions would not fit the simple system of explanation which worked for bodily movements.

I asked the question, "What, in addition to being a bodily movement, is an action?" under the influence of this picture of things. Now I have upset all the presumptions from which that question arose. I was trying to see how the difficult to understand, actions, grew out of the easy to understand, bodily movements. And it has been hard to discover the place of bodily movements in the world: we need some education in science for this. I wanted an understanding of the complex, actions, in terms of the simple, bodily movements. I wanted the strange and puzzling, actions, put on the background of the easy and familiar, bodily movements. Of course, nothing is more familiar or easier to talk about than actions. One must have a highly refined interest, and a special semi-technical vocabulary to talk of bodily movements.

I think now that my original question reversed the order of things; and a better question might be, "What, in addition to an action, is a bodily movement?" What is the answer? Take a bodily action, look at it in a diagnostic way as one might look at a tic or spasm. Think of levers, tubes and flows of liquid, wires and electrical currents. Think of the structure of the body in analogous terms, and study the functioning of its parts. Ask how the action could be the outcome of these workings, and then you are speaking of a bodily movement. In short, learn to take a physiological interest in bodily actions. A physiology professor will frequently refer to a bodily movement in the course of outlining an explanation. He may say something like this, "Notice the way I raise my arm. That particular bodily movement is the outcome of the synchronized contraction of six muscles, but chiefly of three: the deltoid, the brachio-radial, and the radial flexor. The unique insertion of the brachio-radial is important in understanding that particular movement." I shall not understand much of what the professor says, but I'm sure he will go on in this way.

If we ask, out of the blue, "In addition to being an action, what is a bodily movement?" the question will be misleading. It suggests that we must add something to an action in order to make it a bodily movement. The original question, when first considered, was misleading in the same way. "What is an action, in addition to being a bodily movement?" It sent us looking for an ingredient in an action like a mental occurrence. The game similes were intended to counter that misleading suggestion and to give us a clearer grasp of the question. Surely the game similes could just as well be invoked to clear up the new question, "What, in addition to an action, is a bodily movement?" We can say that learning to regard an action or a tic as a bodily movement is learning the "rules" of anatomical and physiological investigation and explanation. And the appeal to rules here will be no more, and no less, indirect and figurative than it was intended to be for the first question. It will serve to remind us that a certain educated interest and special training are required for talk of bodily movements.

Having now some idea of what a bodily movement is, can't I return to the original question? Starting from bodily movements, can't I ask, "What is an action? That is, what is an action, in addition to being a bodily movement?" I must say, "No, I can no longer ask that question." I cannot take a bodily movement as a simple, secure, familiar starting place. I cannot, therefore, feel that actions are questionable by contrast. If there were some question about the nature of actions, why would one think of looking to bodily movements as a starting point for the answer. He would be looking the wrong way. He would be taking a viewpoint from which questions about actions cannot arise. If I ask the question, I am supposed to see that this is the answer, "An action requires a special setting: a chess tournament, a ball game, the rules, the rituals, the ways of the tribe." But a bodily movement requires a special setting of its own, and one with which I am not very familiar. If I can comment now at all, I am inclined to say that a bodily movement cannot survive relocation from one setting to the other. I have been misled into thinking that a bodily movement in an action is like a diamond in a new, ornate setting. Perhaps once it was in another setting. Before that, in its simplest state, it was in no setting at all. It was pure and unadorned and could be viewed by itself.

I suppose that a physiologist at a baseball game might give explanations under his breath of many of the bodily movements taking place on the field, while at the same time following the game, cheering and booing the players and their plays. In that way he could see an action in a bodily movement, and a bodily movement in an action. I suppose that all of us could learn to do this. In learning this, surely we should not become estranged from actions, feeling that they were complex and question-provoking while bodily movements are plain and simple. If we learned to behave as this physiologist at the ball game, we could not ask, "What is an action, in addition to being a bodily movement?"

Then who can ask the question, "What besides a bodily movement, is an action?" Perhaps someone who has been swallowed up in physiology, someone who has lost his bearings. As he walks from the physiology laboratory, the actions on the street about him may seem mystifying. It may seem to him impossible that he is raising his arm to wave at a friend. As I say this, though, it sounds fantastic. Perhaps no person can, in this way, be swallowed up in the physiological point of view. I do not know whether physiology could make any person lose his bearings in that way. But philosophy can make a person lose his bearings in something of that way. Philosophy can make almost anything in heaven and earth seem somewhat mystifying.

POSTSCRIPT : ON PERSONS AND THEIR BODIES

If I am right, human actions seem mystifying because I have a view of things which leads me to think of bodily movements as simple things and actions as complex. We talk of bodily movements with simple words, and we explain them in a straightforward, scientific way. Actions require complex words, and their explanations are suspiciously unscientific.

The same view of things seems to contribute to other philosophical problems. We wonder about "personal identity" : we wonder what makes "one person" out of a lifetime of actions, happenings, thoughts, and dreams. We think that memory is important, but we cannot ignore the body. A person has a body which undergoes changes like any other body, like a rock or a pond; and it is the same body at death as at birth. Bodily continuity is simpler and more basic than memory. A person could not remember his past unless he could remember being here and there, doing this and that. He could not remember without remembering where he was, what he had done. Where he was, of course, is where his body was; and what he did involves the movements of his body. We ask, "What is a person?" And we assume that we should begin from the simple thing. The question becomes "What is a person in addition to a human body?" We point at persons; we point them out. When puzzling over the philosophical question, I think that one could not point to a person. Pointing is a "logically simple" thing. I learned to point as a small child : I learned to point at blocks and balls, chairs and houses. "When I point to a person, I am really pointing at his body." We can point at a person all right, but that is a sophisticated thing. In the appropriate social context, we can point at a person, but we do so in pointing at his body.

"We point at people in pointing at their bodies." I say to a friend, "Will you pick up that domino?" "What?" he says. I repeat, now pointing, "Will you pick up that domino—there?" "You're pointing at a black piece of wood." "Yes. Don't you know what a domino is?" "No." "That black piece of wood is a domino." Later, in a philosophical mood, my friend reflects, "In pointing at a domino, he pointed at a black piece of wood." Can he now generalize, "We point at dominos in pointing at pieces of wood"? If he does generalize, he must be careful not to read anything into the generality which is not present in the particulars it is meant to cover. My pointing at the domino is the kind of particular he must keep in mind. If one wanted to be safe, he would put the generality this way: "Whenever anyone points to a domino and I don't know what a domino is, I will naturally suppose that he is pointing at the piece of wood I see. I will guess that a domino is a piece of wood."

"We point at people in pointing at their bodies." Am I to understand this in an analogous way? "Whenever anyone points at a person and I do not know what a person is, then I will naturally suppose that he is pointing at a human body. I will guess that a person is a human body."

My philosophical question about persons does seem to grow out of an assumption such as this: the word "person" is related to the word "body" the way the word "domino" is related to the word "wood." A child may ask, "What is a domino?" We can show him one, "This piece of wood is a domino." We can explain the game to him. If a child asks, "What is a person?" we cannot give the same sort of answer. We must say, "The word 'person' refers to anyone: your mother, your father, your friends—everyone. They are persons. Each one is a person. You are a person." In this explanation there is reference only to persons, not to bodies. We teach the child that "person" is a general word. It is related to "mother" and to "Uncle Joe," but it is not related to "mother" the way "domino" is related to "wood."

"Then he must have learned that 'mother' is related to 'body' the way 'domino' is related to 'wood'." A child's mother is a person, of course; and in learning to call his mother and point to his mother he is taking the first step in understanding the idea of person. But even this first step is complex. Before he can begin to get the idea of a person, he must have the idea of a body. He must be able to pick out bodies, see bodies, and point to bodies.

At this point, I have misrepresented entirely the way we think and talk of bodies, the way we use the word "body." A child will surely never think or speak of his mother's body. Perhaps during her lifetime, he will never hear anyone speak of his mother's body. As a child he may first hear the word "body" used in talking of Uncle George, lying in his casket. When do we speak of bodies? The coroner might say, "We have room for only two more bodies." An anatomist might wire, "Ship me another body—an older female this time, please." One of the boys on the street corner might say, "Wow! Would you look at that body." "His body has shriveled away to nothing," we may say of a very sick old man. An artist teaching painting or sculpture might say, "Study the human body in all its forms and postures." Police, investigating a homicide, note carefully the position of the body. They issue orders, "Do not move the body."

Talk about bodies requires very special contexts. One has to know something about physical culture, art, girl-watching, undertaking, anatomical study, or police-investigation before he knows how to point to a human body. He has to be engaged in one of these businesses before he can point to or talk about a human body.

We do not speak of the body of an animal except when we have personalized the animal. We dissect a dog. But we prepare the body of faithful old Bowser for burial. Compare: "Look at the *body* of that weight-lifter." "Look at the body of that cat." What could I mean by "the body of that cat"? I should most likely be calling attention to something like this: the cat has an orange body contrasting with black head and tail. The body of a cat is the mid-portion—excluding head and tail. I was not thinking of "body" in the sense of trunk or mid-part. A person excitedly reports, "I found a body in the bushes." Shouldn't we be surprised if we found it to be a dead cow. Shouldn't we think it a joke if the finder knew all along it was a cow? "Body," in the relevant sense, seems to apply only to persons or animals personalized.

If I had to summarize, I should say something like this: A domino is a piece of wood seen from a special point of view. A person is not a body seen from a special point of view. Rather, a body is a person seen from a special point of view. My picture of things leads me to reverse the order. Of the words "body" and "person," if I had to decide which is simple and which complex, I should have to say "person" is simple, and "body" complex. But I do not want to say that, because these words "simple" and "complex," in this connection, are given to me by my misleading picture of things.